COMPLETE
CHOLESTEROL
COUNTER

Also by Peter Cox & Peggy Brusseau

LifePoints
LifePoints Diet
LifePoints for Kids
LifePoints Cookbook
LifePoints Counter & Meal Planner
Linda McCartney's Home Cooking
(with Linda McCartney)
The Complete Fat Counter

THE COMPLETE CHOLESTEROL COUNTER

Peter Cox & Peggy Brusseau

BLOOMSBURY

Publisher's Note
The information in this book was correct to the best of the Editor's and Publisher's belief at the time of going to press. While no responsibility can be accepted for errors and omissions, the Editor and Publisher would welcome corrections and suggestions for material to include in subsequent editions of this book.

This book may include words, brand names and other descriptions of products which are or are asserted to be proprietary names or trade-marks. No judgement concerning the legal status of such words is made or implied thereby. Their inclusion does not imply that they have acquired for legal purposes a non-proprietary or general significance nor any other judgement concerning their legal status.

Please note that food products frequently change in composition, and this may substantially affect the ratings herein. A free update to the information in this book can be obtained from: BM Box Superliving, London WC1M 3XX, England. Please enclose a stamped addressed envelope.

First published in 1999 by
Bloomsbury Publishing Plc
38 Soho Square
London W1V 5DF

Copyright © 1999 by Peter Cox & Peggy Brusseau
International management by the Alta Vista Corporation Ltd
A copy of the CIP entry for this book is available from the
British Library

The right of Peter Cox & Peggy Brusseau to be identified as the authors
of this work has been asserted in accordance with the Copyright,
Designs and Patents Act 1988.

ISBN 0 7475 3647 3

1 3 5 7 9 10 8 6 4 2

Typeset by Palimpsest Book Production Ltd., Polmont, Stirlingshire
Printed and bound in Great Britain by Clays Ltd, St Ives plc

CONTENTS

IMPORTANT NOTICE

The recommendations made in this book are for adults only. If you suspect you may suffer from a raised cholesterol level, we strongly advise you to seek medical treatment. Do not attempt self-treatment without first discussing and agreeing the proposed treatment with your doctor. Diagnosis and treatment of medical conditions is a responsibility shared between you and your doctor and neither the authors nor publisher of this book can accept responsibility for the consequences of treatment based on the recommendations described herein.

PROPRIETARY NAMES

This book may include words, brand names and other descriptions of products which are or are asserted to be proprietary names or trade marks. No judgement concerning the legal status of such words is made or implied thereby. Their inclusion does not imply that they have acquired for legal purposes a non-proprietary or general significance nor any other judgement concerning their legal status.

PART ONE:

WHAT YOU REALLY NEED TO KNOW ABOUT CHOLESTEROL

ALL ABOUT CHOLESTEROL

Every day, your heart will beat 100,000 times (two-and-a-half thousand-million times in a lifetime) as it provides the motive power to supply thousands of kilometres of minute capillaries, larger arteries (which transport oxygen-rich blood away from the heart) and veins (which carry blood back to the heart again).

Every minute, your heart circulates your body's entire volume of blood, about five litres, once round your system (pumping 200 million litres in a lifetime). If your heart stops beating for more than three minutes, permanent brain damage will occur. Being a hard-working muscle, the heart also supplies itself with vital oxygen and nourishment through its own pumping actions and again, if the blood flow through the life-giving coronary arteries is stopped for more than a few minutes, the heart will be damaged to such a great extent that it may be irreversibly stopped. So you see, with such a complex and awesome circulatory system, when something happens to interrupt or diminish your blood flow, the situation can become very serious, very quickly.

As cholesterol builds up on the walls of your arteries it begins to narrow them. No one can *feel* their cholesterol level as it builds up, and even when an artery becomes more than half blocked by this fatty, cholesterol-rich sludge known as 'atheroma', you still may not be aware of any warning signs to tell you that something is badly wrong. In fact, an artery usually has to be more than 75 per cent blocked before blood flow is seriously reduced. But by this stage, time is definitely running out. If allowed to continue, this process will ultimately deprive vital organs of their blood supply, and you will die.

But don't make the mistake of thinking that a high cholesterol level in your blood is only associated with heart disease. In fact, the same cholesterol which forms deposits that build up on artery walls can also act to reduce the flow of blood causing what we commonly know as a 'stroke'. Most strokes are caused by a narrowing or blockage of an artery, leading to a 'cerebrovascular accident', involving damage to the brain.

Of course, those who survive a heart attack or stroke *can* make a good recovery, if they are prepared to change their lifestyles sufficiently. But wouldn't it be more sensible to take *preventative* action now, rather than fighting for your life later on?

That's what this book is about.

WHAT IS CHOLESTEROL, ANYWAY?

Imagine yourself using a sharp knife to perform a task which requires all your attention. Your mind wanders for a moment and – *ouch!* Clumsy... you've pricked your finger! A drop of blood forms... no more than one cubic millimetre in volume, yet, inside it there exists the most complex mixture of substances you could imagine. In round terms, there are roughly five and a half million red blood cells in that minuscule droplet, and each one contains haemoglobin, the oxygen-carrying protein which so efficiently transports its load from the lungs outwards to all the tissues. Each one of these red blood cells takes about a week to manufacture inside the red bone marrow that lies at the very centre of your ribs and vertebrae. During its short but hectic life, this little blood cell speeds around your body about once every 45 seconds. Fresh from the lungs, it takes on a bright red colour, which later changes to a bluish tinge after having delivered its oxygen to all parts of the body. After four hectic months, it will be consigned to the body's multi-purpose recycling plant located inside your liver and spleen, where it will be taken to bits and its component parts recycled.

In that same drop of blood, there also exist about 10,000 white cells. These are the front-line troops in the body's defence force against invading foreign bodies. Specific types of white cells have special defensive tasks assigned to them – some can engulf and devour invading bacteria. Some of them can manufacture antibodies (which also have specific defensive jobs) and other white cells can target and destroy many other kinds of microscopic aggressors.

Also present in that drop of blood are about half a million disk-shaped characters called platelets, whose task in the body's defence system is to close ranks and stick to any damaged area, thus helping the blood to clot and keep out unwelcome visitors. In fact, as you examine that little pin-prick closely, you will see those platelets start to perform their main task in life as the blood clots before your very eyes.

All these tiny particles, and more besides, are kept in a state of movement and circulation because they are suspended in a watery substance called plasma. This is a rich chemical and biological soup, containing not only the cells mentioned above, but also various nutrients and hormones, as well as waste matter on its way to be disposed of.

As you continue to examine this tiny drop of blood, which has already started to clot, you can actually see different parts of it begin to separate out. As the clotting agents begin their work, so they detach themselves from the medium in which they have been transported to the site of your minor injury. Look closely and you will see a pale yellow fluid around the wound. This liquid is called serum, and it consists of the remains of plasma after the clotting agents have gone to work. Now we're getting to the really important part, because this yellow liquid is of especial interest to us. Because, in addition to all its other transport functions, plasma also provides the medium in which cholesterol circulates inside us.

But it is here that the body faces a major problem. Cholesterol is a fat-like substance. Blood, on the other hand, is water-based. How, then, is the body to transport cholesterol in a watery fluid?

The body's answer is characteristically ingenious. It does not try to mix fats directly with water, but instead, packages them into tiny little parcels, which can then be washed around in the bloodstream with the rest of the fluids. At this point we need to use a few scientific labels, because there are several different types of packages, all with different functions and different names.

Your liver does most of this packaging work, and it does it by combining cholesterol with various substances (proteins) which *are* soluble in water. The medical name given to fat-like substances is 'lipid'. Therefore, when these fats, or lipids, are combined with proteins, the resulting substance is called a 'lipo-protein'. In a moment, we'll look at some of these lipoproteins in more detail.

First, let's mention something very similar to lipoproteins, but with a name that sounds as if it comes from a bad science fiction movie. Meet the chylomicron (pronounced ky-lo-my-kron). After you eat a fat-containing meal, vast numbers of chylomicrons surge into your bloodstream as your body begins to take apart the latest culinary offering. At first, a typical chylomicron only contains a small proportion of cholesterol, some of which will come from your food, and some of which will be made mainly by your liver (but is also capable of being made elsewhere throughout your body). The main component, however, of a chylomicron is simply fat. To begin with, this little globule of fat mixed with a little cholesterol and a dash of protein circulates quite happily for a certain time, without being much disturbed by any bio-chemical process going on inside the liver. However, fat cells elsewhere in your body sense a free lunch approaching, and pretty soon most of the fat contained within the chylomicron has been scavenged, just leaving a saggy, cholesterol-rich particle referred to as a remnant. It is now up to the liver to recover the cholesterol from this remnant, and thus remove some cholesterol from your serum. If it does its job effectively, your serum cholesterol level will not increase. But if your liver becomes slightly inefficient, the tendency will be for your serum cholesterol level to rise over time. Which is bad news.

Next on our suspect list are two real lipoproteins. The first is called 'pre-beta lipoprotein', or 'very low density lipoprotein', abbreviated to VLDL, and consists of 8 per cent protein, 20 per cent cholesterol, and a large amount of other fatty substances. The other is called 'beta lipoprotein' or 'low density lipoprotein', abbreviated to LDL, and consists of about 20 per cent protein and 45 per cent cholesterol. Most of the cholesterol you take in dietary form seems to make its first (but quite brief) appearance in your bloodstream in VLDL form. However, VLDL decays in the same way as chylomicrons do, and eventually their remnants become incorporated into LDLs (via an intermediate substance called 'intermediate-density lipoprotein').

Now LDLs are the *main* carriers of cholesterol in your plasma. And as such, they are heavily under suspicion for complicity in elevating your cholesterol level. One of their functions seems to be to transport cholesterol away from the liver to other parts of the body. Now clearly, the liver (and other parts of the body, but mainly your liver) needs some method of keeping your LDL level under control, otherwise you would choke up with cholesterol sludge in a very short space of time. The way it does it is to have specific receptor sites located on cell membranes whose job it is to first bind the LDL particle to the cell, and then absorb it *into* the cell. These incredibly useful devices are called 'LDL receptors'. If you don't have enough of them, or if they aren't working very efficiently, your cholesterol level will climb.

Once the LDL particle has been absorbed into the receptor-containing cell, the protein is stripped away, generating free cholesterol. Well, not quite free, because the free cholesterol is quickly processed to a stable form and simply stored. At the same time, a chemical switch is thrown telling the cell that it now has enough cholesterol for its immediate needs, and it can stop producing it internally. This all sounds fine, but there is a problem. You see, biologically speaking, one of the functions of the LDL is to obtain cholesterol supplies – if there's not enough in the bloodstream, then a message is sent ordering some to be made internally. But when cholesterol exists in abundance, as it does in many of us, there is less need for LDL receptors to thrive and flourish everywhere. Fewer are needed, because fewer receptors can grab as much cholesterol as they need from a rich supply floating by in the bloodstream. To put it simply, they get downright lazy! Consequently, an *excess* of serum cholesterol may actually *decrease* the number of LDL receptors! Which is precisely what we *don't* need. Again, the end result may be the accumulation of more and more cholesterol in the blood.

Amongst all these highly suspicious particles, it comes as a relief to find one whose function is definitely benign. Let us introduce you to 'alpha lipoprotein', or high density lipoprotein (HDL). This type of fat-protein complex has the highest percentage of protein of all – consisting approximately of 50 per cent protein and about 20 per cent cholesterol. Scientists believe that this substance is a 'good' lipoprotein, because one of its functions seems to be to scavenge for cholesterol in the arteries, on the artery walls, and from other tissues, and to transport it back again to the liver for safe disposal.

So you can see, if you have proportionately more functional LDL than HDL, you could be in trouble. Because it's rather like having a six-lane motorway feeding a constant stream of traffic *into* a small town, yet having only one small country road to allow the congestion to *escape* from the town. Having too much LDL keeps cholesterol circulating in your blood – not having enough HDL stops it from being reclaimed and expelled.

Now you know that cholesterol is transported around your body in a number of different forms. From this, it is easy to see that when you have a test for the amount of cholesterol in your blood (sometimes called serum cholesterol) it is also necessary to find out precisely *how* that cholesterol is being transported. Is it in 'good' HDL form? or 'bad' LDL form?

That's why, when you have a cholesterol test, and the results show a higher than healthy level, your doctor will suggest that further tests be done to find out in *precisely* what form your cholesterol is circulating. At this point also, your doctor may well suggest another test for something called triglycerides. These fatty substances are, like cholesterol, both taken in with food and manufactured in the liver. They are used by the body to provide energy, and help us to store fat in our fat tissues. But triglycerides are not free from suspicion. As we eat more food containing triglycerides, it has been found that the rate of cholesterol absorption increases. Also, since they have an effect on blood clotting, someone with high triglyceride levels and with artery-narrowing atherosclerosis may suddenly suffer from a blocked artery due to a blood clot, resulting in a heart attack or stroke.

- LDL (Low Density Lipoprotein) is the main carrier of cholesterol in your plasma. HDL (High Density Lipoprotein) scavenges for cholesterol and transports it back to the liver for safe disposal.

- Having too much LDL keeps cholesterol circulating in your blood – not having enough HDL stops it from being reclaimed and expelled.

- Lowering your total cholesterol, and lowering the cholesterol carried in LDL form (about two thirds of your body's cholesterol is carried like this) will reduce your risk of atherosclerosis.

WHAT'S GONE WRONG?

You will be shocked to learn that the very first clear, clinical account of someone having a heart attack was recorded only as recently as 1912. Today, of course, heart disease is the commonest cause of death in the Western world. This means that heart disease is an *epidemic of the last hundred years*. It means that over the past century, something has happened to make a once rare and unusual form of death so common that by the age of 65, one man out of every five has had a heart attack, and of those, one in ten has died. Although two-thirds of heart attacks happen to men, this still means that, in the United States for example, about 400,000 women have a heart attack every year.

So what exactly have we been doing wrong? We put this question to one of the most eminent researchers in this field, Professor Michael Crawford. This is what he told us:

> What has happened is that we all started from a common baseline of wild foods. This is the sort of 'primitive' diet which humans have eaten throughout most of their evolution, over the past five million years. However, in the last few centuries, things have gone haywire. In Europe, our diets have gone in one direction, in Africa and India they've gone in a different direction.
>
> In Western Europe we've focused on consuming foods which are very rich in non-essential types of fat, but pretty miserable sources of essential fats. Our diets have also become rich in processed and refined carbohydrates. In fact, the problems are quite easy to identify – it's taking corrective action that seems to be difficult for some of us.

Sometimes, we hear about a 'genetic' factor in heart disease – that people with a history of heart disease in the family are more likely to contract heart disease themselves. Scientific evidence shows that this is true, and doctors have termed this inherited high level of blood cholesterol as 'familial hypercholesterolaemia' or FH for short. However, it would be a great mistake to assume that either you are 'doomed' to suffer from heart disease simply because one member of your family has suffered from it, or, alternatively, that you will miraculously escape it because no close relative has succumbed. Bear in mind:

- First, FH is not a diagnosis you can make for yourself. Just because a relative has died from heart disease doesn't mean that you have FH.

- Second, only 1 in 500 people has FH, whereas 1 in every 5 people has an excessively high level of blood cholesterol, and *two-thirds* of the

population should modify their diet, according to one leading authority.[1]

• Third, if you do have a history of heart disease in your family, it is
  even more important that you take steps – including dietary ones – to
  reduce your cholesterol level.

And lastly, we went to visit a top specialist who treats hundreds of
people with high blood cholesterol every year, and asked him how many
of his patients' high blood cholesterol was caused by genetic reasons.
'Very few', he said. 'The vast majority are as a result of years of inappro-
priate diet'. Get the message?

HOW CHOLESTEROL OVERLOAD HAPPENS

As you've already begun to appreciate, cholesterol is a complex
substance. Your body deals with it in a myriad subtle and inter-
connected ways, and the processes we describe here are over-simplifica-
tions. Although we know *for certain* that cholesterol gradually builds up
on artery walls, narrowing them until the odds are heavily against us,
precisely *how*, *why*, and *when* are not quite so clear yet. But let's review
a little more of the evidence.

It is remarkable to think that, in our society, few people can reach
adulthood without having, deep within their bodies, the first but unmis-
takable signs of atherosclerosis – 'furred-up' arteries. From then
onwards, most of us are simply playing for time – either hoping to put
off further narrowing as long as possible, or maybe succumbing to
another common illness before our arteries close in on us.
Atherosclerosis is so common today that many of us perhaps consider it
to be inescapable. But the truth is, in societies which lead different
lifestyles and eat better diets than we do, coronary heart disease is
almost entirely absent. In Kenya, for example, the first case of coronary
heart disease was only diagnosed half way through the twentieth
century. Since then, however, Kenyan diets and lifestyles have become
closer to our Western 'ideal', and deaths from coronary heart disease
have become a much more frequent event. This same pattern has been
repeated in many, many other countries as they seek to emulate our
Western way of life – and death. It is, therefore, important for us to
remember in all that follows that atherosclerosis, and coronary heart
disease, is *not* inevitable. We can fight it.

One thing most investigators are agreed upon is that atherosclerosis
consists of an accumulation of fats, primarily cholesterol, both on the
surface wall of the arteries, and also inside ' foam' cells (cells which are
swollen with cholesterol). Around this deposit proliferate an aggregation of smooth muscle cells, steadily growing, enlarging and blocking

the artery. There are many theories as to how and why these crucial events take place, and the truth of the matter is probably that there a number of major causes, acting together. For example, if some smooth muscle cells are penetrated by an external enemy – such as an invading virus or chemical – they may reproduce themselves very quickly, leading to a breach in the artery wall which then becomes an 'anchor' for cholesterol deposits and further cell growth. Another possibility is that blood platelets may stick together, deposit themselves on the lining of the artery, and so, again, produce a roughened surface on which cholesterol may accumulate. Yet another possibility is that high blood pressure may itself damage the lining of the artery, and again, make it easier for lipids to be deposited there. There are probably a multitude of fundamental causes or precipitating factors.

So some form of damage to the lining of your arteries may be the first stage in producing atherosclerosis. But additionally, a high concentration of LDL in your blood, may, *all by itself*, be responsible for damaging your artery walls. If the amount of LDL in your blood rises above a certain level, then it may manage to breach the artery wall. Normally, the cells lying on the wall, and just under its surface, will have their own ways of excreting cholesterol as it is produced or absorbed. However, if the concentration of LDL is so high as to prevent these cells from coping in the normal manner, then the cells themselves may be damaged, and turned into 'foam cells' which then go on to do so much damage to the lining of the artery itself.

The other crucial event in the development of atherosclerosis is the accumulation of a higher-than-healthy level of cholesterol in your bloodstream. But how does this 'cholesterol overload' happen? There is no one easy answer. You've already seen how the liver plays a crucial role in cholesterol control. It is continually stripping cholesterol out of the bloodstream, and replacing it with newly packaged cholesterol which it then sends all over the body to perform its proper functions in cells. But just think – if you continually eat a high fat diet, the liver will be *forced* to cope with this additional burden of fat processing, and one of the ways in which it will do this is to send the excess fat out into the fatty tissues of the body for storage (of course, this is one way in which people who consume fatty foods put on weight and become fat themselves). And as the liver assembles all this fat into little packages for transport, so it includes a little *cholesterol* in each one. The result? More and more little packages containing cholesterol circulating in your blood. And it will go on circulating until it's eventually reclaimed by your liver. But – here comes a serious problem.

One of your liver's duties is to make cholesterol if there's not enough to be found elsewhere (remember, we *need* some cholesterol). Now with so much cholesterol being taken in with your food (because a high-fat diet is usually a high-cholesterol diet) and with a fair bit of spare cholesterol already circulating in the bloodstream, there is absolutely no need for your liver to produce any homegrown cholesterol. There's masses already! So it cuts back on cholesterol production. Your liver now believes that there is more than enough cholesterol in the world for everyone, so it doesn't need to be so impressively efficient in reclaiming and recycling the cholesterol already circulating in your blood. Which is a big mistake, but at least you can understand how it happens. And the result of this decreasing efficiency of your liver will be a slow but sure build up of cholesterol circulating in your bloodstream.

Now, if this theory is correct, then it might be possible to encourage the liver to become more efficient at cholesterol management simply by eating a diet which is lower in fats and extremely low in cholesterol. In this way, your liver would start to become more efficient in its own management of cholesterol, and become a good recycler of cholesterol in your bloodstream. The happy result of this would be a decrease in your blood cholesterol level.

And here's another good reason to start eating a low-fat, low-cholesterol diet. People who are overweight have a lot of fatty tissue, which may *itself* be producing a significant amount of cholesterol. Normally, cholesterol effectively regulates its own production in cells, but it may not be able to do this in fatty tissue. Fat cells are precisely what they sound like – a huge greasy globule of fat sitting in the middle of a small cell. There's not room inside for much else besides that fat globule, so any cholesterol which is produced is immediately dissolved in fat. Unfortunately, there simply may not be sufficient time for this freshly produced cholesterol to shut down the cell's cholesterol production mechanism – so the cell is deceived into thinking that it needs to produce *even more*. And this is how fatty tissue may be a significant source of serum cholesterol. Therefore, if you lose weight and reduce your fatty tissue, you may well *also* cut your cholesterol level into the bargain.

These are just a few ways in which some scientists speculate that a low-fat, low-cholesterol diet works to cut back the level of cholesterol in your blood. Although the final answers may not be discovered for some time, there is absolutely no doubt that such a diet *can* be used to control cholesterol, and that it should be your first line of attack.

CAN THE DAMAGE BE UNDONE?

Your body contains an impressive collection of systems, many of which continually restore and repair the damage you inflict on yourself simply by living. If your body can successfully repair the cut finger we so cunningly gave you at the beginning of this section, you may be wondering whether it can't also repair a rip in an artery?

Right now, the interest in many scientific circles has shifted towards answering precisely this question. Does the body have the capability to repair existing damage to an artery wall? If we lower a high cholesterol level, can we reverse the process of atherosclerosis? Can damage that has already been done to your arteries be *undone* just by lowering your blood cholesterol? The jury is still out on this one, but the signs are encouraging. There are already some interesting case histories where it seems to have happened, and some experts are beginning to admit that it may indeed be possible.

Apart from 'regression' (as scientists tend to call it), it is very encouraging to note, as well, that there *are* cases where the growth of atherosclerosis seems to have been been halted in its tracks – even though existing damage to the arteries may not have been reversed. But the first case we could find concerning the regression of atherosclerosis occurred in 1977, when 25 patients (all suffering from high levels of blood lipids) were treated by a special diet and also with medication to lower their blood pressure. After just over a year, medical investigators found that 13 patients had continued to develop atherosclerosis. However, three patients showed no change in the state of their disease, and – most excitingly – *nine patients showed 'significant regression'*.[2]

When researchers from the medical school at the University of California recently recruited 162 men to take part in an experiment to see whether the body can reverse the damage done to major blood vessels, they deliberately selected people who had previously undergone coronary bypass operations. Half of them ate a low-cholesterol diet and took cholesterol-reducing medication, while the remainder simply took a placebo. After two years, over 16 per cent of the test group showed 'significant regression' in the coronary arteries.[3]

Another study also seemed to show that about one third of those patients who are given a low-cholesterol, low-fat diet, and who are also receiving drug therapy, *might* succeed in producing some regression of their atherosclerosis. At all events, many original skeptics are now prepared to admit that it *might* occur. The implication, of course, is tremendously exciting – it means that atherosclerosis is well worth fighting, with every weapon in your armoury.

- Regression is possible! The damage that has already been done to your arteries may be undone simply by lowering your blood cholesterol.

Let's answer one more question which may be in your mind at this stage

– and it's a key question. *'Is it worth it? If I reduce my blood cholesterol level, does it mean that I'll be immune to heart attacks and coronary heart disease?'*

Let's try to answer this as honestly and completely as science will currently allow us to. First, no one can *guarantee* that reducing your cholesterol level will prevent you from suffering from heart disease. Life is just not like that. There is no such thing as *absolute* certainty. The man who smokes 60 cigarettes a day *may* just live to be 70 (although the odds are heavily against it). If you try to walk across a busy road wearing a blindfold over your eyes you *may* just reach the other side in one piece. If you play Russian roulette with a loaded gun, you *may* just get lucky and not blow your brains out.

But come on – let's be sensible. Life is already risky enough and full enough of surprises (some of them rather nasty) for us to know that some chances are much riskier than others. Only a fool, an addicted gambler or someone with a death-wish would knowingly take a risk which is overwhelmingly likely to end in their own fatality. And yet, that's precisely what you're doing if you maintain a high blood cholesterol level and do nothing about it. The odds are against you. And even if you like to live dangerously (maybe you're one of those people who thrives on danger, adventure and the smell of catastrophe in your nostrils) why not take up mountain-climbing, parachuting or hang-gliding instead? You'll certainly get more pleasure out of them, and if you reduce your cholesterol level as well, you may stick around a little longer to enjoy them!

When we set out to write this book, we decided to keep it simple and to avoid as many unnecessary figures, percentages, and mathematical calculations as we could, but there is one fundamental little formula which is so important that we're putting it right now. It is, indeed, *so* important that you should memorize it. Here it is:

> *For every one per cent drop in blood cholesterol, there is a two per cent drop in the risk of cardiovascular disease.*

Think about this for a moment. It means that when a population manages to reduce its cholesterol level by – say – a meagre 5 per cent, the risk of cardiovascular disease drops by 10 per cent. And if the level of cholesterol declines by 10 per cent, then the risk drops by 20 per cent. And so on. Now of course, this fact has profound implications for all of us. It means that reducing our blood cholesterol level is one of the most effective ways yet discovered to *dramatically reduce* our risk of suffering from – or being killed by – cardiovascular disease.

There is hard proof of this statement. Since 1960, Americans have on average lowered their cholesterol levels by 3 to 4 per cent – which may not sound very much, until you learn that death rates from heart disease dropped from 286 deaths per 100,000 population in 1960 to 180 per 100,000 in 1985 – actually a reduction of 37 per cent!

'This is the most dramatic trend in death rates in the world', says Dr Patrick L. Remington of the Center for Disease Control. 'The eyes of the entire world's scientific community are on the United States because deaths from heart disease are going down so rapidly.'

How has such a change been achieved? Dr Remington believes that about half the decline in coronary deaths can be attributed to changes in lifestyle, and about a third due to changes in the diet, including the consumption of foods which are beneficial to blood cholesterol levels.

Although the American experience is clearly encouraging and shows the rest of the world just what can be achieved, there is still much more to do. For example, only one out of every ten Americans actually knows what their current cholesterol level is. Do *you* know?

Dr Remington spoke about 'changes in lifestyle' managing to achieve an enormous reduction in deaths. What does this mean? Well, it means that cardiovascular disease is the result of an interplay of factors – of which a high cholesterol level is an important (but not the only) one.

WINNING THE RISK GAME

Life is a gamble – every time you cross the road, you take a risk. Every would-be gambler knows that winning is just a matter of getting the odds stacked in your favour (which is why casinos win more than most punters). A casino, of course, stacks the odds pretty heavily against you, and there's not much you can do about it. But in the casino of life, the odds are much more flexible – and *you* can stack them in *your* favour! Each one of the following important factors can be controlled – by you – to reduce your risk of heart disease. We suggest you take action where appropriate.

HIGH BLOOD PRESSURE

Many people with high blood pressure don't know they have it until it is measured by their doctor. Others suffer from frequent headaches, chronic fatigue or kidney problems which eventually leads them to have a check-up. In fact, the general symptoms of high blood pressure can be quite vague. But there is nothing vague about the *effects* of high blood pressure on your heart and arteries. It is one of the leading causes of heart and circulatory disease and can result in handicap or death from heart attack or stroke. High blood pressure erodes your health, whether you are aware of it or not. It can gradually rise to an unhealthy level without you knowing a thing about it. This is why having your blood pressure measured once each year is a good idea.

Blood pressure is measured (usually by a doctor or nurse) using an inflatable bag which is wrapped round your arm. The inside of this bag is connected by a rubber tube to a mercury-filled pressure gauge. As the bag is inflated, the mercury rises within the pressure gauge, which is marked off in millimetres. When the bag is inflated to the same degree of pressure as that of the blood within your arteries, this flow of blood is briefly interrupted. By listening through a stethoscope it is possible to detect when this interruption occurs and to note the height of mercury within the gauge at this point: this is your *systolic* blood pressure, the first number in your reading. To obtain the *diastolic* blood pressure, the second number in your reading, it is necessary to listen to the pulse as the bag deflates and the mercury drops. Your diastolic pressure is recorded as the point on the mercury gauge when you can no longer hear the pulse. Now you have both figures – they are usually written like this:

$$BP = 120/80 \text{ mm Hg}$$

It is, of course, normal and necessary for your blood pressure to vary according to circumstances, diet or even the time of day. But when your blood pressure is *always* high your health is probably in danger. This state is called hypertension and the person who suffers it is called hypertensive. The arteries and arterioles of a hypertensive person are more narrow and less flexible than in a healthy person. This means that the blood must push through them at greater force in order to circulate and the heart must pump much harder to maintain this circulation. Without sufficient pressure of blood in your arteries you would suffer dizziness, fainting or even death. Therefore, you need a blood pressure that is high enough to ensure proper circulation of the blood, but low enough to avoid damaging your heart and arteries.

Healthy arteries respond to changes in blood pressure by contracting or relaxing. Narrow, unhealthy arteries have lost their flexibility, so that blood circulating through them under high pressure can damage their inner linings. As you already know, when the lining of an artery is damaged, it is vulnerable to the build-up of cholesterol deposits. These deposits will further narrow and harden the artery so that the heart must work harder to circulate the blood through the system. The overall result is that your body *again* increases blood pressure to push all the blood through those restricted arteries. Which is how the vicious cycle of damage, narrowing, increased blood pressure and more damage is set into motion. Unless blood pressure is reduced as early as possible, this cycle of events may be repeated until something catastrophic occurs – such as a stroke or heart attack.

Unfortunately, hypertension often appears in company with other personal features or lifestyle habits that not only worsen this condition but can themselves increase your risk of suffering heart or circulatory disease.

SALT

Table salt or sea salt consist largely of sodium chloride. Sodium works with potassium in your body to balance the level of fluid inside and outside each cell. Too much of one or the other of these salts will create an imbalance. An imbalance – and it need only be a very small one – will create health problems particularly focused on the arteries, heart and kidneys. High blood pressure is one of these problems. About 60 per cent of hypertensives are thought to be 'salt sensitive.'[4] Recent studies have pointed to the fact that chloride may actually be as big a culprit as sodium in hypersensitive individuals.

Most of us probably take in more salt than is good for us so a general recommendation here to *reduce your salt intake* is in order. Here are three simple steps which can reduce your salt consumption by as much as half – without it being difficult or tiresome.

- Don't add salt to your food as you cook. Let each person add a little salt to their own meal when it arrives at the table, if they really want it. Taste tests have shown that food *tastes* saltier when the salt is added after cooking – even though less salt is generally used. And make sure that the salt shaker on the table is transparent and only one-quarter full. This seems to encourage people to use rather less than usual.

- Substitute ordinary table salt for a balanced salt, such as Biosalt™, which contains potassium as well as sodium. Then add other condiments to your table, such as celery seed, dried herbs and spices, which will introduce other flavour-enhancing tastes – not necessarily salty ones.

- Shop with an eye for salty foods. Check the labels. Tinned foods, yeast extract and many 'instant' products are all potential salt traps – read the fine print carefully. Thankfully, many manufacturers have responded to consumer interest and produced excellent low-salt versions of many of these food products.

ALCOHOL

Alcohol consumption (especially red wine) at moderate levels has been shown to be inversely correlated with heart disease. The flavonoid antioxidants in wines probably prevent the oxidation of LDL cholesterol. Some wines also contain levels of salicylic acid sufficient to contribute to cardiovascular wellness, in a manner similar to aspirin. However, many healthcare professionals are reluctant to promote the use of alcohol as a public health measure for the prevention of cardiovascular disease because of the prevalence of alcoholism. The positive effects of alcohol are related to moderate consumption (meaning two drinks or less per day), and many people are not able to moderate their alcohol intake. Certainly, when it is part of a lifestyle 'package' that includes over-eating, smoking and lack of exercise, alcohol can contribute to liver and psychological disorders, obesity and, of course, heart and circulatory disease. The evidence implicating moderate alcohol consumption, by itself, in the development of cardiovascular disease is not strong, but there *are* strong indications that alcohol and other lifestyle habits – such as those just mentioned – together *do* cause cardiovascular disease.

It has been suggested that 'teetotallers' are actually at greater risk of cardiovascular disease than their alcohol-drinking friends. However, these benefits seem only to apply (if they exist) to very moderate, or low-level, drinkers who also keep their weight down and don't smoke. Other studies point to alcohol consumption as a probable factor in the development of breast cancer.[5] Certainly, most doctors agree that excessive drinking is not good for any aspect of your health.

Obviously the choice is yours. But if you decide to drink you should know the risks and practice moderation – which is crucial if you wish to preserve your health. So what are the risks? And what is moderation?

Risks

- Alcohol can cause obesity and high blood pressure

- Even moderate drinking during pregnancy can cause low birth weight and premature birth. Heavy drinking can cause deformity, blindness, retardation and heart problems.

- Alcohol taken with aspirin can cause abnormalities in the way your blood clots.

- Women may experience menstrual or gynecological disorders from moderate to heavy drinking. Use of the contraceptive pill may, for some women, compound this effect.

- Men and women who smoke, overeat or are overweight and who also drink will increase their risk of illness – of any sort – from this combination. Heart and circulatory disease is especially likely.

Moderate Drinking

- Women – consume *no more* than two to three units of alcohol, two to three times in a week

- Men – consume *no more* than four to six units of alcohol, two to three times in a week

- All drinkers – have three or four drink-free days in each week

- All drinks should be consumed slowly: one unit per hour, one unit at a time, preferably accompanied by food

One unit of alcohol equals:

- one-half pint of beer

- one measure of spirit

- one glass of wine

- 1 small glass of sherry

- 1 glass of vermouth or aperitif

A final caution: heavy drinking is *definitely* damaging to the heart, liver, stomach and brain. Avoid it!

OBESITY

Today, over thirty-four million Americans are so fat as to be considered 'obese' – that's one in every five adults. In Britain, the government's COMA Report[6] revealed that there has been a progressive increase in the average weight of adults since the war until – currently – more than 40 per cent of middle-aged men and women are overweight. This figure does not include children. Currently, between 50 and 80 per cent of British children are thought to be overweight and underactive – these children are the obese adults of the future. Obesity is linked to the development of many serious illnesses, but in particular, high blood cholesterol levels occur *more than twice as often* in the overweight than in the non-overweight.

In fact, it seems likely that being overweight by only 10 per cent can greatly increase your risk of death from coronary heart disease, and this is especially likely in young men. Diabetes, hypertension and an increased level of blood cholesterol are all more likely to happen to you if you are overweight, and particularly if you have been overweight since childhood.

Many people learn to be obese as children and their bodies simply remain obese for the rest of their lives. This is hardly surprising when, as suggested by one healthcare group[7], nearly one-third of school children eat a lunch-time diet that is so high in fat it virtually *guarantees* they will suffer obesity and raised serum cholesterol levels later in life. Little wonder when, as the Department of Health's own survey (of the effects of abolishing school meals nutrition standards in 1980) has shown, four out of five children are eating an 'unhealthy' diet, including too much saturated fat and too few essential nutrients. They eat more chips, crisps, and other potato products than any other single food, and three times more chips, cakes, and biscuits than the average household.

Many voices have been raised in protest against the unhealthy diet that our children are eating, but not enough positive action seems to emerge. The 95,000-strong Assistant Masters and Mistresses Association produced a report which heavily criticised nutritional standards.[8] 'There is now ample evidence that our national eating habits are unhealthy', it said, 'and it could be that education authorities, however accidentally, are reinforcing bad eating habits which children should be educated out of, not encouraged to carry over into the home.'

What is the answer to this epidemic of fatties? Ultimately, the root of the problem may lie with governments and food manufacturers, and it is perhaps only through developments in public policy that this crisis may be tackled. The fact is, most of us have a well-established diet and lifestyle by the time we're ten years old, and these patterns are often difficult or impossible to change in later life. If we've been taught bad eating habits, then we'll probably go on eating badly all our lives. And if we have been sedentary much of our childhood, we are likely to lead a sedentary lifestyle in adulthood, predisposing us to a wide range of physical and social problems. Sadly, today's children are underactive when compared with the children of earlier generations – especially so considering they have more calories to burn off. Their sedentary lifestyle comprises up to 20 hours spent watching television per week and greatly reduced numbers of hours spent in sports and games. Part of the blame for establishing an unhealthy diet and lifestyle early in life has to be go to those parents who often say 'We'll let our children decide what they want to eat for themselves, when they are older'. Do they think that *any* standards they present to their children are, in some way, impositions and mean deprivation? The real deprivation is this: the future of these children, their health and happiness, is in jeopardy because people who are overweight are more prone to depression, lack of confidence, guilt and frustration, and are often victims of a social prejudice that labels them as 'unattractive', 'greedy' or 'weak-willed'. They are also much more likely to suffer from cancer, hypertension and heart disease.

How have we got into this terrible predicament? Well it seems we are simply taking too much of a 'good' thing and not enough of what *will* do us good.

Our food, the substance which *should* fill us with health and energy, seems to be turning us into diseased blobs who display little of the enthusiasm for activity that most other living creatures do. A diet high in fat is particularly to blame. The average person's intake of fat is approximately 40 per cent of their total calorie intake. Yet most medical recommendations[9] state that a *maximum* of 30 per cent is ideal. Set this against the fact that two-thirds of men and four-fifths of women don't exercise and, presto, there's big trouble in store. On the principle that what goes in must go somewhere, when we eat too much and exercise too little we s p r e a d ! !

The physical, mental and emotional consequences of obesity are clearly very serious indeed. And together they can act to immobilize you and prevent you from taking any corrective action. Yet that is precisely what you must do if you wish to break this vicious cycle. To reduce your weight you must commit yourself to making a gradual but permanent change in your diet and lifestyle. There really is no other way.

For most people, this means losing about 0.7 to 0.9 kg (1.5 to 2 lbs) a week on a diet of about 1,500 calories a day for women and 2,000 calories a day for men. This is a gradual, but effective, approach to weight loss. 'Starvation' diets consisting of much lower calorie intakes may not be safe, and in any case, the most sensible approach to weight loss is to begin with a medical check-up to make certain that you have no special health problems.

You may estimate your degree of overweight by comparing your weight to that recommended for your height, gender and frame size (see the tables in the A-Z section). Generally, a 5 per cent excess implies that you are moderately overweight. Up to a 10 per cent excess means that you are overweight. Between 10 and 15 per cent excess is very overweight. Over 20 per cent excess weight above the ideal is considered obese.

If you are a young man who should weigh a maximum of 160 pounds (72.6 kilograms), for instance, but you in fact weigh 176 pounds (80 kilograms), then you are 10 per cent over your ideal weight (10 per cent of 160 is 16 pounds). This excess weight, however insignificant it may seem to you, *will increase your risk of coronary heart disease by approximately 30 per cent*.[10] This is because being overweight increases your likelihood of suffering high blood pressure and raised blood cholesterol levels. In fact, if you are overweight, you are between three and six times more likely to have high blood pressure and twice as likely to have raised blood cholesterol. Both of these disorders are directly responsible for many cases of cardiovascular disease.

The above example refers specifically to men, but don't think that being a woman offers you complete protection from cardiovascular disease. It is true that, for most women, risk of coronary heart disease is well below the risk to men for most of a woman's life. Her risk increases sharply after the age of 50 however and, with that knowledge, many women may have relaxed into obesity. Don't! The incidence in women of death from coronary heart disease is rising – mostly due to an increase in women smokers, it's true. But it now seems almost certain[11] that women who carry excess weight, especially around their waist in what has been called a 'masculine' manner, run a higher risk of cardiovascular disease than slim women – no matter what their age.

Your risk can be reduced, however. Obviously if you smoke or drink large quantities of alcohol your risk from cardiovascular disease will decrease when you control these habits. Beyond that, it is imperative that you reduce your weight if you exceed the recommended limits by 5 per cent or more. Here is what we recommend:

- First, talk to your doctor and discuss the amount you have to lose. He or she may have advice or encouragement that you find particularly useful to your own circumstances. You can also put your mind at rest concerning any possible health concerns you have.

- Begin an exercise programme (see the Exercise section in this chapter) that will give you three or four thirty-minute sessions each week. Choose exercise that you can succeed at and enjoy. Talk your ideas through with your GP, especially if you are very overweight.

- Begin a change of diet, such as the diet on which this book is based, which will reduce your intake of fat and excess calories.

- Eat at least three times per day so your body doesn't feel starved. Many people try to lose weight by fasting but, with a few food exceptions, *what* you eat is far more important to your health and eventual weight than how much you eat.

- Eat a high-carbohydrate diet so that 60 to 70 per cent of your food comes from whole grains, fruits, vegetables, beans, pulses and seeds. Prepare these without oils or salt.

Now stick with it! You already know that changing your shape and size can change your life. Why not go ahead and change your life – you will naturally change your shape and size as a result.

SMOKING

There is no doubt that smoking causes cardiovascular disease. In addition, smoking compounds the unhealthy effects of obesity, lack of exercise, high blood pressure and high levels of cholesterol so that, if you smoke, your total risk from cardiovascular disease is greatly increased.

Here is how smoking increases your risk:

- Smoking creates *twice* the risk of having a heart attack compared to non-smokers

- Smoking *plus* high blood pressure *and* high blood cholesterol level creates *eight times* the risk of having a fatal heart attack compared to non-smokers

- Heavy smoking (25 or more cigarettes per day) in men under the age of 45 creates *15 times* the risk of having a fatal heart attack compared to non-smokers

- Women who smoke and take the contraceptive pill increase their risk of suffering ill-effects from this medication. Women who smoke and are over 35 years of age or overweight should stop smoking and consider changing their method of contraception. All women using the contraceptive pill should have their blood pressure checked regularly.

   Note: The contraceptive pill is being continually altered in its strength and precise formulation and it is therefore likely that a change in the type of pill used will change the level of risk. It is also possible that new developments will completely or significantly reduce the risk associated with it. Discuss any queries you might have regarding the pill you take with your doctor.

- Eight out of ten deaths from cardiovascular disease in young men are thought to be caused by smoking.

In chronic smokers the oxygen-carrying capacity of red blood cells can be reduced by 15 per cent. The reason is that cigarette smoke contains carbon monoxide which combines with the haemoglobin in your red blood cells to form a compound called carboxy-haemoglobin. Carboxy-haemoglobin increases the permeability, or openness, of your artery walls so that more cholesterol is able to adhere to them. This is the beginning of atherosclerosis and immediately increases your risk of heart attack.

If you are a smoker, your blood contains a poison that causes your arteries to narrow and your heart to work harder. In addition, nicotine, the addictive substance in tobacco, stimulates your nerves so that they constrict your blood vessels. This forces your heart to work *even harder* and faster in order to keep your blood circulating. Smoking creates ideal conditions in which to develop hypertension, atherosclerosis and, eventually, heart attack and death. That is without a mention of lung, throat and respiratory diseases – including cancer.

It really doesn't make sense to carry on smoking, does it? Especially when you realise that when you do stop smoking, your risk of suffering a fatal heart attack will begin to decline *immediately*. And within five to ten years you will have the same level of risk as a life-long non-smoker.

STRESS

Stress is a reaction to a situation, a person, an event. Anything can cause stress, anything can trigger a stressful response. Stress creates a sense of urgency which, though possibly arising from an emotional or mental reaction, nevertheless has physical symptoms too. Here is what happens:

When you feel stressful, your adrenals make a hormone called adrenaline which prepares your body for immediate hard work and urgent action. This is a physical response – often called the 'fight or flight' response – which is an inheritance from our ancestors who used it to deal with dangerous situations. The situations in which we live are significantly different from theirs, but the same mechanisms are at work in our stressful responses.

During stress your body needs additional oxygen in order to help you either beat the problem or beat a fast retreat (fight or flight). To supply this oxygen, your heart beats faster and harder, your blood pressure rises and your rate of breathing increases. You also begin to perspire, anticipating the need to keep cool during your efforts!

To give you the instant energy you will need to fight or flee, your liver gets the stress message and triggers the release of fats and sugars directly into your bloodstream. This set of responses is an excellent means of ensuring self-preservation and will occur even when the stressful situation is left unresolved. In fact, much of our modern experience of stress is because we cannot resolve problems in the simple 'fight or flight' way. We have conditioned ourselves *not* to fight or flee, but to resolve our problems in a more 'civilised' manner. Unfortunately, our bodies haven't got the message yet.

Your body will react to stress in this age-old manner no matter how your social training tells you to respond. So, while you might *appear* cool, calm and collected, your body is still sweating and speeding – a case of 'all revved up and nowhere to go'. Those extra fats released by your liver, for instance, if not used for energy are left circulating in your bloodstream until they become available to line the arteries as atheroma, the stuff of atherosclerosis. Other manifestations of stress are more apparent, and *very* common. They include: asthma, eczema, headache, hostility, indigestion and ulcers.

Psychological and emotional stress are now known to be important contributing factors in cardiovascular disease. It has been shown that people with heart disease can lower their risk of future cardiac events by more than 70 per cent if they learn to manage stress. Epidemiological research has identified specific psychosocial risk factors, such as hostility, lack of social support and job strain, that are associated either with developing the disease or contributing to a worse prognosis once the disease has been diagnosed. Any of these influences could prove fatal in an individual who already has elevated cardiovascular risk factors. Here are some suggestions to start reducing the stress in your life:

• Raise your stress threshold. Decide, and then train yourself, to become stressful only after all other possibilities have been considered.

There really are dozens of options, apart from stress, including:

(a) laughing
(b) crying
(c) walking away from the problem
(d) making an appointment to solve the problem later today or this week
(e) asking someone else to solve it
(f) asking someone to share it with you
(g) telling the perpetrator of it to go elsewhere

- Change the way you react to the stress in your life. If you currently internalize it, why not try hitting cushions instead! Or if you are a person who goes red with rage but still doesn't feel de-stressed, why not try some rhythmic breathing routines to expel the demon from your system. Here is the most basic breathing pattern for this purpose:

(a) take one long, deep breath in
(b) hold it for three seconds
(c) then let the breath out slowly and, if you like, noisily.
(d) repeat this five to ten times – usually long enough to stop the stress reaction from developing fully.

- Take a nap! Researchers from the University of Athens, in Greece, studied people at risk from coronary heart disease and found that a half-hour nap in the afternoon could reduce their risk of heart attack by as much as 30 per cent. Elsewhere, scientists are 'discovering' what many people have known for ages – that holding and stroking a warm, furry animal soothes your *human* cares away too. In fact, it is possible that this gentle, sharing activity actually slows the heart beat and lowers blood pressure. What more encouragement do you need?

- Exercise combines movement, breathing, relaxation and the personal space and time for private contemplation. Just 20–30 minutes per day seems to dissolve worries, muscular tensions and those dreadful headaches that appear out of nowhere and are surely stress induced. See the Exercise entry that follows.

EXERCISE

When the computer company IBM surveyed the health of its UK employees, it found that four fifths of them were classified as 'unfit', and 32 per cent of them had a significant risk of heart disease due to high cholesterol levels in their blood.[12] 'They are not just a bunch of obese slobs', said a medical officer. In fact, IBM's employees tend to live longer than the national average. 'It raises the question,' said the medical officer, 'of what the others are like if these are the results from a relatively healthy company.'

The survey found that 79 per cent of men, and 75 per cent of women, were obese according to standard medical definitions. On an overall measure, 83 per cent of men and 76 per cent of women aged 25 to 44 were found to be unfit. Only six per cent of men and 10.8 per cent of women were judged 'very fit'.

IBM paid for the cost of the health screening programme (about £70 per employee) and is also investing a large sum in healthcare facilities, including running tracks, gymnasiums and healthcare experts. Now if a company such as IBM is prepared to invest considerable sums of money in its employees health – presumably in order to keep them as productive as possible – shouldn't you also consider investing a little time and perhaps money in your own body? After all, an employee can always be replaced, but your body is the only one you're ever likely to be given.

If you can move and breathe and control your posture, then you can exercise, because exercise is only a particular way of combining movement and breath and posture. Virtually every moving activity you engage in can become an exercise if you add a special attention to detail and a special change in attitude. These special additions can be summarised as:

- an awareness of what is correct and appropriate exercise for you

- an eye for opportunities to improve your movement, posture and breath

- a willingness to learn and to achieve exercise skills

- an attitude of care towards your body

For example, walking your dog twice a day can be a chore which brings you slouching and grumbling out into the open air. Or it can be transformed into an opportunity to get a regular, brisk walk that will increase the strength of your heart and lungs, improve your stamina, muscle tone and possibly the health of your skin. It may also enable you to meet people or observe things you would otherwise have missed. Put like that, it sounds appealing, doesn't it? Yet the majority of us simply do not make the most of such opportunities.

An American study[13] found that 87 per cent of women and 68 per cent of men in their mid-forties do not exercise regularly. Here in the United Kingdom, a report[14] on the health of women showed that fewer than 20 per cent of women over the age of 19 take regular exercise, even though most women know that regular exercise will benefit their health. This report was funded by the Association of the British Pharmaceutical Industry who no doubt want to know just how many of us will be in need of medication for cardiovascular ills in the near future. Quite a few, it seems.

That same American study also found that men and women who are not physically fit have nearly three times the risk of dying from heart disease compared to those who are fit. The report states that 'a lower level of physical fitness is associated with a higher risk of death from coronary heart disease and cardiovascular disease'. Apparently, moderate exercise can reduce this risk. A 30-minute exercise session, three times per week will get you fit and, in the words of Dr Basil Rifkind of the National Heart Lung and Blood Institute, which funded the study, 'fitness is protective against cardiovascular disease'.

How is fitness protective? The American study claims that both blood pressure and blood cholesterol levels drop in subjects who follow a fitness programme. In addition, this and many other studies show that regular exercise aids in weight control and stress management, both of which influence cardiovascular health. And exercise that challenges your heart and lungs, often called stamina or aerobic exercise, can literally strengthen the heart muscle and improve the efficiency with which you take in and circulate oxygen.

Regular exercise benefits the cardiovascular system by:

- reducing blood pressure

- reducing levels of cholesterol in the blood

- toning muscles tissue – including heart muscle

- increasing the efficiency of the heart at all times

- keeping the arteries flexible

- improving circulation and heart rate

- reducing stress

- reducing depression, aggression and hostility

These studies don't mention the other, more general, benefits of regular exercise which have been observed from ancient times. Most forms of exercise have the ability to reduce feelings of tension, both mental and muscular, and gently alter the mood so that you feel uplifted and alert a few minutes into your programme. And odd though it may seem, exercise can reduce fatigue. It seems that the energy you expend somehow returns to you in double quantity! Many people also claim an improvement in their balance, co-ordination and confidence after they have exercised for a few weeks, and, of course, many 'insignificant' aches and pains disappear once you begin to give your body the exercise it was designed to enjoy. Headaches, stiffness, sore joints and muscles, even cold toes and fingers can become ailments of the past.

Hopefully, we have convinced you of the hazards of not exercising, as well as the benefits coming if you do. The next step is to find an exercise programme that will suit you – your schedule, your environment, your age and interests. This is easier when you outline what you want in your programme. Here are a few examples:

- a group exercise such as a game or class *or* a solitary exercise

- a morning-only, daytime-only, evening-only, etc. exercise session

- an exercise that is silent *or* accompanied by rhythmic music

- exercise that involves a little expense, to keep you motivated

- exercise that is free except for the clothes you will wear

- a strict routine *or* a lot of variety

- three or four seasonal exercises *or* one year-round exercise

Do you get the idea? There are many more options that could be added to this list, but we're sure you will discover your own preferences once you give it a bit of thought. We must stress, however, that exercise is most effective when it is an integral part of your life, so that you feel something important is missing when you do *not* exercise. For this reason alone, it is best that the exercise programme you select is pleasurable.

Many people start to exercise regularly but then something happens which gets them out of the routine. In fact, this has probably happened to even the most committed athletes, at some time or other. The difference is, the committed people start up again, but the rest of us say something like 'I just can't find the time any longer'. We found our reply in an old quip which states: 'if you don't have time for exercise, you'll certainly have time for illness.'

We urge you to pick two or three types of exercise and practice them on a rota basis, to accommodate sudden changes in your schedule or circumstances. For instance, if you take up jogging but can't stand jogging in the rain, you could skip rope in your front room on the mornings that it rains. Similarly, you can cycle indoors all the winter, walk spring and autumn and swim in the summer. And if the babysitter doesn't turn up on the day you are scheduled to go swimming, you can spend 20 minutes on the rowing machine or take to that skip rope again.

Here is a summary of essential considerations when planning or beginning an exercise programme:

Pick exercises that cause:

- the muscles to both stretch and contract
- the joints to move
- the brain to deal with co-ordination
- the lungs to open for deep breathing
- the heart to pump strongly and regularly

Exercise a minimum of:

- three times each week
- 30 minutes per session

Each 30 minute session includes:

- warm-up movements
- the exercise of your choice
- cool-down movements

Exercise to the point where:

- you become *slightly* breathless
- but are always able to speak clearly

Do NOT exercise if:

- you are ill
- you are injured
- you are undernourished
- you are *very* tired, physically, mentally or emotionally
- you have already exercised today
- you have a medical condition which requires a doctor's advice – get his or her opinion on the exercise programme you wish to follow

Here are a selection of activities that can provide effective exercise for your heart and lungs. Please follow the guidelines just listed when performing any of these exercises. The summary for each exercise follows the format:

- Where or how is it done?

- How long is it done for?

- Why or for whom is it especially beneficial?

- What are its special attractions?

- What are the clothing requirements?

- What are the drawbacks or disadvantages?

Cycling

- indoors on a stationary bicycle *or* outdoors on a geared bicycle

- minimum of 20 minutes without stopping

- especially good for the elderly or those with hip or back problems

- little likelihood of injury to muscle, tendon, ligament, etc.

- wear non-chafe clothing and a helmet for outdoor cycling

- outdoor cyclists should plan a safe, non-stop route with few hills

Dancing

- ballroom, rock 'n roll, disco, folk, Scottish country or any other

- minimum of 12 minutes without a complete break

- very social and pleasant for those who like music and rhythm

- an attractive activity which makes one feel competent and controlled

- wear flat, comfortable shoes to avoid foot injury

- dance with a partner who can also dance for 12 minutes!

Games

- volleyball, squash, tennis, golf or similar

- minimum of 30 minutes as these are usually stop–start activities

- especially good for those who like to compete or follow a set of rules

- social yet with a chance for individual accomplishment and skill

- wear shoes and clothing suited to the game, allowing free movement

- play with a partner who will challenge you, but not too much

Jarming

- sitting in a chair and 'jogging' with your arms
- minimum of 15 minutes without stopping
- particularly for those who are elderly or in any way infirm
- achieves cardio-respiratory goals safely and effectively
- may be performed to rhythmic music
- maintain a size and pace of 'jarm' that will allow adequate breath

Jogging

- in an indoor court *or* outdoors on track or field
- minimum of 15 minutes without stopping
- for those who are able to exercise strenuously without pain
- may be social or solitary with scope for competition if desired
- select very supportive shoes and non-chafe clothing
- weather, dogs and mud are always hazards

Keep Fit

- in a class or at home using an audio cassette or video tape
- minimum of 30 minutes
- for a complete fitness programme of stretch, strength and mobility
- for all ages; classes are usually very social and full of variety
- wear loose or stretchy clothing
- make sure your teacher is qualified and gives you personal attention

Rowing

- on an indoor machine or join an outdoor rowing club!
- minimum of 15 minutes without stopping
- an excellent way to exercise the whole body
- for all ages; having particular effect on arms, legs, back and abdomen
- wear minimum, non-chafe clothing
- indoors, select a machine with a sliding seat

Skiing or Skating

- cross-country skiing or ice or roller skating
- minimum of 20 minutes without stopping

- all the benefits of running or jogging, without trauma in the joints
- mostly lower-body exercise, though arm movement improves breathing
- wear stretchy, non-chafe clothing and appropriate skis or skates
- skiing is seasonal, and you need to find rink space for skating

Swimming

- in this country, usually an indoor exercise
- minimum of 20 minutes without stopping
- excellent to loosen joints and muscles and improve heart and lungs
- a variety of strokes ensure the majority of joints and muscles are used
- wear minimum clothing
- finding a clean, uncrowded pool is sometimes difficult

Walking

- an anywhere, anytime activity
- minimum of 20 minutes without stopping
- an excellent exercise for heart, lungs, back and lower body
- for all ages; a no-trauma way to travel, entertain yourself or exercise
- wear high-quality supportive shoes
- it is necessary to maintain a brisk pace for maximum benefit

Weight Training

- using a multi-gym or poly-gym arrangement in a sports centre
- aim for 20–30 minutes of sustained training
- improves strength, muscle tone and posture in specific body parts
- for all ages; provides an opportunity to become more physically aware
- wear supportive shoes and loose or stretchy clothing
- a qualified coach is essential in your first month of training

Yoga

- at home from memory or at a class run by a certified teacher
- most classes last at least 1 hour, some up to 2½ hours
- increases your mobility, suppleness, posture and improves breathing

- for all ages; also gives you time and mental space to contemplate

- wear loose or stretchy clothing and have an extra layer at hand

- it can take time to find the teacher and type of yoga class that suit you

PSYCHOLOGICAL ADJUSTMENT

Any change in your lifestyle, even one that you invite, is bound to require a degree of effort on your part. In all of the aspects of lifestyle just discussed, most of the emphasis was placed on physical changes – on how this or that will affect your body – and physical effort. Certainly much of what we discuss and recommend in this book has physical consequences, but we feel it is important to mention the psychological – the mental and emotional – effort and changes that can also occur.

It is a fact that when you change your diet, your sleeping habits, your level of fitness or any of the other influences mentioned, you automatically alter your inner self too. When your body feels better, for instance, your outlook improves. And the reverse is also true: when you improve your outlook, you usually feel better physically. It seems sensible then, to use this link between your body and your inner self to help make the change to a healthy lifestyle more effective and more pleasureable.

We have devised a simple check-list which will help you recognize the role your inner self can assume during your change to a state of low-cholesterol good health.

- *Learn the facts* – give your brain some work to do while your body is making changes to diet, drinking and exercise habits. Read and listen to what you can about each subject so that you become familiar with the terminology and the most current research.

- *Learn to listen* – each physical change affects you mentally and emotionally, if you just listen to your feelings. Sometimes long-standing issues are resolved by dropping alcohol, cigarettes or obesity from your life. When you have seen this happen once, you are more likely to believe it can happen again.

- *Learn to choose* – sometimes you need to make one change at a time in order to change successfully. There is nothing wrong in this. In fact, many people find the change is more likely to be permanent if it is done one step at a time. It is up to you to choose which step to take first... and second, and third...

- *Learn to plan* – when you at last spring into action, it is important to have a plan. Your inner self is especially good at these. Write down the action you will be taking, when you will start and what your goals are. Then pin it to your wall and go!

- *Learn to forgive* – when you make a mistake, lose your way or just plain turn your back on the whole thing you commit a very human act. But don't let yourself fail just because of that! Forgive yourself and then start up again, now!

- *Learn to reward* – when you achieve a goal, however small, treat yourself to praise and a present. You deserve it.

- *Learn to take charge* – the decisions and junctures in your life are yours to determine for yourself. Take possession of and responsibility for your life, your body, your thoughts and feelings. Accept your life as your own and enjoy even those elements of life over which you have no control. Taking charge leaves you in a position to *create* change and opportunity and to determine the course your life will take.

CHECKING YOUR CHOLESTEROL LEVEL

Before we outline the very practical dietary steps which you may take to reduce your risk of cardiovascular disease, you should arrange to have your cholesterol level and your blood pressure checked by your doctor. If you have a family history of heart or vascular disease, if you smoke or are obviously overweight then you become a member of the 'high risk group' as far as cardiovascular disease is concerned. Your risk of suffering heart attack, for instance, is considered greater than in someone who does not display these obvious signs of risk.

However, many people do not visit their doctor very often or may not feel that they fall into these high-risk categories. Nevertheless, they may be at great risk! Both blood pressure and cholesterol are renowned for rising gradually and 'silently' to dangerously high levels – without you knowing anything about it until something drastic happens.

The fact is that *most* of us in this country are at significant risk from cardiovascular disease. Approximately 60 per cent of us have cholesterol levels which place us in the high risk category.[15] We know *why* so many of us fall into the high risk category, but we have done little about it – perhaps because poor diet, obesity, smoking and general ill-health has become 'normal' to us. What a state!

We are certain that you will find yourself interested in and motivated towards a healthier diet and lifestyle if you simply know these two basic facts about your own health. Here's what to do:

Ring your doctor's surgery (today!) and make an appointment. Tell the receptionist that you want to have your cholesterol level measured and your blood pressure checked. It's that easy. No one will ask you embarrassing questions over the phone. Then just turn up and roll up (your sleeve!).

You should ask the receptionist, when you make the appointment, whether the doctor will want you to fast or not. Many doctors feel that your triglycerides might as well be measured at the same time and, for this test, you have to fast for a period of approximately 16 hours. This usually means that you don't eat anything after 8 o'clock the evening before your appointment and nothing during the morning on the day of your appointment.

A growing number of health centres in this country are acquiring a machine which is able to give a fairly immediate cholesterol level measurement just by taking a finger-prick blood sample. If you attend one of these centres, you can get your results within a few minutes of shedding that drop of blood. On the other hand, if you have a standard blood sample taken from your arm you could have to wait up to ten or fourteen days before the results come through to your doctor. This means that you will need to make another appointment to learn the results. And you *must* learn the results!

When you attend your second appointment, ask your doctor to write down your blood cholesterol level on a slip of paper for you. If your triglycerides were measured, ask for that result to be noted down as well. It is very important that you know these figures. When your doctor sees your interest, he or she may offer you advice on diet or lifestyle. Take this opportunity to discuss the implications of your cholesterol level and to inform your doctor that you intend to try reducing your blood cholesterol level through diet, if you haven't informed them already.

How do you interpret the numbers when they arrive? Obviously, this is primarily a matter for your doctor. Your doctor must interpret your cholesterol numbers based on other risk factors. For your interest, we show below broad guidelines used by the National Cholesterol Education Program, and endorsed by the American Heart Association. There are two ways of expressing cholesterol levels: as millimoles per litre (Mmols) which is used in the UK, and as milligrams per deciliter of blood (mg/dL) which is used in America. Milligrams per deciliter can be converted to millimoles per litre by dividing by 38.66. Knowing your total blood cholesterol level is an important first step in determining your risk for heart disease. However, a critical second step is knowing your HDL or 'good' cholesterol level.

Total cholesterol less than 200 mg/dL (5.2 Mmols) *and* HDL 35 mg/dL (1 Mmols) or higher

- Unless you have other risk factors for heart disease, your chance of heart attack is relatively low.

- It is still a good idea to eat a low-saturated-fat, low-cholesterol diet and stay physically active to help maintain a desirable cholesterol level.

- You should have your cholesterol levels rechecked within 5 years or at your next physical examination.

Total cholesterol less than 200 mg/dL (5.2 Mmols) *and* HDL less than 35 mg/dL (1 Mmols)

- You should have your LDL ('bad' cholesterol) level checked. Your doctor will interpret these numbers for you and tell you when to have your cholesterol levels rechecked.

- Work with your doctor to control any other risk factors you have.

- Take steps to modify your diet and increase your physical activity to reduce your risk.

Total cholesterol 200 to 239 (5.2 – 6.2 Mmols), HDL 35 mg/dL (1 Mmols) or higher *and* fewer than 2 risk factors

- You may have twice the risk of heart disease as people whose levels are less than 200.

- Work with your doctor to control any other risk factors you have

- Have your cholesterol levels rechecked in 1–2 years.

- Take steps to modify your diet and increase your physical activity to reduce your risk. Not every person whose cholesterol level is in the 200 to 239 range is at increased risk.

Total cholesterol 200 to 239 (5.2 – 6.2 Mmols), HDL less than 35 mg/dL (1 Mmols) or 2 or more risk factors

- You may have twice the risk of heart disease as people whose levels are less than 200.

- You should have your LDL ('bad' cholesterol) level checked. Your doctor will interpret these numbers for you and tell you when to have your cholesterol levels rechecked.

- Work with your doctor to control any other risk factors you have.

- Take steps to modify your diet and increase your physical activity to reduce your risk.

Cholesterol 240 (6.2 Mmols) and above

- Your risk of heart disease may be substantially high.

- You need to have your LDL ('bad' cholesterol) level checked. Your doctor will interpret these numbers for you and tell you when to have your cholesterol levels rechecked.

- Have your doctor test you for other risk factors. Ask for advice on how to help reduce your risk.

Men between the ages of 40 and 59 can also answer the following questionnaire:[16]

1 How many years have you smoked? Multiply this by 7.5	
2 What is your systolic* blood pressure? Multiply this by 4.5	
3 Has a doctor ever diagnosed angina or a heart attack? If yes, add 265	
4 Has a doctor ever diagnosed diabetes? If yes, add 150	
5 Do you have angina (chest pains while walking uphill or hurrying)? If yes, add 150	
6 Have your parents had heart trouble? If yes, add 50	
TOTAL SCORE	

SCORE	Risk of heart attack within 5 years
Over 1000	1 in 10
Over 890	1 in 30
Over 805	1 in 40
Over 690	1 in 100
Over 625	1 in 250

* Systolic blood pressure is the increased pressure which occurs with each beat of the heart, and is the higher of the two figures given when your blood pressure is taken.

THE INSIDE GUIDE TO CUTTING YOUR CHOLESTEROL

The comprehensive listing of foods in *The Complete Cholesterol Counter* shows you how to quickly and easily compare one food with another, with the aim of choosing the food which is lower in fat and cholesterol. However, canny cholesterol counters know that certain 'magic' foods can actually have a beneficial effect on your cholesterol level, too. Here's a briefing:

SOLUBLE FIBRE IS THE SECRET

There can hardly be a person left alive who hasn't heard of the benefits of eating a diet rich in fibre. Even so, some people still don't seem to have got the message – or at any rate, aren't acting upon it. In Britain alone, it is estimated by those people who make it their business to know about these things that four out of every ten people suffer from constipation, and two out of every ten suffer so severely that they have to use laxatives frequently. And yet, much of this heaving and straining could probably be prevented if they only ate a diet that was higher in natural forms of fibre!

One of the earliest advocates of the advantages of eating more natural fibre was Dr Denis Burkitt, who undertook much pioneering work in this area, and is recognized as one of the world's leading authorities on the subject. He once compared the diets of several different groups of people, ranging from rural Africans through to enlisted naval seamen, and found a remarkable difference in the so-called 'transit time' (i.e. the average time it took for food to pass all the way through their bodies, from one end to the other). For rural Africans, and other groups such as vegetarians who ate a naturally high-fibre, high complex carbohydrate diet, the average transit time was in the region of 36 hours. But for those eating a low-fibre, high-fat diet (such as the seamen) the transit time was well over 80 hours!

Apart from the obvious discomfort of constipation, this sort of transit time is unhealthy because it keeps toxins (including possible carcinogens) trapped inside the body long after they should have been expelled. But this isn't the only benefit that comes from eating a higher fibre diet. We asked Dr Burkitt to explain:

> There are basically two types of fibre, insoluble fibre and water-soluble fibre. The classic insoluble fibre is wheat fibre, with bran and all the bran products. That is highly effective for combating constipation, increasing stool weight, and and preventing things like haemorrhoids and diverticular diseases. Its very good for the guts. But it does almost nothing for what we call the 'metabolic diseases' associated with lack of fibre, particularly diabetes, and coronary heart disease. Now soluble fibre, on the other hand, does have an effect on combating constipation, but it *also* has an effect on lowering raised serum lipid [i.e. fats in your blood] levels, and also on glucose tolerance, so that it has a profoundly beneficial effect on diabetes. Now, as to *how* this fibre works in lowering the blood lipids, there are many suggestions. It has effects on bile acids and so on, but the main way in which soluble fibre is beneficial for diabetes is that it enormously slows down the absorption of energy from the gut. So instead of all the energy being absorbed, as it would be in sugar products, if you have a high-fibre product it makes the intestinal content into a sort of a gel, so that the energy is only absorbed into the circulation very slowly, and so you don't have great and sudden demands on insulin, and so on.

From what Dr Burkitt says, you can see that *soluble* fibre is the sort to choose if you want to use it to lower your blood cholesterol level. But before you get too excited and eat all the soluble fibre within grabbing range, it is important to understand that only *certain forms* of soluble fibre seem to have this cholesterol-lowering effect. Not all soluble fibre seems to work like this. Unfortunately, some books and magazine articles don't make this sufficiently clear, and can leave you with the impression that *any* kind of soluble fibre should lower your cholesterol level. To try and understand more about this effect, we spoke to another world-recognized expert in his field, Dr David Southgate, a scientist who has had a method of dietary fibre analysis named after him – the 'Southgate Method'. This is what he told us:

> The first thing to understand, of course, is that not all soluble

fibres have this effect. It looks as if the effect is related to the physical properties of the soluble fibre, and it seems as though you need a soluble fibre that produces a *viscous* [i.e. gluey] solution. A lot of the soluble materials in plant cell walls do produce viscous solutions, like pectin, guar gum and oat gum – they thicken the solution up and make it more viscous.

Now, as for the mechanism whereby they do this, that's not really known for certain at the present time. But there are two theories as to how it might work. One is that it affects cholesterol metabolism by binding bile salts. Bile salts are cholesterol derivatives, and if you bind bile salts in the gut, you will prevent them from being re-absorbed lower down, thus affecting the metabolism of cholesterol in the liver.

They may in fact work in that way, but there's no really clear evidence that some fibres do cause an increased excretion of bile salts and some don't. The other possible way that viscous, soluble fibres affect serum cholesterol is that these viscous materials can affect the absorption of *many* nutrients – they tend to slow the process of absorption down. In the case of fats and cholesterol it may lower the overall rate of absorption of cholesterol. By partially interfering with this process, it may produce its effect that way.

It's not a simple story by any means. I think in the beginning, people hoped that it would be, but it doesn't look as if it is. In the whole area of dietary fibre research, there's always the added complication that most high-carbohydrate diets also tend to be low-fat diets as well. So some of the effects of a high-fibre diet may be a combination of the effects of not just eating more fibre, but also of lowering fat intake. Dietary fibre is such a complex mixture of different types of material, with different physical properties, that it's very difficult to generalise.

So although we don't yet know for certain precisely how viscous, soluble fibre manages to lower blood cholesterol, that really isn't so important. What we do know is that it *does seem to work*, and – equally importantly – a number of cheap and easy to obtain foodstuffs seem to contain important amounts of it.

SOME GOOD SOURCES OF SOLUBLE FIBRE

Food	Grams of soluble fibre in 100g
Broccoli, frozen	13.36
Carrots, raw	11.32
Brussels sprouts, frozen	10.86
Cauliflower, frozen	8.92
Cabbage, raw	8.68
Spinach, frozen	6.56

OATS – THE GERM OF A GOOD IDEA

It was observed at least as long ago as 1963 that oats could have a cholesterol-lowering effect. However, it was only in recent years that, as part of the quest for the answer to coronary heart disease, scientists have again re-examined this humble and inexpensive product. Today, many experiments have shown that oat bran can and does act to significantly lower blood cholesterol. Here are the results of some recent, highly encouraging studies:

Researchers at the University of California, Irvine, asked test subjects to eat two oat bran muffins a day over a month-long period. The results showed that an average drop in total blood cholesterol of just over 5 per cent, and a nearly 9 per cent reduction in LDL (low density lipoprotein). There was also an 8 per cent cut in triglycerides.

A report published in Scandinavia showed that a low-fat, low-cholesterol diet managed to reduce the blood cholesterol level of its subjects by 20 per cent. When foods containing soluble fibre (e.g. pulses, oats, fruits and vegetables) were added to the diet, an additional fall of 10 per cent serum cholesterol was observed.[17]

When a group of 18 healthy volunteers agreed to add either 23 grams of wheat bran or one 15 gram oat fibre tablet to their usual diet, the researchers found that the oat fibre was more effective in lowering both total cholesterol and LDL cholesterol. Interesting, the 'beneficial' HDL (high density lipoprotein) level remained unchanged. 'The oat fibre tablet also proved easier to take and caused fewer side-effects', reported the scientists.[18]

A group of 20 men with high blood cholesterol were admitted to a metabolic ward for 21 days. Some were fed a 'control' diet (with no oat bran) and others were fed exactly the same diet, but with added oat bran. After just three weeks, the men receiving oat bran supplementation had lowered their serum cholesterol concentrations by 19 per cent and had slashed their LDL concentrations by 23 per cent.[19]

When eight men with hypercholesterolemia (high blood cholesterol) were fed 'control' and oat bran diets in alternation, it was found that while they were eating 100g of oat bran per day they managed to reduce their total serum cholesterol by 13 per cent, and LDL level by 14 per cent. HDL was not affected.[20]

Scientists recruited volunteers from the Continental Illinois National Bank in Chicago to see whether adding oat bran to a low-fat diet could enhance its cholesterol-lowering effect. The experiment lasted 12 weeks, and, after four weeks on a restricted fat diet, half of them were told to add 56g of oat bran to their diets every day. After eight weeks of oat bran supplementation, their average blood cholesterol had dropped by about 10 per cent.[21]

In the above experiments, the actual amounts by which cholesterol drops seems to vary quite considerably. Of course, even a 5 per cent drop in your cholesterol level is worth achieving (remember the rule of thumb from Chapter One – 'for every one per cent drop in blood cholesterol, there is a two per cent drop in the risk of cardiovascular disease'. So even a 5 per cent decrease translates to a 10 per cent reduction in risk – which is well worth working for. In fact, the average range of total cholesterol reduction is in the region of 10 to 25 per cent, and probably depends to some extent on the degree of elevation of serum cholesterol to begin with, whether a low-fat diet is also being consumed at the same time, and how much oat bran is being consumed. A diet which includes about 100g of oat bran and lasts for at least three weeks (the longer the better) should show a useful improvement.

But are there any side-effects? Oats are a natural substance, which have been eaten for thousands of years, so any adverse reactions should be known by now. There may be a softening of your stools, which shouldn't be objectionable (it might be a welcome change!). You may have more wind, which should calm down after a short time. It is possible that, if you are taking more than 50g per day, some bloating or abdominal pain could occur, in which case you should reduce your intake and consult your doctor. As with all new diets, it would be advisable to consult your doctor prior to adding this amount of oat bran to your daily diet, so that your personal medical history can be taken into consideration. Perhaps the only real disadvantage is that it simply seems *too* easy. If you can achieve a useful reduction in blood cholesterol simply by adding oat bran to your normal food, then you may not take further steps to improve the rest of your diet. This would be a mistake. As Dr Basil Rifkind, chief of lipid metabolism and atherogenesis at the National Heart Lung and Blood Institute in Bethesda, says: 'It would be wrong for people to start consuming oat bran and forgetting about everything else. The main thing you want to do is increase complex carbohydrates in the diet and reduce the amount of fat you consume.'[22]

CORN BRAN

Just recently, there has been some speculation that corn bran (not available as widely as oat bran) may also be able to lower cholesterol. Researchers at Georgetown University Hospital found that when people ate raw corn bran their serum cholesterol was lowered by 20 per cent and triglycerides by 31 per cent. They about 40g daily to seven people suffering from hypercholesterolemia, and to make it palatable, flavoured it with garlic powder, black pepper and celery seed, and sprinkled it over tomato juice or soup. Apparently there were no serious side effects.

NIACIN

It has been known for some time that niacin – also called vitamin B3 – can lower cholesterol levels if taken in large amounts, and it is probably one of the safest cholesterol-lowering drugs because of its long track record. Niacin is naturally found in foods such as yeast, milk, eggs, green vegetables and cereal grains, and your daily requirement of it comes to something in the region of 16 milligrams. However, when used clinically to lower cholesterol, it is often taken in doses which are enormously larger – one to three *grams* – 200 times the recommended daily allowance. Only niacin in its nicotinic acid form has been found useful to lower cholesterol; nicotinamide does not have the same effect.

In one study, 37 patients (25 male, 12 female) with seriously high blood cholesterol were given both diet therapy and niacin tablets. With diet therapy only, the average cholesterol reduction was about 17 per cent, and although 12 patients managed to get down to the goal of 5.2 millimoles, none of them managed to maintain their cholesterol at that low level. On the other hand, those patients receiving both diet therapy and niacin supplementation managed to reduce their average levels by 28 per cent, 22 of them reached the target level, and seven of them succeeded in staying down there.[23]

For those people who suffer from very high blood cholesterol, doctors sometimes prescribe niacin combined with one or more other types of drug (perhaps something called a bile acid sequestrant, such as cholestyramine) and additional diet therapy. Under these conditions, it is not uncommon to find a huge reduction in cholesterol of 45 to 60 per cent!

You should remember, however, that your first line of attack against cholesterol should be to reduce your total and saturated fat and cholesterol intake, to control your weight, to increase your physical activity, and to control any disease (such as diabetes or hypothyroidism) which may be elevating your cholesterol. Drug therapy should only be used when all these measures have failed, and under the supervision of your doctor.

It is not known for sure how niacin works to reduce serum cholesterol – it is definitely metabolised in the liver, and probably exerts its beneficial effect on the way your liver reprocesses cholesterol and deals with LDL and VLDL. Also, niacin may partly stop fatty tissues in other parts of the body from secreting fats.

When given in large doses, niacin also opens up blood vessels, and this can cause something called the 'niacin flush' – an intense reddening and itching of the face and upper body. Occasionally it may also cause headache, nausea, dizziness, vomiting and diarrhoea. The 'niacin flush' usually goes away after your body has been taking niacin for a couple of weeks. Slow-release niacin may minimize this effect in some people, which may be uncomfortable but is harmless.

Rarely, niacin may cause rapid beating of the heart. It may interfere with liver-function tests, and increase blood-sugar levels, which is important for diabetics because it may affect their medication requirement. It may also interfere with medications used for high blood pressure. Before you take niacin, tell your doctor if you have diabetes, coronary artery disease, gallbladder disease or a history of jaundice or liver disease, gout, peptic ulcer or allergy. Tests to assess your liver's state of health may be necessary periodically.

Niacin is a safe, useful and powerful weapon in our armoury against cholesterol, but like all weapons, it should be used at the right time and in the right hands. So speak to your doctor first.

BEANS

Beans can be just as effective as oat bran in lowering cholesterol, because they contain useful amounts of the same soluble fibre. One hundred grams of oat bran contains nearly eight grams of soluble fibre. By using the following table, you can see how several different types of beans compare.[24]

Food	Grams of soluble fibre in 100g
Green beans, tinned	8.13
Navy beans, cooked	7.76
Pinto beans, cooked	7.52
Baked beans, tinned	6.3
Kidney beans	5.26

When researchers gave ten men suffering from hypercholesterolemia (high blood cholesterol) a diet containing half a cup of tinned beans every day for three weeks, they found that cholesterol levels had dropped by an average of 13 per cent and triglycerides had sunk by 12 per cent.[25] And this was on an 'average' diet which included a considerable amount of dietary fat and cholesterol! When British researchers carried out similar experiments, they also found that beans could cut cholesterol levels by about one third.[26] The researchers used plain, ordinary tinned Baked Beans, and asked volunteers to eat one 500g tin a day. Within three days of starting, the subjects showed a 10 to 12 per cent drop in cholesterol! It seems, therefore, that eating some beans every day is a healthy, and easy, way to increase your cholesterol-loss.

GUAR GUM

Guar gum is made from the ground-up seed of the tree cyamopsis tetragonolobus (the tender cluster bean pod), and is used to bind pills and tablets together, and enables them to disintegrate on contact with moisture. It has also been used as a 'slimming pill', intended to be taken with water because it swells up in the stomach thus producing a feeling of fullness and, hopefully, a decreased appetite. However, there have been safety fears about its use in this manner, since it could swell up in the gullet causing a dangerous obstruction. Nevertheless, when used to reduce serum cholesterol levels, guar gum is known to be effective – when researchers studied 50 men all of whom showed a moderately elevated cholesterol level, they found that after eight weeks' use, total cholesterol fell by an average of one millimole! The researchers found a greater decrease in cholesterol when using a high viscosity mixture rather than medium or low viscosity.[27]

In another experiment, scientists used diets enriched with both wheat bran and guar gum to produce cuts in total cholesterol and LDL ranging from 10 to 20 per cent, and found that these reductions applied equally to people with normal and elevated serum cholesterol readings.[28] The scientists concluded:

Foods should be selected with moderate to high amounts of dietary fibre from a wide variety of choices to include both soluble and insoluble types of fibre. Insufficient data are available on the long-term safety of high-fibre supplements. People at risk for deficiencies, such as postmenopausal women, the elderly, or growing children, may require supplements of calcium and trace minerals. People with upper gastrointestinal dysfunction are at risk of bezoar formation and cautioned against a diet high in fibre of the leafy vegetable type.

They also suggested that diabetics should pay careful attention to insulin doses, 'because hypoglycemia can result if there is a radical change in fibre intake and insulin dose is not reduced appropriately.'

A further experiment on 14 volunteers, all of whom had been diagnosed as having hypercholesterolemia, produced a baffling result.[29] The experiment lasted 12 weeks, during which time the volunteers received daily supplements of 15g of guar gum. Half way through the trial, the results were very encouraging – showing an average reduction of about one millimole, about a 12 per cent drop. But after this midway point, the cholesterol levels began to climb again, and at the end of the trial, there was no difference. Puzzling though this is, there was at least one encouraging result – the scientists observed no severe side effects during the course of the experiment, and calcium, magnesium, phosphate, and iron levels in the body were not affected by guar gum supplementation. However, another study also using 15g of guar gum supplementation a day *did* find a sustained reduction after three months, although the average drop in total cholesterol was rather modest – about half a millimole, or 5 per cent.[30]

One of the largest reductions in cholesterol due to guar gum supplementation we could discover occurred in 19 patients diagnosed as being hypercholesterolaemic, who received guar gum every day, and who averaged a 15 per cent reduction in serum cholesterol after three months' treatment. The reduction was maintained after a year on the supplement, and the fall in LDL was 20 per cent on average. There was no reduction in triglycerides, nor in 'good' HDL. Two patients had to withdraw from the experiment because of severe diarrhoea.[31]

PECTIN

Pectin is made from apples or citrus fruits, and is the gelling agent used to make fruit jams and jellies. It has also been used to treat diarrhoea. Like guar gum and oat bran, pectin is a good source of soluble fibre, and has demonstrated its ability to lower serum cholesterol. In one trial, six men with familial hypercholesterolemia were alternately treated with diet therapy plus cholestyramine (cholesterol-lowering drug) and diet therapy, cholestyramine and additional pectin. After eight weeks on each regime, it was found that with pectin added, total serum cholesterol was lowered by 31 per cent and LDL fell by 35 per cent. This was an improvement of 20 per cent above and beyond the effect of diet and cholestyramine alone. The amount of pectin added was quite small – 12g a day, or about one scant tablespoon.[32] In another experiment, volunteers were given a daily dose of 15g of pectin combined with 450mg of ascorbic acid (vitamin C) for six weeks, at the end of which it was found that their total serum cholesterol had fallen by more than 8 per cent.[33] In the same trial, it was noticed that for other subjects suffering from more severe hypercholesterolemia, the drop was more pronounced – up to 18 per cent.

Pectin is probably a useful adjunct to the dietary control of cholesterol, and since a small amount seems to produce a beneficial effect, one tablespoon a day could be easily incorporated into most diets.

PSYLLIUM

Psyllium seeds (from the psyllium plantain, sometimes called ispaghula) has been used in bulk laxative preparations because when wettened, they swell up into a viscous mass, stimulating intestinal activity. There is also evidence that psyllium, like some other gel-producing gums, can act favourably on blood cholesterol levels. Twenty-six men were recruited by researchers, who gave them 3½ grams of psyllium at mealtimes, three times a day. No other dietary restrictions were imposed. After eight weeks of treatment, total cholesterol levels had fallen by nearly 15 per cent, and LDL had dropped by 20 per cent. The researchers observed no adverse effects, and concluded that 'psyllium is an effective and well-tolerated therapy for mild to moderate hypercholesterolemia'.[34] In another trial, fibre made from psyllium husks was given to 12 elderly patients for four months, after which time it was found that blood cholesterol had dropped by 20 per cent, but triglycerides were not lowered.[35]

However, some adverse reactions have been noted following psyllium usage, including allergic reaction (anaphylaxis)[36] and hypersensitivity leading to anaphylactic shock.[37] You should therefore check with your doctor if you notice any unusual symptoms if you use psyllium, and should avoid it if you are likely to be allergic.

MAGNESIUM

Magnesium deficiency is associated with an increased incidence of atherosclerosis, hypertension, strokes, heart attacks and diabetes. Low levels of magnesium can cause stiffness in the vasculature, which elevates blood pressure, and a contraction or spasm in the heart muscle that can result in sudden death.

Magnesium single-handedly influences many of the activities associated with a wide variety of cardiac medications. For example, magnesium inhibits platelet aggregation, thins the blood, blocks calcium, and relaxes blood vessels. Magnesium also increases oxygenation of the heart muscle by improving cardiac contractibility.[38]

When magnesium (400mg per day) was given to individuals with elevated cholesterol and low HDL for four months, the average cholesterol level fell from 297 to 257mg/cu, while the good HDL cholesterol level increased by 33 per cent.[39] More than 30 clinical trials have reported that magnesium can lower elevated blood pressure, although these results have not been consistently proven to date.

VITAMIN E

Vitamin E has been shown to play a powerful role in the prevention of heart attacks because it can reduce platelet adhesion and prevent oxidation of LDL cholesterol. In the Cambridge Heart Antioxidant Study, patients with coronary atherosclerosis were randomly given vitamin E (400 IU or 800 IU per day) or a placebo. Compared with placebo controls, vitamin E treatment resulted in a 47 per cent reduction in cardiac-related deaths or non-fatal heart attacks. It is unlikely that the average Western diet can provide all the vitamin E we need, so taking a supplement is a good idea.

FOLIC ACID

Folic acid is gaining recognition in the scientific community as one of the most important 'heart healthy' nutrients. It is necessary for the metabolism and elimination of homocysteine, which can damage blood vessels and promote atherosclerosis. It has been shown that that modest intakes of folic acid (400 to 650 mcg/day) are effective in reducing elevated homocysteine levels.

COENZYME Q1O

Coenzyme Q1O was first recognised by the Japanese, and is now one of the most common methods of treating cardiovascular disease in Japan. Coenzyme Q10 is intimately involved in the production of energy at the cellular level and is a key nutrient for the heart.

Current theory suggests that a significant portion of congestive heart failure may be due, at least in part, to a coenzyme Q10 deficiency. In one double-blind study, 641 individuals with severe CHF were given 150 mg per day of coenzyme Q10. Coenzyme Q10-treated patients had a 38 per cent decrease in hospitalizations due to worsening of heart failure compared to the control group.[40]

POTASSIUM

Potassium has been shown to be effective in preventing both hypertension and strokes. Although having no direct correlation to cholesterol, adequate potassium levels play an important role in the prevention of cardiovascular incidents.

An analysis of 19 clinical trials evaluating the relationship between blood pressure and dietary intake of potassium revealed that increasing potassium intake lowers both systolic and diastolic blood pressure (the effect is greater in patients with higher blood pressure).

Results of a 12-year study revealed that individuals who died from strokes had significantly lower potassium intake than survivors of strokes and individuals who died from other causes. This study emphasized that, regardless of other risk factors, increased intake of potassium decreases stroke risk, while decreased intake of potassium increases the risk.[41] The study also found that eating just one serving of a potassium-rich fresh fruit or vegetable daily provides a 40 per cent reduction in stroke risk. Some potassium-rich foods include avocado, banana, chard, citrus fruit, lentils, nuts, parsnips, sardines and spinach.

HAWTHORN BERRY

Hawthorn berry works in a variety of ways to increase cardiovascular health. It increases blood supply to the heart and improves its metabolic function. These benefits enhance the efficiency of the heart by allowing it to pump more blood to the body. It has a tonifying effect on the cardiovascular system, meaning it has a positive effect on both hypotensive and hypertensive episodes. Hawthorn berry increases cardiac output and dilates coronary vessels. It has been used for arrhythmias and tachycardias, as well as being used in Europe in mild heart failure. The active ingredients in hawthorn also provide strong antioxidant protection throughout the cardiovascular system. It may help to regulate cholesterol and reverse some plaque formation. It is believed that the proanthocyanidin bioflavonoids in hawthorn are responsible for the majority of its cardiovascular activity. Hawthorn berry should be used under a doctor's supervision, especially if you are taking lanoxin or ACE inhibitors.

GARLIC

Garlic is a herb that effectively lowers elevated serum cholesterol and triglycerides, inhibits platelet aggregation and increases fibrinolysis. Several meta-analyses have shown that garlic intake reduces LDL cholesterol levels by up to 9 per cent and produces a small rise in HDL cholesterol levels; one medium-sized garlic clove daily or capsules with 900 to 1,800 mg of dried fresh garlic are sufficient.[42,43] Garlic has no known side effects. So far, no clinical trials have proved that increased intake of garlic decreases cardiac-induced mortality or morbidity, yet its use appears safe and potentially beneficial. Garlic has also been shown to provide a mild antihypertensive effect, as well as antioxidant activity.

GRAPE SEED EXTRACT

Grape seed extract (proanthocyanidins) and bilberry (anthocyanosides) can be considered when attempting to improve capillary fragility and altered permeability associated with atherosclerosis and hypertension. They act as powerful antioxidants to reduce free radical damage to the vasculature and also improve circulation and delivery of oxygen to the periphery.

GINKGO

Ginkgo biloba has no direct effect on lowering cholesterol, but is an invaluable herb to recommend to those who are suffering from the long-term effects of cholesterol buildup. When plaque leads to inter-mittent claudication, ginkgo may help to improve circulation to the legs. Additionally, ginkgo may be beneficial in improving blood flow to the heart, making it invaluable after a heart attack or in cardio-myopathy.

GREEN TEA

Green tea has myriad health benefits, including anti-carcinogenic, immune enhancement, anticariogenic and, in addition, may be a power-ful preventive agent in the progression of atherosclerosis and hyperten-sion. Green tea's polyphenols are known to block lipid peroxidation, and it has been shown in human models to block the increase in serum cholesterol levels, even in atherogenic-inducing diets. Recent studies also suggest that ingestion of 10 cups of green tea a day, or the equiva-lent, not only reduces VLDL, LDL cholesterol and triglycerides, but also raises HDL cholesterol. Those who are sensitive to caffeine may need to limit themselves.

SOYA PRODUCTS AND LEGUMES

Eating soya products decreases LDL and total cholesterol levels without decreasing HDL cholesterol levels.[44] Legume intake has also been shown in studies to decrease LDL and total cholesterol levels without decreas-ing HDL levels. Soya and bean products can serve as a protein source in a meal and can further reduce LDL cholesterol levels if they are substituted for fatty animal products.

MONOUNSATURATED-RICH NUTS

Nuts are a rich source of n-3 fatty acids, monounsaturated fats and vitamin E. Studies have shown that an increased intake of nuts is associated with improved lipid levels and decreased mortality and heart attacks.[45,46] Nuts rich in monounsaturated fats and omega-3 fats (e.g., hazelnuts, almonds, pecans, cashews, walnuts and macadamia nuts) appear preferable to nuts containing polyunsaturated fats, such as peanuts and pine nuts.

ALL ABOUT OILS AND FATS

Many people are confused about fat. Is margarine better than butter? Or should we all be eating olive oil instead? We seem to get one message one week, and the opposite the next. This makes it very difficult for anyone to understand what to do any more. So let's start with some basics...

WHAT IS FAT?
Fats are solid at room temperature, oils are liquid. But scientists now use the term 'fat' to include all oils and fats, whether or not they're solid or liquid. So we will, too.

Chemically, fats are made up of three molecules of fatty acids and one of an alcohol called glycerol. What's a fatty acid? We'll come to that in a moment. You'll also hear the word 'triglycerides' used to describe fat – it means three fatty acid molecules ('tri') plus glycerol... tri-glyceride.

WHAT'S A FATTY ACID?
Fatty acids are – not surprisingly – acids that are found in fats. That's why they're called fatty acids! There are four major fatty acids: palmitic, stearic, oleic and linoleic. Remember, each molecule of fat contains three of these four fatty acids. Now it's the *combination* of these acids in the fat molecule that determines whether the fat is saturated, unsaturated, or polyunsaturated – words we've all heard a great deal in the past few years. So let's explain them.

All fats consist of long chains of carbon and hydrogen atoms. When all the available sites on the carbon atoms are filled with hydrogen atoms, the fat is saturated. If there are unfilled spaces, the fat is unsaturated. The more empty spaces, the more unsaturated the fat is.

Saturated
Palmitic fatty acid has 16 carbon atoms and no unsaturated carbon bonds. So it's called 'saturated'.

Stearic fatty acid has 18 carbon atoms and no unsaturated carbon bonds. So it's also called 'saturated'.

Saturated fat is known to raise the level of cholesterol in your blood and intake of saturated fat increases the rates of strokes and heart attacks. It is well established that reducing intake of saturated fat reduces LDL cholesterol levels and that reductions in LDL cholesterol levels decrease the risk of coronary artery disease. Studies have also shown that the causal relationship between saturated fat intake and coronary artery disease may be stronger than the relationship between coronary artery disease and hypertension, diabetes or tobacco use.[47]

As a guide, saturated fat is usually sold at room temperature – animal fat contains lots of saturated fat – lard, meat, butter and so on. A few plant fats also contain significant amounts – principally coconut and palm oil. As a quick rule of thumb, simply reducing or eliminating the animal fat in your diet is a quick and painless way to reduce your saturated fat intake.

Monounsaturated

Oleic fatty acid has 18 carbon atoms and one unsaturated carbon bond. So it's called 'mono-unsaturated'.

In contrast to the dominant use of polyunsaturated fat in most of the Western world, the Mediterranean diet uses predominantly mono-unsaturated fatty acids and omega-3 fats as fat sources. An important scientific study from France has shown that patients who have suffered a heart attack can benefit simply by switching from polyunsaturated fat to monounsaturated.[48,49] The investigators randomly divided 605 heart attack patients into two groups, one of which ate a Western diet with 30 per cent of total calories from fat, and the other consuming a Mediterranean diet, based around olive oil and a special margarine made from canola oil. Significant reductions in heart attacks, unstable angina, heart failure, stroke and thromboembolic events were noted in the patients on the Mediterranean diet. Over five years, total mortality decreased by 70 per cent in the patients who followed the Mediterranean diet compared with the patients who followed the Western diet. These results are important because they indicate that dietary changes, independent of cholesterol levels, can affect the health of patients with coronary heart disease.

Polyunsaturated

Linoleic fatty acid has 18 carbon atoms and two unsaturated carbon bonds. So it's called 'poly-unsaturated'.

The more polyunsaturated an oil is, the more it can be damaged by excess heat, air and light. Most polyunsaturated oils should only be used raw, because once damaged, they form free radicals. Good sources of polyunsaturated fats include sunflower and corn oil. We all need a little linoleic acid in our diets every day, because of the four major fatty acids, this is the only one we can't synthesise for ourselves internally.

Both monounsaturated and polyunsaturated fatty acids decrease LDL and total cholesterol levels and produce a small increase in triglyceride levels. However, there is growing evidence that increased intake of polyunsaturated fatty acid increases the oxidation of LDL cholesterol, leading to increased LDL uptake by macrophages, damage to the artery walls and development of coronary artery obstruction.[50] Polyunsaturated fatty acids also increase platelet aggregation, which can increase thrombus formation and the risk of stroke and heart attack.[51] These factors make the intake of monounsaturated fats (such as canola oil, monounsaturated-rich safflower oil and olive oil) preferable to polyunsaturated fats (such as corn oil, soybean oil and many margarines).

TRANS-FATTY ACIDS

By bubbling hydrogen through vegetable oil, food manufacturers can add some hydrogen to the fatty acids, in a process called hydrogenation. The result – partially hydrogenated vegetable oils – can be used in a semisolid spread like margarine. Because of the particular chemical configuration they take, some of the fatty acids in hydrogenated oils are known as trans-fatty acids, or trans fat. Trans fatty acids increase LDL cholesterol levels and decrease HDL cholesterol levels.[52,53] The official advice is not to increase trans fat in the diet any further.[54] Studies have shown that people can reduce their intake of saturated fat and trans fatty acids by nearly 50 per cent by cutting out three dietary sources: butter and margarine, fatty meats and dairy products made from 2 per cent or whole milk.[55]

BUTTER OR MARGARINE?

Fierce advertising wars have tried to persuade us over the years that one or other of these fats is healthier. In fact, some margarines can contain as much total fat as butter, although their saturated fat content would be less. Advertising has also tried to persuade us to increase the amount of polyunsaturated margarine we eat which, if we didn't reduce our other fat consumption, would simply result in us eating more fat than ever. So what should you do?

In reality, there is probably little practical difference between butter and most of the mass-market margarines. Butter will certainly be higher in saturated fat, but margarines can contain hydrogenated oils (see trans fats, above). The process of hydrogenation fills some unsaturated bonds of the fat molecule with hydrogen atoms, making it more similar to a saturated fat. For example, soybean oil in its natural state is only 15 per cent saturated, but when it's partially hydrogenated it's closer to 25 per cent saturated, similar to vegetable shortenings. We think it's prudent to avoid hydrogenated fats where you can.

One alternative is to buy margarines which specifically state they are *not* hydrogenated and often contain high-quality oils such as cold-pressed sunflower oil and olive oil. Another is simply to cut down your usage of both types of fat. For example, do you really need to eat quite so much margarine or butter? If you want something to put on your toast in the morning, why not try lightly brushing a little olive oil on to it? Similarly, when cooking, use our low-fat sauté (see recipe section).

CHOOSING OILS

There are three methods of extracting oil from plants:

- Cold pressing. This is the traditional hydraulic pressing process where the temperature is kept low throughout and which therefore preserves temperature-sensitive vitamins. The end product is expensive, mainly because there is a high percentage of waste in the discarded pulp, but the oil is nutritious and tastes and smells good. Buy it – so what if it's more expensive – you consume less! Which is what we all need to do, in any case!

- Screw or expeller. This process involves high pressure pressing which generates high temperatures. Vitamins are destroyed during this process and although it enables more oil to be extracted it is dark, strong smelling and needs further refining and deodorising.

- Solvent extraction. This is the most common process because it produces the highest yields. The grains or seeds are ground, steamed and then mixed with solvents. The solvents used are either the petroleum based benzene, hexane or heptane. The mixture is then heated to remove the solvents and then washed with caustic soda. This has the effect of destroying its valuable lecithin content. After this it is bleached and filtered which removes precious minerals as well as any coloured substances. Finally it is heated to a high temperature to deodorise it. One other aspect of vegetable oils produced by solvent extraction is that they have lost their vitamin E. This vitamin helps stop the oil from going rancid. Rancid oils are dangerous because they provide the raw material for producing free radicals in our bodies. Sometimes chemical retardants are added to stop the oil from turning rancid, but it would seem to be much more sensible to stick with the cold-pressed oils which can keep well, if properly stored, for up to six months.

ESSENTIAL FATTY ACIDS

The two classes of essential fatty acids (EFAs) are named omega-6 and omega-3. They are both necessary for good health because they provide the catalysts for various metabolic functions (e.g. they can activate prostaglandins, or cell regulators). Through a complicated transformation process, essential fatty acids become biologically active and there-fore become useful links in many metabolic systems. They are called 'essential' because the body cannot make them, and they must be obtained from food sources. Most vegetable oils provide the EFAs to a greater or lesser extent, but they are not significantly present in meat.

- Omega-6 fatty acids (e.g. linoleic acid) are found in vegetable seeds and the oils produced from them. Good sources include oils made from safflower, sunflower, corn, soya, evening primrose, pumpkin, walnut, and wheat germ.

- Omega-3 fatty acids (e.g. alpha linolenic acid) are found in deep-water fish oils and are alleged to have near-miraculous properties – hence the popularity of fish-oil supplements. They are also, however, found in linseed, rapeseed (canola) green leafy vegetables, soybean products, walnuts and hazelnuts, so vegetarians do not need to consume fish if they wish to increase their omega-3s. The food supplement spirulina also contains both linoleic and linolenic acids. In fact, flaxseed (linseed) oil actually contains about twice as much omega-3 essential fatty acids as is found in fish oil. According to nutritionist Ann Louise Gittleman, co-author of *Beyond Pritikin*, flaxseed oil's greatest attribute is its ranking as the vegetable source highest in omega-3 fatty acids. 'Fish is the best-known source of the omega-3s', she says, 'but flaxseed oil contains 55 to 60 per cent omega-3 – about twice as much as is found in fish oil'.[56] Flaxseed is also rich in omega-6 fatty acids.

Increased intake of foods rich in alpha-linolenic acid decreases LDL cholesterol levels.[57] Intake of linolenic acid is strongly associated with a decreased risk of coronary artery disease.[58] In one study of 43,757 health professionals, the protective cardiac effect achieved with linolenic acid was more significant than a reduction in saturated fat intake.[59] Of particular interest in this study was the finding that plant sources of omega-3 fatty acids exhibited a significant protective effect, while seafood sources of omega-3 fatty acids did not.

THE BOTTOM LINE

- Reduce your total fat intake
- Reduce your saturated fat intake
- Reduce butter and margarine – favour olive oil instead
- Increase your consumption of vegetables and fruits
- Increase your consumption of dietary sources of vitamin E and omega-3s.

PART TWO:

NO-CHOLESTEROL COOKING

RECIPES

Well, you're in for a treat! Here are some of our favourite recipes, and they're not just low-cholesterol – they're *no*-cholesterol! If you've scratched your head and wondered just how it's possible to enjoy eating low-fat, no-cholesterol cuisine, here's the answer! The proof that you don't have to give up on taste when you're cutting down on your cholesterol.

For your convenience, every recipe has been nutritionaly analysed for total fat, saturated fat, cholesterol, and calories. By reducing your intake of fatty foods, you will automatically be reducing the number of calories you take in your diet, because fat is the greatest single source of calories. However, don't forget that calories are still important and should be considered when planning your meals. Some carbohydrates can stimulate the body to manufacture fats called triglycerides which are, like cholesterol, under suspicion as a cause of coronary heart disease. Since they have an effect on blood clotting, someone with high triglyceride levels and with artery-narrowing atherosclerosis could suffer from a blocked artery due to a blood clot. So remember, particularly if you have a raised triglyceride level or if you have a weight problem, your calorie intake is still important and should be counted.

Enjoy!

BREAKFASTS

Fruity Breakfast Bowl
Serves 4
Calories per serving: 306
Grams saturated fat per serving: 0.6
Milligrams cholesterol per serving: 0
Preparation time: 15 minutes

50g (2 oz) dried dates, finely chopped
50g (2 oz) dried figs, finely chopped
2 eating apples, finely chopped
1 orange, peeled and sliced
1 grapefruit, peeled and sliced
50g (2 oz) raisins or currants

300ml (10 fl.oz) apple juice
50g (2 oz) rolled oats
2.5ml (½ tsp) ground cinnamon
230ml (8 fl.oz) soya milk concentrate (optional)

Mix the fruits and juice together in a large bowl.

Stir the oats and cinnamon together and spread out on a baking tray. Place under a hot grill for 2 minutes, stir well and return to the grill for a further 2 minutes. Divide the fruit mixture into 4 large bowls and sprinkle each serving with the oat mix. Serve at once, with a little soya milk concentrate over each serving if desired.

Fruity Oatbran Porridge
Serves 4
Calories per serving: 193
Grams saturated fat per serving: 0.6
Milligrams cholesterol per serving: 0
Preparation time: 15 minutes

90g (6 tbsp) oat bran
55g (2 oz) raisins or currants
2.5ml (½ tsp) ground cinnamon
285ml (10 fl.oz) water
285ml (10 fl.oz) soya milk
4 small pitted dates, finely chopped
1 eating apple, finely chopped

Measure the oat bran into a saucepan with the raisins and cinnamon. Add the water and soya milk, stir well and place over a low flame. Bring to a low simmer, stirring frequently.

When the porridge is quite thick, after 3–5 minutes, add the dates and apple and stir well. Serve hot.

Spicy Fruit Scones
Makes 12 scones
Calories per 2 scones: 224
Grams saturated fat per 2 scones: 1.5
Milligrams cholesterol per 2 scones: 0
Preparation time: 30 minutes

170g (6 oz) flour
10ml (2 tsp) baking powder
5ml (1 tsp) ground cinnamon
2.5ml (½ tsp) ground allspice

115g (4 oz) raisins or currants
85g (3 oz) oil or margarine
230ml (8 fl.oz) water

Pre-heat the oven to 180°C/350°F/Gas Mark 4 and lightly oil a baking tray.

Measure the dry ingredients together in a large mixing bowl and stir well. Add the oil or margarine and work in to a fine, crumbly consistency. Add the liquid, adjusting as necessary to make a firm, sticky dough. Roll the dough out on a lightly floured board to a thickness of ¾ inch and cut into large rounds. Arrange on the baking tray and bake for 15 minutes. Cool on a wire rack before serving with Speedy Applesauce (page 131) or your favourite jam.

Cinnamon & Raisin Tea Ring
Serves 8
Calories per serving: 200
Grams saturated fat per serving: 1.4
Milligrams cholesterol per serving: 0
Preparation time: 40 minutes

170g (6 oz) flour
10ml (2 tsp) egg replacer
5ml (1 tsp) baking powder
60ml (2 fl.oz) oil or margarine
140ml (5 fl.oz) water
55g (2 oz) brown sugar
5ml (1 tsp) ground cinnamon
55g (2 oz) raisins
30g (2 tbsp) margarine

Pre-heat the oven to 170°C / 325°F / Gas Mark 3.

Mix the flour, egg replacer and baking powder together in a mixing bowl. Work in the oil to a fine, crumbly consistency, then add the water and stir well. Roll the dough into a rectangle on a lightly floured board to a thickness of ½ inch.

Sprinkle the rectangle with the brown sugar, cinnamon and raisins, making sure to leave the edges of the dough clear. Now drop tiny pieces of the margarine onto the raisin filling. Carefully roll the rectangle in on itself along the long edge. Use a little water to help seal the edges, then form the roll into a ring and pinch the ends together.

Place the ring on a baking tray. Slice the outer edge of the ring to one-third its depth and two-thirds its diameter at 1 inch intervals. Bake for 25 minutes. Serve warm with Speedy Applesauce (page 131), Tofu Cinnamon Cream (page 134) or Sweet Orange Sauce (page 132).

Hot Berry Muffins
Makes 24 muffins
Calories per 4 muffins: 202
Grams saturated fat per 4 muffins: 1
Milligrams cholesterol per 4 muffins: 0
Preparation time: 40 minutes

170g (6 oz) flour
55g (2 oz) oat bran
10ml (2 tsp) egg replacer
5ml (1 tsp) baking powder
5ml (1 tsp) ground allspice
60ml (2 fl.oz) oil
115g (4 oz) berries, tinned, frozen or fresh (i.e. blackberries, blueberries, bilberries, blackcurrants), drained
285ml (10 fl.oz) apple juice

Pre-heat the oven to 180°C / 350°F / Gas Mark 4 and line 24 tartlet tins with paper baking cases.

Mix the first five ingredients together in a mixing bowl then work in the oil to a fine, crumbly consistency.

Measure the berries into a small bowl and sprinkle a little flour over them. Shake the berries until they are well coated in the flour then discard the excess flour and add the berries to the dry mix, stirring well but gently. Pour the apple juice over the mixture and stir briefly until the ingredients are just moist. Spoon the batter into the baking cases (about two-thirds full) and bake the muffins for 25 minutes. Turn out onto a wire rack to cool. Serve warm or cold with Speedy Applesauce (page 131), Tofu Cinnamon Cream (page 134) or Sweet Orange Sauce (page 132).

Scrambled Tofu
Serves 2
Calories per serving: 205
Grams saturated fat per serving: 1.8
Milligrams cholesterol per serving: 0
Preparation time: 20 minutes

15ml (1 tbsp) oil
1 small onion, finely chopped
5ml (1 tsp) turmeric
1 medium carrot, thinly sliced
1 medium courgette, sliced
55g (2 oz) mushrooms, quartered
285g (10 oz) firm tofu
5ml (1 tsp) freshly ground black pepper

15g (½ oz) fresh parsley, finely chopped

Heat the oil in a frying pan and sauté the onion until tender. Add the turmeric and stir well to make an even colouring. Now add the carrot, courgette and mushrooms and continue the sauté for a further 3–5 minutes.

Crumble the tofu into the sauté and add the black pepper. Stir well over a medium heat while the tofu warms and absorbs the colour, about 5 minutes. Add the chopped parsley, stir for 1 minute, then serve onto hot plates. Serve with toast, Bubble 'n Squeak or grilled tomatoes.

BREADS & BISCUITS

Basic Sourdough Bread
Makes 2 loaves
Serves 8
Calories per serving: 280
Grams saturated fat per serving: 0
Milligrams cholesterol per serving: 0
Preparation time: 3 days!

for the starter
45ml (3 tbsp) plain flour
75ml (5 tbsp) water

Stir the flour and water into a paste. Cover the bowl first with a paper towel and then a small plate and leave for 2–3 days. It will become more liquid and bubbly.

for the bread:
1 kilo (2 lbs) whole wheat flour
30ml (2 tbsp) sugar, dissolved in a little warm water
the *Sourdough Starter*
710 – 850ml (1¼ – 1½ pints) water

Stir all the ingredients together, knead the dough and then shape it into loaf tins or rounds on a baking tray.

Allow to rise, covered, for 12 hours or overnight. Uncover and bake at 160°C / 300°F / Gas Mark 3 for 40 minutes. Allow to cool on a rack.

Simple Rye Bread
Makes 2 loaves
Serves 8
Calories per serving: 289
Grams saturated fat per serving: 0.4
Milligrams cholesterol per serving: 0

Preparation time: 2 hours

850ml (1½ pints) tepid water, approximately
30ml (2 tbsp) molasses
1 × 23g sachet dried yeast *or* 25g (1 oz) fresh yeast
30ml (2 tbsp) oil
450g (1 lb) rye flour
450g (1 lb) whole wheat flour

Measure half the water into a jug and dissolve the molasses in it. Then add the yeast to the liquid, stir well and leave to work for 10 minutes.

Pour the oil in with the remaining water.

Mix the rye and wheat flours together in a large bowl.

When the yeast has worked, stir it into the flour mixture with a large wooden spoon. Gradually add the oil and water, stirring constantly.

When the dough is too thick to stir, use your hands and knead it to a firm consistency. The amount of water needed will vary – adjust as necessary to make a firm, non-sticky dough.

When you have kneaded the dough for about 5 minutes, form it into a ball in the bowl, cover the bowl with greaseproof paper and a clean tea towel and leave in a warm place to rise for 45 minutes.

Knead the dough again and shape into loaves. Place them in an oiled bread tin and leave to rise in a warm place for 30 minutes.

Bake at 170°C / 325°F / Gas Mark 3 for 35 minutes. Leave to cool in the tins for 10 minutes, then turn out onto a wire rack to cool completely.

Quick Pumpkin Bread
Makes 1 large loaf
Serves 8
Calories per serving: 279
Grams saturated fat per serving: 0.9
Milligrams cholesterol per serving: 0
Preparation time: 1 hour

115g (4 oz) raisins *or* sultanas
85g (3 oz) brown sugar
60ml (2 fl.oz) oil
340g (12 oz) whole wheat flour
10ml (2 tsp) baking powder
30ml (2 tbsp) egg replacer
5ml (1 tsp) ground cinnamon
2.5ml (½ tsp) ground nutmeg *or* allspice
285g (10 oz) tinned, prepared pumpkin
140ml (5 fl.oz) water

Warm the oven to 170°C / 325°F / Gas Mark 3 and lightly oil a 900g (2 lb) loaf tin.

Mix the raisins, sugar and oil together in a small bowl and stir well.

Measure the flour, baking powder, egg replacer and spices into a separate mixing bowl and stir together.

In another bowl, mix the pumpkin and water and whisk briskly. Stir the three mixtures together in the largest bowl and blend for 2–3 minutes.

Turn the mixture into the loaf tin and bake for 45 minutes. Cool on a wire rack and serve the same day.

Raisin Banana Bread
Makes 1 large loaf
Serves 8
Calories per serving: 218
Grams saturated fat per serving: 0.9
Milligrams cholesterol per serving: 0
Preparation time: 1 hour

225g (8oz) whole wheat flour
10ml (2 tsp) baking powder
30ml (2 tbsp) egg replacer
5ml (1 tsp) ground cinnamon
2.5ml (½ tsp) ground cloves
60ml (2 fl.oz) oil
2 ripe bananas
115g (4 oz) raisins
230ml (8 fl.oz) water

Pre-heat the oven to 170°C / 325°F / Gas Mark 3 and lightly oil a 900g (2 lb) loaf tin.

Mix the dry ingredients together in a bowl.

Whisk the remaining ingredients together in a separate bowl. Combine the two mixtures, stir well, adding more water if necessary to make a thick, moist batter, and turn into the loaf tin. Bake for 30–40 minutes. Cool for 10 minutes in the tin before turning out onto a wire rack. Slice and serve the same day.

Pepper Herb & Onion Loaf
Makes 1 large loaf
Serves 8
Calories per serving: 140
Grams saturated fat per serving: 0.5
Milligrams cholesterol per serving: 0

Preparation time: 1 hour and 10 minutes

1 × 23g sachet dried yeast *or* 25g (1 oz) fresh yeast
15ml (1 tbsp) sugar
285ml (10 fl.oz) tepid water
30ml (2 tbsp) oil
3 cloves garlic, finely chopped
1 small onion, finely chopped
285g (10 oz) flour
15ml (1 tbsp) mixed sweet dried herbs
5ml (1 tsp) freshly ground black pepper

Pre-heat the oven to 180°C / 350°F / Gas Mark 4 and lightly oil a 900g (2 lb) loaf tin.

Dissolve the yeast and sugar in the tepid water and leave in a warm place to soften.

Heat the oil in a small frying pan and sauté the garlic and onion until just tender, about 5 minutes. Remove from the heat.

Mix the flour, herbs and pepper together in a mixing bowl. Stir very well then add the sauté, including the oil and work to an even consistency. Finally, add the yeast and water. Stir the dough, then knead it for 5 minutes, adding more flour or water as necessary to make a firm dough.

Shape the dough into a loaf and place in the tin. Leave to rise in a warm place then bake for 30–40 minutes. Leave to cool in the tin for 10 minutes before turning out onto a wire rack. Serve the same day.

Apple Bread
Makes 2 small loaves
Serves 8
Calories per serving: 281
Grams saturated fat per serving: 1.1
Milligrams cholesterol per serving: 0
Preparation time: 1 hour

225g (8 oz) whole wheat flour
115g (4 oz) oat bran
10ml (2 tsp) egg replacer
5ml (1 tsp) baking powder
5ml (1 tsp) ground cinnamon
2.5ml (½ tsp) ground nutmeg
55g (2 oz) sugar
60ml (2 fl.oz) oil
285ml (10 fl.oz) apple sauce or puree
140ml (5 fl.oz) apple juice

Pre-heat the oven to 180°C / 350°F / Gas Mark 4 and lightly oil two 455g (1 lb) loaf tins.

Stir the dry ingredients (first seven) together in a mixing bowl. Work in the oil to an even, crumbly consistency.

Now stir in the apple sauce and apple juice, adding more juice if necessary to make a batter. Turn the batter into the loaf tins and bake for 20 minutes. Reduce the heat to 160°C / 300°F / Gas Mark 2 and bake for a further 15–20 minutes, until a toothpick inserted in the loaves comes out clean.

Leave the loaves to cool in the tins for 10 minutes before turning onto a wire rack. Serve within 3 days.

Carob Crunch Cookies
Makes 24 cookies
Calories per 4 cookies: 257
Grams saturated fat per 4 cookies: 1.5
Milligrams cholesterol per 4 cookies: 0
Preparation time: 30 minutes

115g (4 oz) flour
60g (2 oz) carob powder
10ml (2 tsp) egg replacer
5ml (1 tsp) baking powder
60g (2 oz) sugar
60ml (2 fl.oz) oil or margarine
5ml (1 tsp) vanilla extract
140ml (5 fl.oz) water
60g (2 oz) walnut halves

Pre-heat the oven to 160°C / 300°F / Gas Mark 2.

Mix the first five ingredients together in a mixing bowl. Add the oil or margarine and work into the dry mix to a crumbly, even texture. Stir in the vanilla extract and the water, adding more water if necessary to make a firm dough.

Roll the dough into 24 large balls and arrange on baking trays. Use the bottom of a glass to gently press each ball flat, to about ½ inch thickness. Press one walnut half onto each cookie and bake for 12–15 minutes. Cool on a wire rack before serving.

Currant Oat Biscuits
Makes 24 biscuits
Calories per 4 biscuits: 206
Grams saturated fat per 4 biscuits: 1.1
Milligrams cholesterol per 4 biscuits: 0
Preparation time: 30 minutes

85g (3 oz) currants or raisins
170ml (6 fl.oz) water
115g (4 oz) flour
60g (2 oz) rolled oats
10ml (2 tsp) egg replacer
5ml (1 tsp) baking powder
10ml (2 tsp) ground cinnamon
60g (2 oz) sugar
60ml (2 fl.oz) oil or margarine

Measure the currants and water into a small mixing bowl, stir well and leave to one side.

Pre-heat the oven to 170°C / 325°F / Gas Mark 3.

Measure the dry ingredients into a large mixing bowl and stir well. Now add the oil or margarine and work together to an even consistency. Next add the currants and water and stir the mixture well.

Drop large spoonfuls of the dough onto a lightly oiled baking tray and bake for 15 minutes. Cool on a wire rack before serving.

Marmalade Biscuits
Makes 24 biscuits
Calories per 4 biscuits: 157
Grams saturated fat per 4 biscuits: 1.3
Milligrams cholesterol per 4 biscuits: 0
Preparation time: 30 minutes

115g (4 oz) flour
10ml (2 tsp) egg replacer
5ml (1 tsp) baking powder
5ml (1 tsp) ground coriander
60g (2 oz) sugar
60g (2 oz) candied peel
60g (2 oz) margarine
140ml (5 fl.oz) orange juice

Pre-heat the oven to 180°C / 350°F / Gas Mark 4.

Mix the first six ingredients together in a large mixing bowl. Now work in the margarine to a fine, even consistency. Finally, add the orange juice and work to a firm dough, adding more liquid if necessary.

Roll the dough out to ¼ inch thickness and cut into shapes with a biscuit cutter. Arrange on baking trays and bake in the hot oven for 10 minutes. Cool on a wire rack before serving.

Three-Grain Bread
Makes 2 small loaves
Serves 8

Calories per serving: 250
Grams saturated fat per serving: 0.6
Milligrams cholesterol per serving: 0
Preparation time: 2 hours and 30 minutes

1 × 23g sachet dried yeast or 25g (1 oz) fresh yeast
15ml (1 tbsp) sugar
285ml (10 fl.oz) tepid water
30ml (2 tbsp) molasses
30ml (2 tbsp) oil
285ml (10 fl.oz) hot water
455g (1 lb) whole wheat flour
115g (4 oz) rye flour
60g (2 oz) oat bran

Pre-heat the oven to 160°C / 300°F / Gas Mark 2 and lightly oil two
455g (1 lb) loaf tins.

Dissolve the yeast and sugar in the tepid water and leave to one side
while the yeast softens. Dissolve the molasses, with the oil, in the hot
water and leave to one side to cool slightly.

Mix the flours and oat bran together in a large mixing bowl and
make a well in the centre. When the yeast has softened and the molasses
mixture is tepid, add both mixtures to the dry mix and stir well. Then
knead to a firm dough, shape into a ball in the mixing bowl, cover the
bowl and leave in a warm place to rise.

After about 45 minutes, knead the dough again, shape into two
loaves and place in their tins. Leave the loaves in a warm place to rise,
then bake for 45 minutes. Turn the loaves out of the tins to cool on a
wire rack before serving.

Simple Corn Bread
Serves 8
Calories per serving: 128
Grams saturated fat per serving: 0.6
Milligrams cholesterol per serving: 0
Preparation time: 45 minutes

170g (6 oz) flour
340g (12 oz) corn meal
15ml (1 tbsp) egg replacer
5ml (1 tsp) baking powder
45ml (3 tbsp) oil
500ml (1 pint) water

Pre-heat the oven to 180°C / 350°F / Gas Mark 5 and lightly oil a 20cm
(8-inch) or 23cm (9-inch) cake tin.

Measure the dry ingredients together in a mixing bowl and stir well. Add the oil and water and stir briskly for 1 minute then turn the batter into the cake tin. Bake for 35 minutes.

Leave the bread to cool in the pan. Cut into chunks and serve with a savoury meal, with sauce or gravy, New Mexican Chilli or even a dollop of jam. Keeps for 2 days.

Nourishing Potato Bread
Makes 2 small loaves
Serves 8
Calories per serving: 369
Grams saturated fat per serving: 0.5
Milligrams cholesterol per serving: 0
Preparation time: 3 hours

455g (1 lb) potatoes, peeled and chopped
500ml (1 pint) water, approximately
1 × 23g sachet dried yeast *or* 25g (1 oz) fresh yeast
15ml (1 tbsp) sugar
285ml (10 fl.oz) tepid water
30ml (2 tbsp) oil
900g (2 lbs) whole wheat flour

Pre-heat the oven to 160°C / 300°F / Gas Mark 2 and lightly oil two 455g (1 lb) loaf tins.

Put the potatoes in a saucepan, cover with the water and place over a medium heat. Boil until tender, then purée the potatoes and their cooking water together. Leave to cool to blood temperature.

Meanwhile, dissolve the yeast and sugar in the tepid water and leave to one side while the yeast softens.

Add the oil, then the yeast mixture into the potato purée and stir well. Gradually add the flour to this mixture, stirring first, then kneading to make a firm dough. Shape the dough into a ball and leave, covered, in a warm place to double in size.

Knead the dough again, shape into loaves (using a litle more flour if necessary) and place in the prepared tins. Put in a warm place to rise then bake for 50 minutes. Leave to cool on a wire rack before serving.

Sweet & Speedy High-Fibre Bread
Serves 8
Calories per serving: 230
Grams saturated fat per serving: 1
Milligrams cholesterol per serving: 0
Preparation time: 45 minutes

115g (4 oz) flour
85g (3 oz) oat bran
85g (3 oz) rolled oats
15ml (1 tbsp) baking powder
45ml (3 tbsp) sugar
45ml (3 tbsp) oil
425ml (15 fl.oz) apple juice

Pre-heat the oven to 180°C / 350°F / Gas Mark 4 and lightly oil a 900g (2 lb) loaf tin.

Stir the dry ingredients together in a large mixing bowl, then add the oil and work to an even consistency. Add the apple juice, stir well and leave to sit for 3 minutes. Stir again, quite vigourously, and turn into the loaf tin.

Bake for 35 minutes. Leave to cool in the pan for 10 minutes before turning onto a wire rack. Serve within 3 days.

SOUPS

Easy Bean & Broccoli Soup
Serves 4
Calories per serving: 180
Grams saturated fat per serving: 0.5
Milligrams cholesterol per serving: 0
Preparation time: 30 minutes

2 cloves garlic, finely chopped
1 medium onion, finely chopped
15ml (1 tbsp) oil
1 × 425g (15 oz) tin whole tomatoes
1 × 455g (1 lb) tin white beans (i.e. haricot, butter), drained
1 litre (2 pints) vegetable stock or water
5ml (1 tsp) yeast extract
5ml (1 tsp) dried basil
10ml (2 tsp) dried parsley (or 1 tablespoon fresh parsley, chopped)
10ml (2 tsp) freshly ground black pepper
225g (½ lb) chopped broccoli

Sauté the garlic and onions in the oil over a medium flame. When tender, add the tomatoes, breaking them as you stir the sauté.

Add the beans to the tomato and onion sauté, then add the stock and yeast extract. Stir often as you bring the mixture to a simmer. Adjust the heat to maintain a gentle simmer and add the herbs and black pepper.

Now add the broccoli to the soup. Stir well, cover the pan and simmer for a further 15 minutes, until the broccoli is tender.

Serve hot.

Chunky Leek & Potato Soup
Serves 8 (2 servings each for 4 people)
Calories per 2 servings: 294
Grams saturated fat per 2 servings: 0.5
Milligrams cholesterol per 2 servings: 0
Preparation time: 45 minutes

1 kilo (2 lbs) potatoes
2 litres (4 pints) cold water
4 medium leeks
3 cloves garlic, finely chopped
2 medium onions, finely chopped
15ml (1 tbsp) oil
10ml (2 tsp) yeast extract
10ml (2 tsp) freshly ground black pepper
3 bay leaves
5ml (1 tsp) caraway seed
5 stalks celery, chopped

Peel and cube the potatoes and place them in a large bowl with the cold water. Leave to one side.

Top and tail the leeks then slice into chunks. Wash in a bowlful of cold water, drain and rinse. Leave to drain in a colander.

In a large, deep saucepan, sauté the garlic and the onions in the oil until tender. Now add the potatoes and the water they have been sitting in. Increase the heat, bringing the liquid to a rolling boil, and add the yeast extract. Stir well, reduce the heat and add the leeks, black pepper, bay leaves and caraway seed. Stir well for 1–2 minutes.

Reduce the heat and simmer the soup, covered, for 10 minutes.

Add the celery to the soup and simmer for a further 15 minutes. Serve hot.

Thick Curry Soup
Serves 4
Calories per serving: 324
Grams saturated fat per serving: 0.75
Milligrams cholesterol per serving: 0
Preparation time: 30 minutes

15ml (1 tbsp) oil
5ml (1 tsp) cumin seed
3 cloves garlic, finely chopped
2 large onions, finely chopped
1 × 455g (16 oz) tin chickpeas, drained
450g (1 lb) carrots, thinly sliced

1x 425g (15 oz) tin whole tomatoes
2.5ml (½ tsp) chilli powder
10ml (2 tsp) freshly ground black pepper
1 – 1.5 litres (2–3 pints) vegetable stock or water
1 strip of kombu (optional)
10ml (2 tsp) garam masala
15ml (1 tbsp) cider vinegar

Heat the oil in a large saucepan over a medium heat. Add the cumin seeds, stirring frequently while they sauté. Now add the garlic and onions, continuing the sauté until the onions are tender.

Add the chickpeas, carrots and tomatoes. Stir well before adding the chilli powder and black pepper. Keep stirring while adding the stock, a little at a time until the consistency you desire.

Add the strip of kombu at this point, cover the pan, reduce the heat and simmer for about 15 minutes to allow the soup to thicken.

At the end of this time, stir in the garam masala and the vinegar. Leave over a low heat for a further 5 minutes, or until ready to serve. Serve hot.

Boneless Pea Soup
Serves 4
Calories per serving: 214
Grams saturated fat per serving: 0.5
Milligrams cholesterol per serving: 0
Preparation time: 1 hour

15ml (1 tbsp) oil
3 cloves garlic, finely chopped
1 medium onion, finely chopped
225g (8 oz) dried split green peas
1 litre (2 pints) vegetable stock or water
10ml (2 tsp) yeast extract
1 bunch fresh coriander, finely chopped
10ml (2 tsp) freshly ground black pepper

Heat the oil in a deep saucepan over a medium heat. Add the garlic and onion and sauté until tender, about 5 minutes. Stir frequently.

Wash and drain the peas and add them to the sauté. Now add the stock and yeast extract, stirring the mixture well. Cover the pan, increase the heat and bring the soup to the boil.

When the soup begins to foam, reduce the heat and simmer for 45 minutes, stirring occasionally, until the peas are tender. You may need to top up the soup with a little water.

When the peas are very tender, add the coriander and the black pepper to the soup. Stir well and simmer for a further 10 minutes. Serve very hot with fresh bread.

Wholesome Lentil Soup
Serves 4
Calories per serving: 131
Grams saturated fat per serving: 0.5
Milligrams cholesterol per serving: 0
Preparation time: 45 minutes

15ml (1 tbsp) oil
3 cloves garlic, finely chopped
1 large onion, finely chopped
5ml (1 tsp) chilli powder
225g (8 oz) dried red lentils
1 litre (2 pints) vegetable stock or water
1 whole chilli, fresh or dried
7.5ml (1½ tsp) turmeric
1 small green pepper, finely chopped
1x 425g (15 oz) tin whole tomatoes
juice of 1 lemon

Heat the oil in a large saucepan over a medium heat. Add the garlic and onion and sauté until the onion is tender. Now add the chilli powder to the sauté and stir well.

Wash the lentils very well, drain them and add them to the sauté with the stock. Stir well and bring the mixture to the boil. Add the whole chilli, then cover the pan, reduce the heat and simmer the soup for 20 minutes, until the lentils begin to lose their shape.

Add the turmeric, the chopped green pepper and the tinned, whole tomatoes. Stir well and cook for a further 10 minutes (30 minutes in total) or until the lentils have completely lost their shape and are quite mushy.

Stir in the lemon juice just before serving. Serve hot.

Creamy Spinach Soup
Serves 4
Calories per serving: 175
Grams saturated fat per serving: 1
Milligrams cholesterol per serving: 0
Preparation time: 45 minutes

450g (1 lb) fresh spinach
15ml (1 tbsp) oil

3 cloves garlic, finely chopped
2 medium onions, finely chopped
10ml (2 tsp) freshly ground black pepper
10ml (2 tsp) yeast extract
500ml (1 pint) vegetable stock or water
15ml (1 tbsp) oil
10ml (2 tsp) caraway seed
15ml (1 tbsp) cornflour
500ml (1 pint) soya milk
5ml (1 tsp) ground coriander

Wash the spinach and slice it into coarse strips. Leave to drain in a colander until needed.

Heat the oil in a deep saucepan over a medium heat. Add the garlic and onion and sauté until the onions are tender.

Add the black pepper, yeast extract and stock and bring to a slow boil. Now add the drained spinach, reduce the heat, cover the pan and leave to simmer gently, stirring occasionally.

In a small saucepan, heat the oil and lightly saute the caraway seeds over a low heat.

Sprinkle the cornflour over the oil and stir thoroughly to make a smooth paste (a roux). Keep the pan over the heat as you add the milk – a little at a time – stirring after each addition.

Add the coriander to this sauce and stir until a smooth consistency is reached.

Finally, add the white sauce to the soup and stir together very well. Cook the soup for another 10 minutes, stirring often. Serve hot.

Cream of Vegetable Soup
Serves 4
Calories per serving: 205
Grams saturated fat per serving: 0.8
Milligrams cholesterol per serving: 0
Preparation time: 40 minutes

15ml (1 tbsp) oil
3 cloves garlic, finely chopped
1 medium onion, finely chopped
5ml (1 tsp) paprika
15ml (1 tbsp) cornflour
570ml (1 pint) soya milk
570ml (1 pint) vegetable stock or water
5ml (1 tsp) yeast extract
2 medium carrots, thinly sliced

2 medium courgettes, sliced
1 × 340g (12 oz) tin sweetcorn
15ml (1 tbsp) fresh thyme or marjoram, chopped

Heat the oil in a large saucepan over a low heat. Add the finely chopped garlic and onion and sauté until tender.

Stir the paprika into the cornflour and sprinkle over the sauté. Stir well to make a thick paste, or roux.

Mix the milk and all but 2 fl.oz of the stock together in a jug and gradually add to the roux, stirring well after each addition to make a thick sauce. When all the liquid has been added, remove the pan from the heat and put to one side.

Mix the yeast extract with the remaining stock and place over a medium heat in a separate pan. When the liquid bubbles, add the carrots and courgettes and stir them until they become slightly tender and browned. Add the sweet corn to this sauté and cook for 5 minutes, stirring often.

Now place the thick sauce over a medium heat once again and stir the vegetable sauté into it. Add a little more water if necessary to get the consistency you desire. Then add the fresh herb and leave to simmer over a very low heat for a further 10–15 minutes.

Serve hot with a garnish of fresh herb.

Spiced Carrot Soup
Serves 4
Calories per serving: 132
Grams saturated fat per serving: 0.5
Milligrams cholesterol per serving: 0
Preparation time: 40 minutes

1 large swede, peeled and finely chopped
450g (1 lb) carrots, peeled and thinly sliced
1 litre (2 pints) vegetable stock or water
10ml (2 tsp) yeast extract
15ml (1 tbsp) oil
3 cloves garlic, finely chopped
1 medium onion, finely chopped
10ml (2 tsp) freshly ground black pepper
2.5ml (½ tsp) ground cinnamon
a pinch of ground nutmeg
1 bunch spring onions, sliced into rounds

Prepare the swede and carrots and place them in the stock in a deep saucepan over a high heat. Bring to the boil, then stir in the yeast extract. Now cover the pan, reduce the heat and cook at a simmer for

20 minutes, or until the vegetables are tender.

Remove the pan from the heat and run the vegetables and the liquid through a blender or hand-mouli to make a smooth purée. Add water if necessary to make up for any stock that has boiled away. Then return the puréed soup to the saucepan and then the cooker, placing over a low heat.

Meanwhile, heat the oil in a small pan over a medium heat. Add the garlic and onion and sauté until tender. Sprinkle the pepper, cinnamon and nutmeg over the sauté and stir well. Then add this mixture to the puréed soup and stir while the soup comes to a slow simmer, about 5 minutes.

Add the finely chopped spring onion 5 minutes before you are ready to serve the soup, leaving some aside to use as a garnish if you wish.

Serve hot.

Beetroot & Celery Soup
Serves 4
Calories per serving: 98
Grams saturated fat per serving: 0.5
Milligrams cholesterol per serving: 0
Preparation time: 40 minutes

15ml (1 tbsp) oil
3–5 cloves garlic, finely chopped
2 medium onions, finely chopped
5ml (1 tsp) caraway seed
10ml (2 tsp) yeast extract
1.5 litres (3 pints) vegetable stock or water
2 medium beetroot, peeled and chopped
1 head of celery, chopped
28g (1 oz) fresh parsley, chopped

Heat the oil in a large saucepan over a medium heat. Add the garlic, onion and caraway seed and sauté until the onion is tender.

Add the yeast extract to the sauté, stir well then gradually add the stock. Cover the pan and bring the liquid to a gentle boil.

Meanwhile, prepare the beetroot and celery, then add them to the boiling liquid and stir again. Cover the pan, reduce the heat and leave to simmer for 20 minutes, or until the beetroot is very tender.

Serve the soup hot with a garnish of chopped parsley.

Thick Broccoli Soup
Serves 4
Calories per serving: 129
Grams saturated fat per serving: 0.5

Milligrams cholesterol per serving: 0
Preparation time: 1 hour

55g (2 oz) barley
1 litre (2 pints) vegetable stock or water
15ml (1 tbsp) oil
1 medium onion, finely chopped
2 medium carrots, thinly sliced
450g (1 lb) broccoli
10ml (2 tsp) freshly ground black pepper
15ml (1 tbsp) dried mixed sweet herbs

Wash and drain the barley. Place in a deep enamel saucepan with the stock. Stir well, cover the pan and place over a high heat. Bring the stock to the boil then reduce the heat and simmer the barley for 30 minutes.

Meanwhile, heat the oil in a small pan over a medium heat. Add the onion and sauté until tender. Then add the carrots and continue to sauté for a further 5 minutes.

Stir this sauté into the barley broth towards the end of the 30 minutes.

Wash, trim and finely chop the broccoli and add to the soup. Stir in the black pepper and mixed herbs, cover the pan and cook for 10–15 minutes longer. Serve hot.

Cabbage & Watercress Soup
Serves 4
Calories per serving: 81
Grams saturated fat per serving: 0.5
Milligrams cholesterol per serving: 0
Preparation time: 30 minutes

15ml (1 tbsp) oil
3 cloves garlic, finely chopped
2 medium onions, finely chopped
5ml (1 tsp) caraway seed
450g (1 lb) cabbage, shredded
10ml (2 tsp) yeast extract
1 litres (2 pints) vegetable stock or water
2 bay leaves
10ml (2 tsp) freshly ground black pepper
1 bunch of fresh watercress, coarsely chopped
5ml (1 tsp) ground coriander

Heat the oil in a large, deep saucepan and place over a medium flame.

Add the garlic, onions and caraway and sauté until the onion is tender, stirring often.

When the onions are very soft, add the cabbage to the sauté. Then stir in the yeast extract and gradually add the stock, bay leaves and pepper. Bring to a slow boil over a medium heat, then cover the pan, reduce the heat and simmer for 10–15 minutes.

Finally, add the watercress and ground coriander to the soup. Keep the cover off the pan as the soup continues to simmer a further 5 minutes. Stir well and serve hot.

Thick & Creamy Cauliflower Soup
Serves 4
Calories per serving: 121
Grams saturated fat per serving: 0.5
Milligrams cholesterol per serving: 0
Preparation time: 45 minutes

15ml (1 tbsp) oil
1 medium onion, finely chopped
5ml (1 tsp) chilli powder
10ml (2 tsp) ground coriander
15ml (1 tbsp) cornflour
570ml (1 pint) soya milk
285ml (½ pint) vegetable stock or water
10ml (2 tsp) turmeric
1 large cauliflower, chopped
4 slices lemon, to garnish

Heat the oil in a saucepan over a medium heat. Add the onion and sauté until tender, stirring often.

Mix the chilli powder, coriander and cornflour together and, when the onion is tender, sprinkle over the sauté. Stir well to make a thick paste, or roux.

Now mix the milk and stock together and add to the roux, stirring after each addition to make a smooth sauce. Keep the sauce over a low to medium heat throughout.

When all the liquid has been added, stir in the turmeric and bring the sauce to a simmer.

Add the chopped cauliflower and a little more liquid if desired, cover the pan and simmer over a low heat for 20 minutes, stirring occasionally.

When the cauliflower is tender, remove the soup from the heat and run it through a blender or hand mouli to make a smooth puree. Return the soup to the heat, add liquid or spices to taste and bring back to a low simmer. Serve hot with a slice of lemon floating on top of each bowlful.

Green Bean & Celery Soup
Serves 4
Calories per serving: 82
Grams saturated fat per serving: 0.4
Milligrams cholesterol per serving: 0
Preparation time: 35 minutes

15ml (1 tbsp) oil
3 cloves garlic, finely chopped
1 medium onion, finely chopped
5 stalks celery, chopped
450g (1 lb) fresh green beans, thinly sliced
10ml (2 tsp) yeast extract
1 litre (2 pints) vegetable stock or water
2 bay leaves
10ml (2 tsp) freshly ground black pepper
10ml (2 tsp) dried mixed sweet herbs

Heat the oil a large saucepan over a medium heat. Add the garlic and onion and sauté until the onion is tender. Now add the chopped celery and continue to sauté, over a low heat, for 3–5 minutes stirring often.

Add the green beans and yeast extract and stir constantly as you gradually add the stock. Increase the heat and bring the soup to a low boil.

Add the bay leaves, pepper and sweet herbs and stir well. Cover the pan and simmer over a low heat for 20 minutes. Serve hot.

Vegetable Stock
Serves 4
Calories per serving: 131
Grams saturated fat per serving: 0.1
Milligrams cholesterol per serving: 0
Preparation time: 1 hour and 15 minutes

55g (2 oz) barley or scotch broth mixture
2 litres (4 pints) water
450g (1 lb) root vegetables or parts (i.e. peels, tops & tails, chunks)
225g (8 oz) greens or outside leaves (i.e. unsightly leaves, green parts of cauliflower, leaves of celery, coarse lettuce leaves, cabbage hearts)
2 large onions, coarsely chopped and including the skins
garlic to taste, coarsely chopped and including the skins
2 bay leaves

Measure the barley and water into a large saucepan and place over a high heat. Bring the mixture to a boil, stirring frequently.

Add the remaining ingredients and stir well. Cover the pan, reduce the heat and leave to simmer for 45–60 minutes, stirring occasionally. Top up the liquid once or twice during this time to maintain approximately 2 litres of stock.

Strain the stock through a colander or sieve and discard the vegetable matter. Use the stock at once or measure it into portions for freezing and later use.

Potato & Parsley Soup
Serves 4
Calories per serving: 231
Grams saturated fat per serving: 0.5
Milligrams cholesterol per serving: 0
Preparation time: 35 minutes

15ml (1 tbsp) oil
2 medium onions, finely chopped
700g (1½ lbs) potatoes, peeled and cubed
1 litre (2 pints) vegetable stock or water
1 medium carrot, peeled and grated
2 bay leaves
10ml (2 tsp) freshly ground black pepper
55g (2 oz) fresh parsley, coarsely chopped
5ml (1 tsp) yeast extract

Heat the oil in a large saucepan over a medium heat. Add the onion and sauté until the onion is tender, stirring often.

Add the cubed potatoes and continue the sauté for a further 5 minutes, stirring frequently. The potatoes will begin to soften slightly.

Now add the stock and stir the soup well, ensuring that no onion or potato sticks to the bottom of the pan. Bring the mixture to a low boil, then cover the pan, reduce the heat and simmer for 15 minutes.

Add the remaining ingredients, stir well and continue to simmer for a further 10 minutes. Stir occasionally. Serve hot.

Cream of Asparagus Soup
Serves 4
Calories per serving: 140
Grams saturated fat per serving: 0.7
Milligrams cholesterol per serving: 0
Preparation time: 25 minutes

15ml (1 tbsp) oil
5 cloves garlic, finely chopped
5ml (1 tsp) ground cumin

15ml (1 tbsp) cornflour
570ml (1 pint) soya milk
285ml (10 fl.oz) vegetable stock or water
450g (1 lb) asparagus, steamed and chopped
juice of 2 oranges
zest of 1 orange
freshly ground black pepper to taste

Heat the oil in a saucepan over a medium heat. Add the garlic and cumin and sauté until the garlic is lightly browned. Sprinkle the cornflour over the sauté and stir well to make a thick paste, or roux.

Mix the soya milk and stock together and add to the roux, a little at a time, stirring after each addition. Add more water if desired to give a consistency you will enjoy.

Keep the soup over a medium heat, stirring often, as you add the remaining ingredients. Stir well and leave to simmer, covered, over a low heat for 5–10 minutes. Serve hot.

Creamy Mushroom Soup
Serves 4
Calories per serving: 142
Grams saturated fat per serving: 0.7
Milligrams cholesterol per serving: 0
Preparation time: 30 minutes

15ml (1 tbsp) oil
3 cloves garlic, finely chopped
2 small onions, finely chopped
15ml (1 tbsp) cornflour
570ml (1 pint) soya milk
285ml (10 fl.oz) vegetable stock or water
450g (1 lb) mushrooms, cleaned and finely chopped
10ml (2 tsp) freshly ground black pepper
1.25ml (¼ tsp) grated nutmeg

Heat the oil in a saucepan over a medium heat. Add the garlic and onion and sauté until the onion is tender, stirring often.

Sprinkle the cornflour over the sauté and stir well to make a thick paste, or roux.

Mix the soya milk and stock together and add a little at a time to the roux, stirring well after each addition, to make a creamy sauce.

Add the remaining ingredients and stir well as the mixture begins to simmer. Cover the pan, reduce the heat and simmer gently for 15 minutes. Serve hot.

Malaga Gazpacho Soup
Serves 4
Calories per serving: 229
Grams saturated fat per serving: 2.2
Milligrams cholesterol per serving: 0
Preparation time: 1 hour and 30 minutes, including chilling time

60ml (2 fl.oz) olive oil
1 bunch spring onions, finely chopped
2 cloves garlic, crushed
850ml (1½ pints) vegetable stock
170g (6oz) chopped tomato
1 medium green pepper, finely chopped
1 medium cucumber, peeled and finely diced
1 large sprig fresh parsley, finely chopped
5ml (1 tsp) freshly ground black pepper
a pinch of salt
115g (4 oz) fresh grapes, sliced and de-seeded
20ml (4 tsp) ground almonds

Measure the oil into a small bowl, add the onion and garlic and stir well then leave to one side.

Pour the vegetable stock into a large serving tureen and add the tomato, green pepper, cucumber, parsley and seasoning. Stir well and adjust the seasoning to taste.

Now stir in the oil and onion mixture, cover the tureen and chill for one hour, or until ready to serve.

Ladle the soup into serving bowls and garnish with sliced grapes, topped by a sprinkling of ground almonds. Serve immediately with fresh bread or croutons.

Thick & Spicy Celery Soup
Serves 4
Calories per serving: 106
Grams saturated fat per serving: 0.4
Milligrams cholesterol per serving: 0
Preparation time: 45 minutes

15ml (1 tbsp) oil
3 cloves garlic, finely chopped
1 medium onion, finely chopped
1 head of celery, chopped
1 medium potato (approximately 4–6 oz), peeled and grated
850ml (1½ pints) vegetable stock or water

10ml (2 tsp) freshly ground black pepper
7.5ml (1½ tsp) turmeric
5ml (1 tsp) ground coriander
2.5ml (½ tsp) ground allspice
a pinch of salt or celery salt
juice of ½ lemon

Heat the oil in a saucepan and place over a medium heat. Add the garlic and onion and sauté until the onion is tender, stirring often. Add the chopped celery and continue to sauté for a further 5 minutes, stirring frequently.

Now add the grated potato and vegetable stock. Stir the mixture well and bring to a rolling boil. Reduce the heat and stir in the remaining ingredients. Cover the pan and simmer over a low heat for 20 minutes. Serve hot.

Tangy Spinach & Potato Soup
Serves 4
Calories per serving: 276
Grams saturated fat per serving: 1.2
Milligrams cholesterol per serving: 0
Preparation time: 45 minutes

455g (1 lb) fresh spinach, washed and chopped
10ml (2 tsp) oil
2 medium onions, finely chopped
675g (1½ lbs) potatoes, peeled and chopped
1 litre (2 pints) vegetable stock or water
10ml (2 tsp) freshly ground black pepper
10ml (2 tsp) freshly ground coriander
4 whole cloves, freshly ground
15ml (1 tbsp) smooth peanut butter
zest of 1 orange

Prepare the spinach and leave to one side to drain.

Heat the oil in a saucepan over a medium heat. Add the chopped onion and sauté until the onion is tender, stirring often.

Add the chopped potato and continue the sauté for a further 5 minutes, until the potato becomes slightly tender.

Now add the stock and ground spices and bring the soup to a slow boil.

Next, add spinach and peanut butter. Reduce the heat, stir well and leave to simmer, covered, for 10–15 minutes. Finally, stir in the zest of orange and simmer for a final 5 minutes, then serve hot.

Cauliflower & Sweetcorn Soup
Serves 4
Calories per serving: 149
Grams saturated fat per serving: 0.6
Milligrams cholesterol per serving: 0
Preparation time: 45 minutes

15ml (1 tbsp) oil
3 cloves garlic, finely chopped
5ml (1 tsp) fresh ginger, grated
1 large onion, finely chopped
1 whole cauliflower, washed, trimmed and chopped
1 litre (2 pints) vegetable stock or water
1 × 340g (12oz) tin sweetcorn, drained
5ml (1 tsp) freshly ground black pepper
5ml (1 tsp) garam masala
2.5ml (½ tsp) fenugreek
15ml (1 tbsp) soy sauce (or tamari or shoyu)

Heat the oil in a saucepan over a medium heat. Add the garlic and ginger and sauté until the garlic becomes slightly golden. Then add the onion and continue the sauté until the onion is tender, stirring constantly.

Add the chopped cauliflower to the sauté and stir well for a further 5 minutes. Then add the stock and bring the soup to a slow boil over a medium heat.

Add the remaining ingredients, stir well and cover the pan. Reduce the heat and simmer gently for 20 minutes. Serve hot.

SNACKS, SANDWICHES & STARTERS

Easy Cheesy Popcorn
Serves 4
Calories per serving: 105
Grams saturated fat per serving: 0.8
Milligrams cholesterol per serving: 0
Preparation time: 15 minutes

30ml (2 tbsp) oil
55g (2 oz) popcorn kernels
60ml (4 tbsp) nutritional yeast flakes

Heat the oil in a deep, thick-bottomed saucepan. When very hot, add the popcorn kernels and spread them to thinly cover the bottom of the pan. Cover the pan and place over a medium to high heat. Shake the pan occasionally as the kernels heat and begin popping.

When the popping has stopped, turn the popcorn into a large bowl and sprinkle the yeast flakes over it, while still hot. Use a large spoon to toss the yeast flakes into the popcorn. Serve immediately in individual serving bowls.

Hot Tempeh Sandwiches
Serves 4
Calories per serving: 294
Grams saturated fat per serving: 1.3
Milligrams cholesterol per serving: 0
Preparation time: 25 minutes

225g (8 oz) tempeh, defrosted
15ml (1 tbsp) oil
8 slices whole wheat bread, lightly toasted
10ml (2 tsp) prepared mustard, or to taste
8 lettuce leaves
2 medium tomatoes, thinly sliced

Pre-heat the oven to 180°C / 350°F / Gas Mark 4.

Slice the block of tempeh in half then slice each half into four thin slices along its thickness. Spread the oil in a baking tray and lay the eight tempeh slices on the tray. Bake for 15 minutes, turning once in that time.

Meanwhile, toast the bread and spread each slice with mustard, to taste. Arrange the lettuce and tomato slices onto four bread slices then place two of the tempeh slices on each of these. Close the sandwiches with the remaining bread slices and serve immediately.

Orange & Tahini Filled Sushi
Serves 4
Calories per serving: 109
Grams saturated fat per serving: 0.6
Milligrams cholesterol per serving: 0
Preparation time: 1 hour and 15 minutes

1 sheet toasted Nori seaweed
225g (8 oz) well-cooked rice
30ml (2 tbsp) tahini
juice and zest of 1 orange
2 cloves garlic, crushed
2.5ml (½ tsp) freshly ground black pepper

Lay the sheet of nori on a clean, dry surface and spread the cooked rice to an even thickness over all but the outer ½ inch of the nori.

Mix the tahini, orange juice, zest, garlic and black pepper in a small bowl. Carefully spread this mixture over the rice.

Damp the edges of the nori with water and carefully roll the nori in and over the rice, sealing the edges as you finish. Rest the sushi with the seam down on a plate and chill for 1 hour before serving. Slice into 1 inch thick rounds and serve as a snack or starter.

Savoury Stuffed Celery Snacks
Serves 4
Calories per serving: 138
Grams saturated fat per serving: 1
Milligrams cholesterol per serving: 0
Preparation time: 20 minutes

8 stalks celery, cleaned and trimmed
4 medium gherkins, minced
30g (1 oz) ground walnuts
285g (10 oz) tofu
60ml (2 fl.oz) soya milk
5ml (1 tsp) paprika or chilli powder

Slice the celery into approximately 4-inch-long pieces. Mix the remaining ingredients together in a bowl to an even consistency. Now press some filling into each of the celery pieces, allowing the filling to rise up in a mound. Chill the snacks if desired, or serve immediately as a snack or starter.

Sandwich Select-O-Mat

Peanut Butter & Banana Sandwich
Serves 1
Calories per serving: 376
Grams saturated fat per serving: 3
Milligrams cholesterol per serving: 0

2 slices whole wheat bread
½ ripe banana
30ml (2 tbsp) peanut butter

Simple Salad Sandwich
Serves 1
Calories per serving: 235
Grams saturated fat per serving: 1.2
Milligrams cholesterol per serving: 0

2 slices whole wheat bread
5ml (1 tsp) prepared mustard

15ml (1 tbsp) salad cream (no animal ingredients)
2 lettuce leaves
1 tomato, sliced
¼ cucumber, sliced

Tofu & Beansprout Sandwich
Serves 1
Calories per serving: 237
Grams saturated fat per serving: 1
Milligrams cholesterol per serving: 0

2 slices whole wheat bread
100g (3½ oz) tofu
15g (½ oz) alfalfa or mung bean sprouts
1 medium tomato, sliced
5ml (1 tsp) prepared mustard

Avocado & Watercress Sandwich
Serves 1
Calories per serving: 298
Grams saturated fat per serving: 2.7
Milligrams cholesterol per serving: 0

2 slices whole wheat bread
½ ripe avocado, peeled and thinly sliced
15g (½ oz) fresh watercress, finely chopped
freshly ground black pepper to taste

Melon Starter with Almond, Port & Rosemary
Serves 4
Calories per serving: 135
Grams saturated fat per serving: 0.4
Milligrams cholesterol per serving: 0
Preparation time: 15 minutes

2 melons (i.e.1 honeydew and 1 canteloupe), halved and cleaned
30g (1 oz) ground almonds
5ml (1 tsp) ground coriander
285ml (10 fl.oz) port
4 tiny sprigs fresh rosemary

Scoop out the melon halves to make dozens of little melon balls and put to one side. Save any melon juice that accumulates.

Mix the almonds and coriander together in a small bowl. Sprinkle half of this mixture into the melon shells, dividing it evenly between the four melon halves. Return the melon balls to the melon halves, mixing the two types of melon as you do so. Pour the port over the melon balls, sprinkle the remaining almond mixture over each serving and garnish with a sprig of fresh rosemary. These may be chilled before serving or served immediately.

Grilled Grapefruit Starter
Serves 4
Calories per serving: 70
Grams saturated fat per serving: 0
Milligrams cholesterol per serving: 0
Preparation time: 15 minutes

2 large grapefruit
30ml (2 tbsp) brown sugar

Slice the grapefruits in half and remove the pithy core. Pack the core with a little brown sugar and place the grapefruit halves under a hot grill. Grill for 5–10 minutes, until the top of the grapefruits are beginning to brown and the sugar has melted. Serve immediately, with a slice of melba toast if desired.

Dried Banana Nuggets in Hot Orange Sauce
Serves 4
Calories per serving: 275
Grams saturated fat per serving: 4
Milligrams cholesterol per serving: 0
Preparation time: 15 minutes

8 dried bananas
1 × recipe of Sweet Orange Sauce (page 132)

Cut each dried banana into 1-inch nuggets and arrange on each of four serving plates.

Make up one recipe of Sweet Orange Sauce and pour, while still hot, over each serving of banana. Serve at once.

Radichio with Tofu & Toasted Nori Filling
Serves 4
Calories per serving: 109
Grams saturated fat per serving: 1
Milligrams cholesterol per serving: 0
Preparation time: 20 minutes

8 radichio leaves
15ml (1 tbsp) oil
3 cloves garlic, crushed
285g (10 oz) tofu, finely chopped

15ml (1 tbsp) sesame seeds
50g (1¾ oz) shredded nori

Arrange two radichio leaves on each of four serving plates.

Heat the oil in a large frying pan and sauté the garlic until lightly browned. Add the tofu pieces and stir frequently as they brown. Finally, add the sesame seed to the sauté and stir for a further 3 minutes over a medium to high heat.

Meanwhile place the nori under a hot grill until it goes crispy. Fill each of the radichio leaves with the sauté filling and top with the toasted nori. Serve at once as a snack or starter.

SALADS & DRESSINGS

Easy Potato Salad
Serves 4
Calories per serving: 109
Grams saturated fat per serving: 0
Milligrams cholesterol per serving: 0
Preparation time: 20 minutes, plus chilling time

500g (1 lb) new potatoes, cleaned
5 spring onions, thinly sliced
2–4 sprigs of fresh parsley, finely chopped
1 sprig fresh mint, finely chopped

Steam the potatoes until tender, then allow them to cool. Turn them into a large salad bowl.

Mix the remaining ingredients in with the potatoes and top with the following dressing (or a dressing of your choice). Stir well and serve immediately or cover and chill before serving.

Simple Creamy Dressing
Serves 4
Calories per serving: 69
Grams saturated fat per serving: 1
Milligrams cholesterol per serving: 0
Preparation time: 5 minutes

30ml (2 tbsp) olive oil
30ml (2 tbsp) soya milk concentrate
5ml (1 tsp) prepared mustard
2.5ml (½ tsp) freshly ground black pepper
60ml (2 fl.oz) cider vinegar

Measure all the ingredients into a jar and shake well to make a smooth emulsion. Pour over the salad, stir well and serve.

Colourful Pasta Salad
Serves 4
Calories per serving: 144
Grams saturated fat per serving: 0.2
Milligrams cholesterol per serving: 0
Preparation time: 20 minutes, plus chilling time

225g (8 oz) whole wheat pasta shells
1 × 340g (12 oz) tin sweetcorn
1 large green pepper, finely chopped
2 large carrots, peeled and shredded
30ml (2 tbsp) chives *or* 2 spring onions, finely chopped
15g (½ oz) fresh parsley, chopped

Cook the pasta until just tender, drain well and allow to cool.

Mix the sweet corn, pepper, carrot and chives together in a large salad bowl. Stir in most of the chopped parsley as well.

When the pasta has cooled, stir it into the salad also, along with the following dressing (or a dressing of your choice). Sprinkle the remaining parsley over the tossed salad and serve immediately or chill for one hour before serving.

Mayonnaise-Style Dressing
Serves 4
Calories per serving: 78
Grams saturated fat per serving: 0.7
Milligrams cholesterol per serving: 0
Preparation time: 5 minutes

55g (2 oz) tofu
140ml (5 fl.oz) soya milk concentrate
15ml (1 tbsp) olive oil
garlic to taste, crushed
5ml (1 tsp) freshly ground black pepper
15ml (1 tbsp) cider vinegar or lemon juice

Measure all the ingredients into a blender and puree to a smooth consistency. Chill for use later, or immediately stir into the salad.

Tangy Pickled Salad
Serves 4
Calories per serving: 214
Grams saturated fat per serving: 2
Milligrams cholesterol per serving: 0
Preparation time: 20 minutes, plus chilling time

1 large raw beetroot, shredded

1 medium raw turnip, shredded
115g (4 oz) carrots, shredded
115g (4 oz) white cabbage, shredded
55g (2 oz) raisins or sultanas
1 medium onion, very finely chopped
10ml (2 tsp) fresh ginger, grated
2.5ml (½ tsp) chilli powder
juice and grated peel of 1 lemon
170ml (6 fl.oz) cider vinegar
60ml (2 fl.oz) olive oil

Mix the first 7 ingredients together in a large salad bowl.

Stir the remaining ingredients together in a jug and pour over the salad. Stir well and cover the bowl.

Chill or keep in a cool place for 1–4 hours, stirring occasionally. Stir again and serve with other salads or as a side dish to a hot meal.

Cress & Chicory Salad
Serves 4
Calories per serving: 83
Grams saturated fat per serving: 0.1
Milligrams cholesterol per serving: 0
Preparation time: 30 minutes

450g (1 lb) 'beef' tomatoes, sliced
a little salt
5ml (1 tsp) celery seed
1 × 340g (12 oz) tin water chestnuts, drained and sliced
2 medium sized chicory, washed and separated
15g (½ oz) watercress, washed and coarsely chopped

Arrange the tomato slices on a large plate and sprinkle the salt and celery seed over them. Place to one side for 20–30 minutes, the salt will help to remove the 'bitter' from them.

Mix the remaining ingredients together in a salad bowl and toss in the following dressing (or a dressing of your choice).

Drain the liquid from the tomatoes and arrange the slices on each of four plates. Top with the chicory salad and an extra spoonful of the dressing. Serve at once.

Refreshing Lemon Dressing
Serves 4
Calories per serving: 105
Grams saturated fat per serving: 1.4
Milligrams cholesterol per serving: 0

Preparation time: 5 minutes

45ml (3 tbsp) olive oil
juice of 2 lemons
5ml (1 tsp) sugar
2.5ml (½ tsp) ground allspice
2.5ml (½ tsp) freshly ground black pepper

Mix all the ingredients together in a jar and shake well. Pour over the salad and toss well.

Butter Bean & Beetroot Salad
Serves 4
Calories per serving: 121
Grams saturated fat per serving: 1
Milligrams cholesterol per serving: 0
Preparation time: 15 minutes

1 × 450g (16 oz) tin butter beans, drained
1 medium beetroot, shredded
1 bunch spring onions, thinly sliced
4 large sprigs of fresh parsley, chopped
5ml (1 tsp) freshly ground black pepper
juice and zest of 1 orange
30ml (2 tbsp) olive oil

Stir all the ingredients together in a large salad bowl and serve. A further dressing may be added if desired (i.e. Refreshing Lemon Dressing, page 94). This salad may be stored, covered, in the refrigerator for 2 days.

Bean & Coriander Salad
Serves 4
Calories per serving: 214
Grams saturated fat per serving: 1.5
Milligrams cholesterol per serving: 0
Preparation time: 15 minutes, plus soaking and cooking time if using dried beans

115g (4 oz) dried *or* 1 × 450g (1 lb) tin black-eyed beans
30g (1 oz) fresh coriander
5 stalks celery, thinly sliced
1 medium red pepper, sliced or chopped
45ml (3 tbsp) olive oil
juice of 1 lemon
5ml (1 tsp) freshly ground black pepper
a pinch of salt

Soak the beans and the coriander separately in very cold water overnight if using dried beans. Rinse, drain and pressure cook the beans. Allow to cool. Alternatively, drain the tinned beans.

Wash the coriander and chop quite finely.

Mix the coriander, celery and pepper together in a large salad bowl. Now stir the cool beans into the mix.

Mix the remaining ingredients together in a jug and pour over the salad. Stir well and serve. This salad will keep, covered, in the refrigerator for 2 days.

High-Protein Salad
Serves 4
Calories per serving: 222
Grams saturated fat per serving: 0.5
Milligrams cholesterol per serving: 0
Preparation time: 15 minutes

1 × 450g (1 lb) tin kidney beans
225g (½ lb) carrots, shredded
¼ small head of cabbage, shredded
15g (½ oz) fresh parsley or watercress, chopped
3–5 spring onions, thinly sliced (optional)
55g (2 oz) raisins or sultanas
30g (1 oz) slivered almonds

Mix all the ingredients together in a large salad bowl and stir well. Serve with the following dressing (or a dressing of your choice). This dressing looks appetizing on a bed of lettuce or chicory. One serving of this salad give you about 20 per cent of your daily protein requirement!

Savoury Orange Dressing
Serves 4
Calories per serving: 88
Grams saturated fat per serving: 1
Milligrams cholesterol per serving: 0
Preparation time: 5 minutes

60ml (2 fl.oz) olive oil
juice of 2 oranges
15ml (1 tbsp) cider vinegar
2.5ml (½ tsp) chilli powder or 1 chilli, finely chopped
a pinch of salt

Measure all the ingredients into a jar and shake well. Pour over the salad and serve.

Raw Goodness Salad

Serves 4
Calories per serving: 53
Grams saturated fat per serving: 0
Milligrams cholesterol per serving: 0
Preparation time: 10 minutes

225g (8 oz) sprouted mung beans
1 medium raw beetroot, shredded
115g (4 oz) carrots, shredded
5 stalks celery, finely chopped
2 cloves garlic, crushed
25g (1 oz) fresh parsley, finely chopped

Toss all the ingredients together in a large salad bowl and serve with your the following dressing (or a dressing of your choice).

Two Thousand Island Dressing

Serves 4
Calories per serving: 58
Grams saturated fat per serving: 0.3
Milligrams cholesterol per serving: 0
Preparation time: 10 minutes

140g (5 oz) silken tofu
120ml (4 fl.oz) soya milk concentrate
15ml (1 tbsp) cider vinegar or lemon juice
3 cloves garlic, crushed or to taste
2.5ml (½ tsp) paprika
5ml (1 tsp) freshly ground black pepper
30ml (2 tbsp) capers, chopped

Measure the tofu, soya milk and vinegar into a blender and puree to a smooth, creamy consistency. Add more milk or vinegar if desired.

Spoon the puree into a bowl and stir in the remaining ingredients. Adjust the seasoning to taste and serve immediately.

Endive & Olive Salad

Serves 4
Calories per serving: 157
Grams saturated fat per serving: 1.4
Milligrams cholesterol per serving: 0
Preparation time: 20 minutes

2 sprigs of fresh mint, finely chopped
60ml (2 fl.oz) cider vinegar

juice of 1 lemon
45ml (3 tbsp) olive oil
5ml (1 tsp) freshly ground black pepper
115g (4 oz) olives, thinly sliced
1 whole endive
1 orange
5 spring onions, thinly sliced

Mix the first five ingredients together in a small jug. Pour this dressing over the sliced olives, in a small bowl, and put to one side.

Wash, trim and break the endive and place in a large salad bowl.

Peel the orange very well, divide into segments and slice very thinly. Add to the endive in the salad bowl, ensuring that the juice is also added.

Next, add the spring onions and toss the salad well.

Pour the olive and dressing mixture over the salad. Toss gently and serve.

Minty Mixed Salad
Serves 4
Calories per serving: 48
Grams saturated fat per serving: 0.1
Milligrams cholesterol per serving: 0
Preparation time: 15 minutes

1 × 425g (15 oz) tin green beans, drained
115g (4 oz) beansprouts (i.e. mung, alfalfa)
1 medium red or yellow pepper, finely chopped
115g (4 oz) button mushrooms, cleaned and quartered
15ml (1 tbsp) fresh mint, chopped

Mix all the ingredients together in a large salad bowl and top with your favourite dressing or the juice of one lemon and one orange. Toss well and serve. This salad is good as a filling for baked potato, baps or warm pitta bread.

Refreshing Cucumber Salad
Serves 4
Calories per serving: 89
Grams saturated fat per serving: 0.6
Milligrams cholesterol per serving: 0
Preparation time: 20 minutes

140g (5 oz) plain tofu
285ml (½ pint) soya milk concentrate
3 cloves garlic, crushed

3 spring onions, finely chopped
1 large cucumber, peeled and finely chopped
5 stalks celery, thinly sliced
5ml (1 tsp) freshly ground black pepper
15g (½ oz) fresh mint, finely chopped
1 lemon, to garnish

Blend the tofu and soya milk together in a bowl or blender until of a very smooth consistency. Turn into a large salad bowl, add the garlic and onion and stir well.

Add the remaining ingredients to the tofu mixture and stir gently together. Serve garnished with a wedge of lemon which, when squeezed over the salad, will add an extra tang. Serve immediately or chill for one hour before serving.

Ginger & Chicory Salad
Serves 4
Calories per serving: 94
Grams saturated fat per serving: 0.2
Milligrams cholesterol per serving: 0
Preparation time: 1 hour and 20 minutes

10ml (2 tsp) fresh ginger, grated
30ml (2 tbsp) cider vinegar
juice of 2 lemons
15ml (1 tbsp) brown sugar
225g (8 oz) button mushrooms, cleaned and quartered
1 large eating apple, finely chopped
2 large chicory
225g (8 oz) tomatoes, thinly sliced

Grate the ginger into a salad bowl. Mix the vinegar, lemon juice and brown sugar together and add to the ginger. Stir well.

Now add the mushroom pieces and apple chunks to the ginger mixture. Stir well, cover the bowl and leave to one side, or in the refrigerator, for at least one hour.

Separate the leaves of the chicory and arrange with the sliced tomato on each of four plates. Spoon some of the ginger mixture over each portion and serve immediately. This salad is especially nice served beside a small portion of Refreshing Cucumber Salad (see page 98).

Simple Cucumber Salad
Serves 4
Calories per serving: 25
Grams saturated fat per serving: 0

Milligrams cholesterol per serving: 0
Preparation time: 30 minutes

1 large cucumber, very thinly sliced
5ml (1 tsp) freshly ground black pepper
2 sprigs fresh dill weed, finely chopped
10ml (2 tsp) brown sugar
140ml (5 fl.oz) cider vinegar

Arrange the cucumber in layers in a broad, shallow bowl, sprinkling a little pepper and dill weed in between each layer.

Mix the sugar and vinegar together in a jug and pour over the sliced cucumber. Cover the bowl and place to one side for at least 20 minutes.

Serve chilled, if desired, as a light salad, starter or as part of a large selection of salads.

Simple Tomato Salad
Serves 4
Calories per serving: 104
Grams saturated fat per serving: 1
Milligrams cholesterol per serving: 0
Preparation time: 35 minutes

900g (2 lbs) tomatoes, thinly sliced
5ml (1 tsp) salt
2–3 sprigs fresh basil, finely chopped
1 small sprig fresh tarragon, finely chopped
5ml (1 tsp) celery seed
juice of 1 lemon
15ml (1 tbsp) cider vinegar
30ml (2 tbsp) olive oil

Arrange the sliced tomatoes on a platter and sprinkle the salt over them. Leave to one side for at least 30 minutes so that the salt removes the 'bitter' from them.

Meanwhile, mix the remaining ingredients together in a jar or jug and shake or stir well. Leave this mixture to one side also, to allow the flavours to blend.

When ready to serve, drain the salty liquid from the tomatoes and pour the dressing evenly over the tomatoes. Serve immediately.

Broccoli & Almond Salad
Serves 4
Calories per serving: 128
Grams saturated fat per serving: 0.8
Milligrams cholesterol per serving: 0

Preparation time: 20 minutes

450g (1 lb) fresh broccoli, trimmed and halved
115g (¼ lb) red cabbage, shredded
5 spring onions, thinly sliced
55g (2 oz) slivered almonds
3 sprigs fresh parsley, finely chopped

Steam cook the broccoli until it is just tender, about 12 minutes. Allow to cool.

Mix the remaining ingredients together in a large salad bowl. Add the cooled broccoli and stir all the ingredients gently together.

Serve with the following dressing or a dressing of your choice.

Thick Tahini Dressing
Serves 4
Calories per serving: 127
Grams saturated fat per serving: 1.5
Milligrams cholesterol per serving: 0
Preparation time: 10 minutes

210ml (7 fl.oz) soya milk concentrate
55g (2 oz) tofu
30ml (2 tbsp) tahini
pinch of salt
10ml (2 tsp) ground coriander
freshly grated nutmeg, (optional)

Measure all the ingredients together into a blender and purée to an even consistency. Pour into a serving jug and serve immediately. A more aromatic dressing may be made by adding a little freshly grated nutmeg.

Orange & Asparagus Salad
Serves 4
Calories per serving: 44
Grams saturated fat per serving: 0.1
Milligrams cholesterol per serving: 0
Preparation time: 30 minutes

juice and zest of 1 orange
2.5ml (½ tsp) ground allspice
2.5ml (½ tsp) paprika
450g (1 lb) fresh asparagus
1 orange, peeled and thinly sliced

Stir the orange juice, zest, allspice and paprika together in a small jug and place to one side.

Wash, trim and steam the asparagus until tender; allow to cool.

Peel the remaining orange very well and slice it with a very sharp knife. You should aim to have 8–12 slices. Place an equal number of these onto each of four serving plates. Arrange the cooled asparagus over the orange slices and pour a little of the spicy orange dressing over each serving. Serve immediately or chill until ready to serve.

Cold-Stuffed Pepper Salad
Serves 4
Calories per serving: 132
Grams saturated fat per serving: 1.4
Milligrams cholesterol per serving: 0
Preparation time: 20 minutes

2 medium red or green peppers
115g (4 oz) button mushrooms, finely chopped
1 medium avocado, peeled and finely chopped
30ml (2 tbsp) fresh parsley, finely chopped
1 × 140g (5 oz) tin sweetcorn, drained
5ml (1 tsp) freshly ground black pepper
juice of 1 lemon

Slice each pepper in half along its length and scrape out the seeds. Rinse and leave to drain.

Mix the mushrooms, avocado, parsley, sweetcorn and black pepper together in a mixing bowl.

Fill each of the pepper halves with one-quarter of the mixture and pour a little of the lemon juice over each. Serve immediately on a bed of lettuce or as one of a selection of salads. Top with a further dressing if desired.

Cool & Quick Fruit Salad
Serves 4
Calories per serving: 228
Grams saturated fat per serving: 0.2
Milligrams cholesterol per serving: 0
Preparation time: 45 minutes

225g (8oz) fresh, seedless grapes, rinsed and de-stalked
1 orange, peeled and chopped
1 grapefruit, peeled and chopped
1 eating apple, finely chopped or sliced
115g (4 oz) fresh or dried dates, pitted and chopped
1 banana, thinly sliced

juice of 2 lemons
4 small sprigs of fresh mint
140ml (5 fl.oz) fruit juice (of your choice)

Mix the grapes and pieces of orange, grapefruit, apple, date and banana together in a large salad bowl. Pour over the lemon juice and chill the salad for at least 30 minutes.

Divide the salad evenly between 4 serving bowls and garnish with a sprig of fresh mint. Pour a little fruit juice over each portion and serve immediately.

Overnight Marinade
Serves 4
Calories per serving: 300
Grams saturated fat per serving: 3
Milligrams cholesterol per serving: 0
Preparation time: 45 minutes, plus cooling and chilling time

1 medium cauliflower, cut into florets
455g (1 lb) broccoli, coarsely chopped
1 × 450g (16 oz) tin kidney beans, drained
1 bunch spring onions, thinly sliced
5 cloves garlic, finely chopped
for the marinade:
430ml (¾ pint) cider vinegar
120ml (4 fl.oz) oil
10ml (2 tsp) coarsely ground black pepper
5ml (1 tsp) freshly ground mustard seed
5ml (1 tsp) coarsely ground caraway or fennel seed
juice and zest of 1 lemon

Prepare the vegetables, stir together and place to one side.

Measure the marinade ingredients into a large enamel or glass saucepan and place over a medium heat. Bring to a gentle simmer.

Add the prepared vegetables, stir well and cover the pan. Keep covered over the medium heat for 15 minutes, stirring twice in that time.

Remove the pan from the heat and turn the contents into a heatproof dish. Cover and leave to marinate, while it cools, all day or overnight. You may chill this marinade if desired. Serve as a starter, light lunch or accompaniment to other salads.

Special Five-Bean Salad
Serves 4
Calories per serving: 370
Grams saturated fat per serving: 2.1

Milligrams cholesterol per serving: 0
Preparation time: 30 minutes, plus cooling and chilling time

1 × 440g (16 oz) tin kidney beans, partly drained
1 × 440g (16 oz) tin green beans, drained
1 × 440g (16 oz) tin chickpeas, partly drained
1 × 440g (16 oz) tin butter beans, partly drained
1 × 440g (16 oz) tin borlotti or pinto beans, drained
5 spring onions, thinly sliced
1 eating apple, grated
3 cloves garlic, crushed
10ml (2 tsp) fresh ginger, grated
15ml (1 tbsp) brown sugar
10ml (2 tsp) freshly ground black pepper
juice of 1 lemon
285ml (½ pint) cider vinegar
140ml (5 fl.oz) oil

Measure all the ingredients into a glass or enamel saucepan and stir well. Place the pan over a medium heat, cover and bring to a slow boil. Reduce the heat and simmer, covered, for 10 minutes.

Leave the pan covered and remove from the heat. Allow to cool then, if desired, spoon into a separate dish to chill in the refrigerator. This salad improves as it cools and may be kept, chilled, for up to three days.

New Chef's Salad
Serves 4
Calories per serving: 195
Grams saturated fat per serving: 0.6
Milligrams cholesterol per serving: 0
Preparation time: 15 minutes

1 head crispy lettuce, rinsed and coarsely chopped
3 medium carrots, grated
115g (4 oz) red cabbage, shredded
4 medium tomatoes, quartered
285g (10 oz) plain tofu, cubed
140g (5 oz) Nuttolene nut paté (or similar), finely cubed

Toss all the ingredients together in a large salad bowl and serve with the following dressing, or a dressing of your choice.

Extra Spicy Dressing
Serves 4
Calories per serving: 154

Grams saturated fat per serving: 2.1
Milligrams cholesterol per serving: 0
Preparation time: 5 minutes

60ml (2 fl.oz) olive oil
140ml (5 fl.oz) cider vinegar
3 cloves garlic, crushed
2.5 ml (½ tsp) chilli powder
5ml (1 tsp) prepared mustard
60ml (2 fl.oz) soya milk

Measure the ingredients into a jar or jug in the order given and shake or stir to make a smooth emulsion. Pour over the salad and serve immediately.

SIDE DISHES

Ladies' Finger Saute
Serves 4
Calories per serving: 103
Grams saturated fat per serving: 0.5
Milligrams cholesterol per serving: 0
Preparation time: 25 minutes

450g (1 lb) fresh ladies' fingers (okra)
15ml (1 tbsp) oil
3 cloves garlic, finely chopped
2 small onions, finely chopped
225g (8 oz) button mushrooms, halved
5ml (1 tsp) yeast extract or Rechard or tandoori paste
140ml (5 fl.oz) water
freshly ground black pepper to taste

Wash the ladies' fingers and cut the hard top off each one. Leave to one side to drain.

Heat the oil in a deep frying pan over a medium heat and sauté the garlic and onion until tender. Add the ladies' fingers to the sauté and stir constantly over a high heat for 5 minutes.

Add the mushrooms to the sauté, stir well and cook for another 3–4 minutes over the high heat.

Add the yeast or spicy paste to the sauté with the water and pepper and stir well. Cover the sauté and cook for 5 minutes longer. Serve immediately with rice, pasta, toast or a selection of other vegetable dishes.

Bean & Brussels Sprout Savoury
Serves 4
Calories per serving: 204
Grams saturated fat per serving: 0.6
Milligrams cholesterol per serving: 0
Preparation time: 30 minutes

15ml (1 tbsp) oil
5 cloves garlic, finely chopped
10ml (2 tsp) caraway seed
450g (1 lb) Brussels sprouts, cleaned and halved
1 bunch spring onions, trimmed and thinly sliced
1 × 455g (1 lb) tin kidney beans, drained
5ml (1 tsp) yeast extract, diluted in a little water
5ml (1 tsp) freshly ground black pepper
15ml (1 tbsp) cider vinegar

Heat the oil in a large frying pan and sauté the garlic and caraway seed
for 3 minutes, stirring constantly. Add the Brussels sprouts and continue
the sauté. After 5 minutes, add the spring onions and sauté for 2–3
minutes.

Now add the beans, diluted yeast extract and the black pepper, stir
well and cover the pan. Cook for 5 minutes over a low heat then add
the cider vinegar. Stir well and serve immediately with rice or baked
potato.

Simple Spiced Rice
Serves 4
Calories per serving: 249
Grams saturated fat per serving: 0.4
Milligrams cholesterol per serving: 0
Preparation time: 45 minutes

225g (8 oz) rice, washed and drained
5ml (1 tsp) turmeric
6 whole cardamom
2 medium carrots, diced
15ml (1 tbsp) oil
juice of 1 lemon

Cover the rice in twice its volume of water in a deep saucepan and place
over a high heat. Bring the water to a boil then reduce the heat, add the
turmeric, cardamom, carrots and oil, stir well and cover the pan.
Simmer, covered, until all the water is absorbed – about 35 mintues.

Spoon the rice onto hot plates and pour a little of the lemon juice over each serving. Serve immediately. This dish may be served cold with salads as well.

Delicatessen Rice
Serves 4
Calories per serving: 324
Grams saturated fat per serving: 1.2
Milligrams cholesterol per serving: 0
Preparation time: 50 minutes

225g (8oz) rice, washed and drained
5ml (1 tsp) turmeric
1 bay leaf
1 × 5cm (2 inch) piece cinnamon stick
5ml (1 tsp) mixed sweet dried herbs
15ml (1 tbsp) oil
3 cloves garlic, finely chopped
5 spring onions, thinly sliced
55g (2 oz) sunflower seeds
lemon wedges to garnish

Cover the rice in twice its volume of water in a deep saucepan and place over a high heat. Bring the water to a boil then reduce the heat, add the turmeric, bay leaf, cinnamon and herbs, stir well and cover the pan.

Heat the oil in a small frying pan and sauté the garlic, onion and sunflower seeds for 5–7 minutes. Add them to the rice and stir well. Simmer the rice mixture, with the pan covered, until all the water is absorbed – about 35 mintues.

Garnish each serving with a wedge of lemon. Serve hot or cold with salads or steamed vegetables.

Butter Bean Savoury
Serves 4
Calories per serving: 195
Grams saturated fat per serving: 0.5
Milligrams cholesterol per serving: 0
Preparation time: 25 minutes

15ml (1 tbsp) oil
3 cloves garlic, finely chopped
5ml (1 tsp) cumin seed, crushed
5ml (1 tsp) freshly ground black pepper
455g (16 oz) tin butter beans, drained
455g (1 lb) broccoli, trimmed and thinly sliced
1 bunch spring onions, sliced lengthwise

140ml (5 fl.oz) apple juice

Heat the oil in a large frying pan and sauté the garlic, cumin seed and black pepper for 3 minutes.

Add the butter beans and stir them into the sauté. Arrange the broccoli on top of the sauté and the spring onions over the broccoli. Do not stir. Cover the pan and cook over a low to medium heat for 5–7 minutes. Add the apple juice, cover the pan and cook for a further 5 minutes.

Stir the mixture gently together and serve immediately over rice or pasta or beside a selection of other vegetable dishes.

Sweet Portatoes in Orange Sauce
Serves 4
Calories per serving: 332
Grams saturated fat per serving: 4
Milligrams cholesterol per serving:
Preparation time: 35 minutes

4 large (approximately 900g (2 lbs)) sweet potatoes
15ml (1 tbsp) oil
30g (1 oz) breadcrumbs
5ml (1 tsp) freshly ground black pepper
1 recipe Sweet Orange Sauce (page 132)

Pre-heat the oven to 180°C / 350°F / Gas Mark 4.

Scrub the sweet potatoes and halve or quarter them. Spread the oil in the bottom of a large baking tray. Mix the breadcrumbs and pepper together and sprinkle over the oil in the baking tray. Now lay each potato piece cut-side-down onto the breadcrumb mixture.

Cover the tray with foil and bake for 25 minutes.

Turn the potatoes onto a hot serving plate and cover with the Sweet Orange Sauce. Serve immediately with a Vegetable Loaf and selection of other vegetables.

Seaweed & Vegetable Savoury
Serves 4
Calories per serving: 92
Grams saturated fat per serving: 0.2
Milligrams cholesterol per serving: 0
Preparation time: 45 minutes

50g (2 oz) arami seaweed
450g (1 lb) broccoli, washed and trimmed
1 large (approximately 170g (6 oz)) potato, diced
1 bunch spring onions, thinly sliced lengthwise

60ml (2 fl.oz) soy sauce
5ml (1 tsp) Rechard or tandoori paste
freshly ground black pepper to taste

Rinse the arami in very cold running water. Now soak it in a bowl of clean cold water for 5 minutes. Move the arami around in the water to free any particles of sand, then lift out of the water and drain. Discard that water.

Place the arami in a deep saucepan and cover with water. Cover the pan and bring the water to the boil. Reduce the heat and simmer for 20 minutes.

Steam the broccoli and potato for 15 minutes or until tender.

When the arami has cooked, drain the water from it and add the broccoli, potato and onions. Stir them together over a high heat. Mix the soy sauce with the spicy paste and add to the seaweed mixture. Stir together for 5–10 minutes. Serve immediately with a little black pepper. This is delicious with rice or other vegetable dishes.

Delicate Carrot Sauté
Serves 4
Calories per serving: 91
Grams saturated fat per serving: 0.4
Milligrams cholesterol per serving: 0
Preparation time: 25 minutes

15ml (1 tbsp) oil
3 cloves garlic, finely chopped
5ml (1 tsp) caraway seed
2.5ml (½ tsp) ground allspice
455g (1 lb) carrots, peeled and thinly sliced
1 bunch spring onions, sliced lengthwise
freshly ground black pepper to taste

Heat the oil in a large frying pan over a medium heat and sauté the garlic, caraway seed and allspice for about 3 minutes. Add the carrots to the sauté and stir for a further 3 minutes. Now add the onions to the sauté, laying them on top of the carrots.

Cover the pan and reduce the heat. Leave covered for 10 minutes then remove the cover, stir the sauté well and serve immediately with a sprinkling of black pepper. This dish is good with rice, Vegetable Loaf, or a selection of other vegetable dishes.

Mushroom Burgers in Onion Sauce
Serves 4
Calories per serving: 160

Grams saturated fat per serving: 0.1
Milligrams cholesterol per serving: 0
Preparation time: 45 minutes

1 packet No-Salt VegeBurger dry mix
5ml (1 tsp) freshly ground black pepper
30g (1 oz) tahini
140ml (5 fl.oz) water
225g (8 oz) button mushrooms, cleaned and halved
a little whole wheat flour
Sauce:
15ml (1 tbsp) yeast extract
285ml (10 fl.oz) water
2 medium onions, thinly sliced
3 cloves garlic, finely chopped
5ml (1 tsp) freshly ground black pepper

Pre-heat the oven to 170°C / 325°F / Gas Mark 3 and lightly oil a baking tray.

Stir the VegeBurger mix, black pepper and tahini together in a mixing bowl. Add the water and stir very well. Set to one side for 10 minutes.

Divide the burger mix into 16 parts. Roll each part into a ball then place on a floured work surface and roll each ball flat, into a burger.

Arrange the sliced mushrooms onto eight of the burgers. Wet the edges of all the burgers and press the eight plain burgers over those covered with mushrooms. Press the edges firmly together and place the mushroom burgers (there should be eight) on the baking tray.

Bake the burgers for 15 minutes. Then turn them with a spatula and continue baking for a further 10 minutes.

Dissolve the yeast extract in the water and pour a little of it into a frying pan. Place over a medium heat and add the onions and garlic to this liquid. Once they have softened, add the rest of the liquid and the pepper and simmer gently for 10 minutes.

When the burgers are cooked, place them in a warmed serving dish and pour the hot onion sauce over them. Serve immediately.

Quick & Easy Vegetable Kebabs
Serves 4
Calories per serving: 100
Grams saturated fat per serving: 0.2
Milligrams cholesterol per serving: 0
Preparation time: 25 minutes

2 medium onions, quartered
1 medium red pepper, coarsely chopped
1 medium green pepper, coarsely chopped
115g (4 oz) button mushrooms, cleaned (and the large ones halved)
2 medium courgettes, cut into chunks
115g (4 oz) pitted olives, drained
1 large orange, peeled, divided into segments and halved

Push a selection of these prepared vegetables onto each of eight long kebab skewers (metal or bamboo). Support the kebabs (i.e. across a baking tray) and place under a hot grill.

Grill the kebabs for 2–3 minutes, turn or rotate them and grill them for another 2 minutes.

Serve immediately – two kebabs per person – with rice or salad and a sauce of your choice. (i.e. Rich Tomato Sauce (page 133) or Spicy Peanut Sauce (page 135))

Barbequed Potatoes in Pepper Sauce
Serves 4
Calories per serving: 230
Grams saturated fat per serving: 0.1
Milligrams cholesterol per serving: 0
Preparation time: 1 hour

900g (2 lbs) potatoes, quartered
Sauce:
140g (5 oz) tomato purée
10ml (2 tsp) freshly ground black pepper
5ml (1 tsp) chilli powder
15ml (1 tbsp) molasses (or brown sugar)
170ml (6 fl.oz) cider vinegar

Pre-heat the oven to 180°C / 350°F / Gas Mark 4 or make a barbecue fire!

Take each potato quarter and pierce it several times, all over, with a fork. Place in a bowl of cold water when you have done this.

Mix all the sauce ingredients together, stirring very well to ensure there are no lumps.

Dip each potato quarter into the sauce so that it is well coated and some of the sauce stays in the fork holes. Place each quarter potato on a piece of baking foil and put to one side. When all the potatoes have been treated in this way, pour any surplus sauce onto the baking foil. Now wrap each potato quarter tightly in the foil and bake for 30 minutes. Serve at once.

Sweet Potato Puffs
Serves 4
Calories per serving: 234
Grams saturated fat per serving: 0.4
Milligrams cholesterol per serving: 0
Preparation time: 45 minutes

15ml (1 tbsp) oil
2 large (approximately 675g (1½ lbs)) sweet potatoes
10ml (2 tsp) prepared mustard
5ml (1 tsp) freshly ground black pepper
5ml (1 tsp) ground allspice
55g (2 oz) self-raising flour

Pre-heat the oven to 180°C / 350°F / Gas Mark 4. Pour the oil into 8 or 12 tartlet tins and place these in the oven to warm.

Peel and chop the sweet potatoes and steam until tender, about 15 minutes. Now purée them in a blender with the remaining ingredients to make a light batter. Add a little water if necessary to achieve this consistency.

Pour the batter into the hot tartlet tins and bake the puffs for 20 minutes. Serve hot or cold with brown pickle (i.e. Branston).

Pommes Annabelle
Serves 4
Calories per serving:251
Grams saturated fat per serving: 0.5
Milligrams cholesterol per serving: 0
Preparation time: 1 hour

900g (2 lbs) potatoes, peeled and thinly sliced
1 head garlic, finely chopped
15ml (3 tsp) freshly ground black pepper
Sauce:
15ml (1 tbsp) oil
15ml (1 tbsp) cornflour
350ml (12 fl.oz) vegetable stock
10ml (2 tsp) yeast extract

Pre-heat the oven to 180°C / 350°F / Gas Mark 4.
Layer the potatoes, garlic and ground pepper in a casserole dish. Make the sauce by heating the oil in a saucepan over a medium heat and sprinkling the cornflour over it. Stir well to make a thick paste, or roux. Gradually add the vegetable stock, stirring well after each addition, to make a smooth sauce. Add the yeast extract, stir well and remove the sauce from the heat.

Pour this sauce over the layered potatoes, cover the casserole and bake for 45 minutes. Serve hot.

Sweet Marinated Mushrooms
Serves 4
Calories per serving: 88
Grams saturated fat per serving: 0.1
Milligrams cholesterol per serving: 0
Preparation time: 25 minutes, plus chilling time

455g (1 lb) button mushrooms, cleaned
55g (2 oz) brown sugar
5ml (1 tsp) fresh ginger, grated
2.5ml (½ tsp) chilli powder
230ml (8 fl.oz) cider vinegar

Arrange the mushrooms in a pretty serving dish. (Note: the mushrooms must not be washed for this dish, but rubbed clean).

Mix the remaining ingredients together in a jug and pour over the mushrooms. Cover the mushrooms and leave in a cool place to marinate for 2–6 hours. Serve chilled if possible.

Squash with Herb & Garlic Paste
Serves 4
Calories per serving: 110
Grams saturated fat per serving: 0.4
Milligrams cholesterol per serving: 0
Preparation time: 40 minutes

1 medium squash (i.e. acorn or butternut), halved
Paste:
15ml (1 tbsp) oil
3 cloves garlic, crushed
5ml (1 tsp) freshly ground black pepper
5ml (1 tsp) dried parsley
2.5ml (½ tsp) dried oregano
3 spring onions, thinly sliced

Pre-heat the oven to 180°C / 350°F / Gas Mark 4.
Clean the seeds and stringy pulp from the centre of each half squash and discard. Place each half on a sheet of baking foil. Use a small sharp knife and cut deep scores into the hollow of each half squash.

Mix the paste ingredients together in a small bowl then spread the paste into the scored hollows of both squash halves. Sprinkle the spring onions into the two halves. Wrap the foil round each half and place them on a baking tray. Bake for 25 minutes. Cut each half in half again and serve immediately.

MAIN DISHES

Winter Casserole
Serves 4
Calories per serving: 160
Grams saturated fat per serving: 0.8
Milligrams cholesterol per serving: 0
Preparation time: 50 minutes

1 large cauliflower, cut into florets
450g (1 lb) Brussels sprouts, trimmed and halved
Sauce:
15ml (1 tbsp) oil
3 cloves garlic, finely chopped
1 small onion, finely chopped
7.5ml (1 ½ tsp) freshly ground black pepper
5ml (1 tsp) paprika
15ml (1 tbsp) cornflour
425ml (15 fl.oz) soya milk
Topping:
30ml (2 tbsp) nutritional yeast flakes (optional)
4 matzoes, crumbled

Pre-heat the oven to 170°C / 325°F / Gas Mark 3. Mix the cauliflower and sprouts together in a deep casserole.

Heat the oil in a saucepan and sauté the garlic and onion.

Stir the pepper, paprika and cornflour together in a small bowl then sprinkle over the sauté and stir to a thick paste, keeping over the heat all the while. Gradually add the milk, stirring constantly to make a smooth sauce.

Cover the casserole and bake for 30 minutes. Mix the yeast flakes and crushed matzoes together and sprinkle over the casserole. Then bake, uncovered, for a further 5 minutes. Serve immediately.

Pasta with Spicy Spinach Sauce
Serves 4
Calories per serving: 124
Grams saturated fat per serving: 0.5
Milligrams cholesterol per serving: 0
Preparation time: 25 minutes

225g (8 oz) pasta

Sauce:
15ml (1 tbsp) oil
3 cloves garlic, finely chopped
1 medium onion, chopped
140ml (5 fl.oz) tomato purée
270ml (10 fl.oz) water
10ml (2 tsp) freshly ground black pepper
5ml (1 tsp) Rechard or tandoori paste
450g (1 lb) fresh spinach, washed, trimmed and coarsely chopped

Cook the pasta in a large pan of boiling water until just tender.

Heat the oil in a deep pan and place over a medium heat. Add the garlic and onion and 'sauté' until just tender.

Mix the tomato purée and water together in a jug. Add the tomato mixture, the pepper and spicy paste to the sauté and stir well as you bring the mixture to a simmer. Cover the pan and reduce the heat.

Prepare the spinach then pack it into the pan with the tomato sauce, cover once again and leave untouched for 15 minutes over the low heat.

At the end of this time, stir the spinach into the tomato sauce. Serve the sauce over the pasta on heated plates.

Broccoli Almond Bake
Serves 4
Calories per serving: 182
Grams saturated fat per serving: 1
Milligrams cholesterol per serving: 0
Preparation time: 45 minutes

900g (2 lbs) broccoli
2 small onions, thinly sliced
3 cloves garlic, finely chopped
30g (1 oz) slivered almonds
Sauce:
15ml (1 tbsp) oil
15ml (1 tbsp) cornflour
5ml (1 tsp) turmeric
10ml (2 tsp) freshly ground black pepper
290ml (10 fl.oz) soya milk
140ml (5 fl.oz) water

Pre-heat the oven to 170°C / 325°F / Gas Mark 3. Wash and drain the broccoli.

Arrange the sliced onions in the bottom of a deep casserole dish. Sprinkle the chopped garlic over the onions, then arrange the broccoli pieces over the garlic. Sprinkle the slivered almonds over the broccoli.

Heat the oil in a saucepan. Mix the cornflour, turmeric and pepper together in a small bowl, then sprinkle over the hot oil. Stir constantly over a medium heat to make a thick paste. Gradually add the soya milk and water, stirring constantly, to make a smooth sauce. Add a little more water if a less thick sauce is desired. Pour the sauce over the broccoli, cover the casserole and bake for 20 minutes. Uncover and continue baking for a further 10 minutes. Serve immediately with a green vegetable or a salad.

Tomato Vegetable Rice
Serves 4
Calories per serving: 221
Grams saturated fat per serving: 0.5
Milligrams cholesterol per serving: 0
Preparation time: 40 minutes

225g (8 oz) rice
Sauce:
15ml (1 tbsp) oil
5 cloves garlic, finely chopped
2 small onions, finely chopped
115g (4 oz) carrots, peeled and finely chopped
115g (4 oz) parsnip, peeled and finely chopped
1 medium potato, peeled and finely chopped
1 × 455g (16 oz) tin whole tomatoes
140g (5 oz) tomato purée
5ml (1 tsp) freshly ground black pepper
10ml (2 tsp) dried parsley *or* 2 sprigs chopped fresh parsley
5ml (1 tsp) dried basil

Wash and drain the rice and cook in twice its volume of water.

Heat the oil in a large pan and sauté the garlic and onion until tender. Add the chopped vegetables and continue the sauté, stirring frequently for 5 minutes, or until the vegetables begin to brown.

Add the remaining ingredients, stir well and bring to a simmer over a medium heat. Cover the pan, reduce the heat and leave to simmer for 15 minutes, until the vegetables are tender.

Serve the cooked rice onto heated plates, cover with the vegetable sauce and serve immediately.

Sweet & Savoury Casserole
Serves 4
Calories per serving: 321

Grams saturated fat per serving: 0.2
Milligrams cholesterol per serving: 0
Preparation time: 1 hour and 15 minutes

455g (1 lb) potatoes, thickly sliced
455g (1 lb) carrots, thickly sliced
1 large onion, thinly sliced
455g (1 lb) parsnips, thickly sliced
10ml (2 tsp) freshly ground black pepper
115g (4 oz) raisins or sultanas
15ml (1 tbsp) yeast extract
450ml (¾ pint) water

Warm the oven to 180°C / 350°F / Gas Mark 4.

Place the first six ingredients in rough layers in a deep casserole: potato, carrot, onion, parsnip, pepper, raisins, etc. until they are all used.

Mix the yeast extract and water together and pour over all. Cover the casserole dish and bake for 55 minutes. Serve immediately.

Tempeh Marinade
Serves 4
Calories per serving: 333
Grams saturated fat per serving: 2.9
Milligrams cholesterol per serving: 0
Preparation time: 50 minutes, plus marinating time

225g (8 oz) tempeh, defrosted
170ml (6 fl.oz) cider vinegar
90ml (3 fl.oz) oil
60ml (2 fl.oz) soy sauce
5ml (1 tsp) mustard seed
12 whole cloves
12 whole peppercorns, partly crushed
3–6 cloves garlic, finely chopped
2 small onions, finely chopped

Cut the tempeh into 1-inch cubes and place in a casserole dish.

Mix the remaining ingredients together in a jug. Stir well and pour over the tempeh pieces.

Cover the casserole and leave the tempeh to marinate for 4–8 hours. Bake, covered, at 170°C / 325°F / Gas Mark 3 for 30 minutes. Remove the cover and bake for a further 10 minutes. Serve with rice and green vegetables.

Creamy Tomato Pasta Casserole
Serves 4
Calories per serving: 174
Grams saturated fat per serving: 0.8
Milligrams cholesterol per serving: 0
Preparation time: 55 minutes

225g (8 oz) pasta shells
15ml (1 tbsp) oil
3–6 cloves garlic, finely chopped
2 medium onions, finely chopped
140g (5 oz) tomato purée
5ml (1 tsp) each dried basil, parsley and oregano
10ml (2 tsp) freshly ground black pepper
350ml (12 fl.oz) soya milk concentrate
350ml (12 fl.oz) water

Pre-heat the oven to 180°C / 350°F / Gas Mark 4. Measure the pasta into a deep casserole.

Heat the oil in a saucepan and sauté the garlic and onion until tender. Remove from the heat and add the tomato purée, herbs and black pepper.

Stir well, then gradually add the milk and water.

Pour the sauce over the pasta shells and bake, covered, for 45 minutes. Serve immediately.

Sweet & Sour Mushrooms Over Rice
Serves 4
Calories per serving: 340
Grams saturated fat per serving: 0.5
Milligrams cholesterol per serving: 0
Preparation time: 25 minutes

225g (8 oz) rice
15ml (1 tbsp) oil
3 cloves garlic, finely chopped
1 medium onion, finely chopped
455g (1 lb) button mushrooms, quartered
2–3 large prunes, finely chopped
15ml (1 tbsp) nutritional yeast flakes
10ml (2 tsp) freshly ground black pepper
30ml (2 tbsp) vinegar

Wash and drain the rice and cook in twice its volume of water, until tender.

Heat the oil in a large frying pan and sauté the garlic and onion until tender. Add the mushrooms and continue to sauté over a medium heat, stirring frequently.

Stir in the prunes, yeast and pepper, stir well and simmer, covered, over a low heat for 10 minutes. Add the vinegar, stir well and simmer, uncovered, for a further 5 minutes. Serve immediately over the cooked rice.

New Mexican Tostadas
Serves 4
Calories per serving: 355
Grams saturated fat per serving: 0.8
Milligrams cholesterol per serving: 0
Preparation time: 40 minutes

12 corn-meal tostadas
225g (8 oz) carrots, shredded
1 medium beetroot, shredded
1 medium onion, thinly sliced
½ head crispy lettuce, thinly sliced
1 bunch fresh parsley, finely chopped
Paste filling:
2 × 455g (1 lb) tins red or pinto beans
15ml (1 tbsp) oil
3 cloves garlic, finely chopped
1 small onion, finely chopped
10ml (2 tsp) chilli powder
10ml (2 tsp) soy sauce
15ml (1 tbsp) cider vinegar
Sauce:
see the Quick Thick Catsup recipe (page 134)

Warm the tostadas in a hot oven for 2–3 minutes on a baking tray.

Prepare the vegetables as advised and arrange them on separate dishes.

Prepare the paste filling: drain half of the liquid from the tinned beans and purée the remaining liquid and the beans in a blender. Heat the oil in a saucepan and sauté the garlic and onion until tender. Add the puréed beans and the remaining ingredients and stir together over a medium heat. Leave covered over a low heat while you finish preparations.

Prepare the Quick Thick Catsup recipe (page 134).

Spoon a little bean paste onto each tostadas and spread to the edges.

Then sprinkle a little of each of the salad ingredients over the bean paste and finally top with the sauce. Serve immediately.

Green Bean Curry
Serves 4
Calories per serving: 264
Grams saturated fat per serving: 0.4
Milligrams cholesterol per serving: 0
Preparation time: 35 minutes

225g (8 oz) rice
15ml (1 tbsp) oil
3 cloves garlic, finely chopped
2 small onions, thinly sliced
10ml (2 tsp) cumin
5ml (1 tsp) yeast extract
2 × 455g (16 oz) tins green beans, drained
140ml (5 fl.oz) water
1 whole chilli pepper, fresh or dried
5ml (1 tsp) Rechard paste or tandoori paste
10ml (2 tsp) garam masala

Wash, drain and cook the rice in twice its volume of water, until tender.

Heat the oil in a frying pan and sauté the garlic and onion until tender.

Add the cumin and yeast extract and stir well. Now add the beans and stir frequently over a medium heat for 5 minutes.

Add the remaining ingredients, *except* the garam masala, cover the pan and allow the mixture to simmer for 10 minutes.

Stir in the garam masala and leave to simmer for a further 5 minutes before serving hot over the rice.

Cold Millet & Vegetable Compote
Serves 4
Calories per serving: 155
Grams saturated fat per serving: 1
Milligrams cholesterol per serving: 0
Preparation time: 1 hour

1 litre (2 pints) boiling water
225g (8 oz) millet, rinsed and drained
1 × 455g (16 oz) tin green beans, drained
115g (4 oz) pitted olives, sliced
1 bunch spring onions, thinly sliced
1 bunch watercress, chopped

1 large sprig fresh mint, finely chopped
5ml (1 tsp) freshly ground black pepper
30ml (2 tbsp) olive oil
juice of ½ lemon
a pinch of paprika

Bring the water to a hard boil and add the millet. Stir well and leave to simmer rapidly for 20 minutes, covered.

Measure the next six ingredients together in a large salad bowl and stir them gently.

Place the millet in a steamer lined with cheesecloth. Steam for 20 minutes. Allow to cool.

Stir the millet into the prepared vegetables. Mix the oil and lemon juice together and pour over the mixture. Sprinkle the paprika over the top and serve immediately or chill until ready to serve.

Hot Bulghur with Coriander
Serves 4
Calories per serving: 167
Grams saturated fat per serving: 0.1
Milligrams cholesterol per serving: 0
Preparation time: 20 minutes

710ml (1 ¼ pints) water
15ml (1 tbsp) yeast extract
3 cloves garlic, crushed
5 spring onions, thinly sliced
225g (8 oz) bulghur wheat
1 whole chilli, fresh or dried
28g (1 oz) fresh coriander, washed and chopped
soy sauce, to taste

Measure the water into a deep saucepan and bring to the boil. Stir in the yeast extract until it is dissolved.

Add the garlic and onion to the water, then add the bulghur and whole chilli, stir well and cover the pan. Cook over a low heat for 2 minutes.

Stir the fresh coriander into the bulghur and cover the pan again. Leave over a low heat for a further 10–15 minutes, without stirring, until the bulghur is tender. Serve immediately, with a little soy sauce if desired, accompanied by a selection of steamed or salad vegetables.

Vegetable Loaf
Serves 4
Calories per serving: 360

Grams saturated fat per serving: 0.3
Milligrams cholesterol per serving: 0
Preparation time: 1 hour and 10 minutes

55g (2 oz) red lentils, washed and drained
2 packets No-Salt VegeBurger dry mix (or similar)
55g (2 oz) rolled oats
5ml (1 tsp) chilli powder
10ml (2 tsp) dried parsley
400ml (14 fl.oz) water
Sauce:
30ml (2 tbsp) tomato purée
140ml (5 fl.oz) water
10ml (2 tsp) mixed sweet dry herbs

Lightly oil a 900g (2 lb) loaf tin and warm the oven to 170°C/325°F/
Gas Mark 3.

Stir the first five ingredients together in a mixing bowl.

Add the water, stir well and leave the mixture to sit for 10 minutes.

Make the sauce by mixing the tomato purée, water and herbs
together in a small bowl.

Stir the loaf mixture once again then press firmly into the loaf tin.
Bake for 10 minutes then remove from the oven and pour the sauce over
the loaf. Cover the loaf in kitchen foil and return to the oven. Bake for
a further 40 minutes.

Leave the loaf on a cooling rack for 5–10 minutes, then turn it out
onto a serving platter. Serve in slices – hot with vegetables, or cold in
sandwiches.

Greek Spinach & Chickpea Saute
Serves 4
Calories per serving: 202
Grams saturated fat per serving: 0.7
Milligrams cholesterol per serving: 0
*Preparation time: 35 minutes, plus soaking and cooking time for the
dried chickpeas*

115g (4 oz) dry chickpeas
900g (2 lbs) fresh spinach, washed and trimmed
15ml (1 tbsp) oil
3–5 cloves garlic, finely chopped
2 medium onions, finely chopped
10ml (2 tsp) freshly ground black pepper
5ml (1 tsp) crushed cumin

10ml (2 tsp) yeast extract (or Rechard or tandoori paste)
140ml (5 fl.oz) water

Wash the chickpeas and soak them in cold water all day or overnight. Cook them over a medium heat until tender, adding water to cover.

Coarsely chop the spinach and leave to drain.

Heat the oil in a deep frying pan or saucepan and place over a medium heat. Add the garlic and onion and sauté them until tender, stirring frequently. Add the pepper and cumin and sauté for a further 3 minutes.

Next, add the cooked chickpeas to the sauté and stir well as they brown slightly. Mix the yeast extract with the water and add to the sauté.

Now place the spinach on top of the chickpea mixture, cover the pan and leave over a low heat for 10–15 minutes. Do not remove the cover.

At the end of this time, stir the spinach into the chickpeas and serve immediately by itself, or with rice or steamed vegetables.

New Mexican Chilli
Serves 4
Calories per serving: 225
Grams saturated fat per serving: 0.5
Milligrams cholesterol per serving: 0
Preparation time: 40 minutes

15ml (1 tbsp) oil
5 cloves garlic, finely chopped
1 medium onion, finely chopped
55g (2 oz) soya mince (TVP)
570ml (1 pint) water
140g (5 oz) tomato purée
1 × 400g (14 oz) tin chopped tomatoes
15ml (1 tbsp) soy sauce
2.5ml (½ tsp) chilli powder
1 × 450g (16 oz) tin kidney beans
30ml (2 tbsp) cider vinegar

Heat the oil in a deep saucepan and place over a high flame. Add the garlic and onion and sauté for 5 minutes, until tender. Add the soya mince to the sauté and stir for a further 2–3 minutes.

Mix the water, tomato purée and the chopped tomato and stir into the sauté.

Reduce the heat and add the soy sauce, chilli powder and the beans. Stir well, then cover the pan and leave to simmer for 20 minutes.

Five minutes before serving, add the vinegar and stir once again.
Serve in bowls with a side salad.

All Vegetable Shepherd's Pie
Serves 4
Calories per serving: 181
Grams saturated fat per serving: 0.2
Milligrams cholesterol per serving: 0
Preparation time: 1 hour and 15 minutes

55g (2 oz) red lentils, rinsed and drained
55g (2 oz) soya mince (TVP)
10ml (2 tsp) freshly ground black pepper
15ml (1 tbsp) mixed sweet dry herbs
710ml (1¼ pints) water
15ml (1 tbsp) yeast extract
455g (1 lb) potatoes, peeled and quartered
15ml (1 tbsp) oil
3–5 cloves garlic, finely chopped
2 medium onions, finely chopped
225g (8 oz) carrots, peeled and sliced
225g (8 oz) Brussels sprouts, trimmed and halved
170ml (6 fl.oz) soya milk
15ml (1 tbsp) margarine

Pre-heat the oven to 180°C / 350°F / Gas Mark 4.

Stir the lentils, soya mince, pepper and herbs together in a mixing
bowl.

Measure the water and dissolve the yeast extract in it. Pour this over
the lentil and soya mixture and stir well. Leave to one side.

Steam the potatoes until tender.

Heat the oil in a frying pan and sauté the garlic and onion until
tender. Add the carrots and brussels sprouts to the sauté and stir
frequently for a further 5 minutes. Now stir this sauté in with the lentil
mixture.

Turn the mixture into a deep casserole dish or large baking tin.

Mash the cooked potatoes with the milk and margarine and spread
the mash over the mixture in the casserole. Draw a fork across the top
of the mash to give it texture.

Cover the dish and bake for 30 minutes then remove the cover and
bake for a further 10 minutes to brown the top. Serve hot.

Spinach & Lentil Lasagna
Serves 4
Calories per serving: 324

Grams saturated fat per serving: 1
Milligrams cholesterol per serving: 0
Preparation time: 1 hour and 15 minutes

450g (1 lb) lasagna sheets
15ml (1 tbsp) oil
3–5 cloves garlic, finely chopped
2 medium onions, finely chopped
455g (1 lb) fresh spinach, washed and coarsely chopped
1 × 400g (14 oz) tin chopped tomatoes
140g (5 oz) tomato purée
340ml (15 fl.oz) water
10ml (2 tsp) dried basil
10ml (2 tsp) dried oregano
10ml (2 tsp) freshly ground black pepper
115g (4 oz) red lentils, washed and drained
1 bunch fresh parsley, finely chopped
285g (10 oz) tofu, thinly sliced

Pre-heat the oven to 170°C / 325°F / Gas Mark 3.

Bring some water to boil in a deep saucepan and half-cook the lasagna noodles in it – they should only begin to become pliable. Drain and put to one side.

Heat the oil in a frying pan and sauté the garlic and onion until tender. Add the spinach to the sauté, cover the pan and leave over a low heat for 10 minutes, stirring occasionally.

Mix the tomatoes, purée and water together in a jug. Add the basil, oregano and black pepper and stir well.

Arrange three or four lasagna sheets in the bottom of a broad casserole dish or baking tray. Spoon some of the lentils over the noodles. Spread a large spoonful of spinach and onion sauté over the lentils. Sprinkle some chopped parsley over this and pour a little of the tomato sauce over the parsley. Now arrange a few slices of tofu over the sauce.

Repeat the layers two or three times more: lasagna, lentils, spinach sauté, parsley, sauce, tofu.

Finish with a layer of sauce and bake for 45 minutes. Serve hot or cold, with salad or steamed vegetables.

Double Stuffed Peppers
Serves 4
Calories per serving: 201
Grams saturated fat per serving: 1.1
Milligrams cholesterol per serving: 0
Preparation time: 1 hour

15ml (1 tbsp) oil
2 small onions, finely chopped
55g (2 oz) soya mince (TVP)
15ml (1 tbsp) yeast extract
285ml (10 fl.oz) water
10ml (2 tsp) freshly ground black pepper
2 medium red peppers
2 medium green peppers
115g (4 oz) carrots, peeled and grated
115g (4 oz) button mushrooms, cleaned and quartered
25g (1 oz) fresh parsley, finely chopped
285g (10 oz) tofu, crumbled
55g (2 oz) fresh breadcrumbs
juice of 1 lemon

Pre-heat the oven to 180°C / 350°F / Gas Mark 4.

Heat the oil in a frying pan over a medium heat and sauté the onion until tender. Add the soya mince and continue to sauté for 2 minutes. Dissolve the yeast extract in the water and add this liquid to the sauté. Add the black pepper, stir well and leave to simmer gently for 10 minutes, stirring occasionally. Remove from the heat.

Wash the sweet peppers and slice them in half along their length. Remove the seed cluster and arrange the pepper shells in a baking tray.

Stir the remaining ingredients together in a separate bowl. Now stir three-quarters of this mixture into the soya mince sauté. Fill each half-pepper with this stuffing and top with a layer of the tofu mixture. Sprinkle a little lemon juice over each filled pepper.

Cover the tray and bake the peppers for 25 minutes. Uncover the tray and bake for a further 10 minutes. Serve immediately with rice or salad – one red and one green half-pepper per person.

Nine-to-Five Stew
Serves 4
Calories per serving: 485
Grams saturated fat per serving: 0.5
Milligrams cholesterol per serving: 0
Preparation time: 1 day

455g (1 lb) swedes, cubed
455g (1 lb) carrots, chopped
455g (1 lb) parsnips, cubed
455g (1 lb) turnips, cubed
455g (1 lb) potatoes, cubed
455g (1 lb) very small onions, peeled

15ml (1 tbsp) whole cloves
12 whole peppercorns
455g (1 lb) chestnut purée
2 litres (4 pints) water

Pre-heat the oven to 140°C / 275°F / Gas Mark 1 – or a very low temperature of your choice.

Mix the first five ingredients together in a large bowl or pan.

Prepare the onions and press one whole clove into each end of each onion.

Mix the vegetables, onions and peppercorns together and turn into a large enamel or cast-iron stew pot.

Blend the chestnut purée and water together in a jug and pour over the vegetable mixture.

Cover the pot tightly and place in the oven for 6–8 hours. Don't lift the lid! At the end of this time, serve the stew hot with lots of fresh bread.

Chunky Winter Pie
Serves 4
Calories per serving: 243
Grams saturated fat per serving: 0.8
Milligrams cholesterol per serving: 0.5
Preparation time: 1 hour and 15 minutes

700g (1½ lbs) potatoes, peeled and quartered
15ml (1 tbsp) oil
5 cloves garlic, finely chopped
1 medium onion, finely chopped
3 medium carrots, peeled and cubed
115g (4 oz) soya chunks (TVP)
425ml (15 fl.oz) vegetable gravy
10ml (2 tsp) freshly ground black pepper
5ml (1 tsp) dried thyme
10ml (2 tsp) dried parsley
15ml (1 tbsp) soya sauce
285ml (10 fl.oz) soya milk

Pre-heat the oven to 180°C / 350°F / Gas Mark 4.

Steam the potatoes until tender, about 20 minutes.

Heat the oil in a large pan over a medium heat and sauté the garlic and onion until tender, about 5 minutes. Add the carrots and soya chunks and continue the sauté for a further 5 minutes, stirring often.

Now add all the remaining ingredients, except the soya milk, to the sauté and bring to a simmer. Leave to simmer, stirring occasionally, while the soya chunks soften, about 10 minutes.

Mash the steamed potatoes with the soya milk to make a smooth purée.

Turn the carrot and soya chunk mixture into a casserole dish. Spread the mashed potato over it and draw a fork across the top of the potato to add texture.

Cover the pie and bake for 30 minutes then uncover and bake a further 10 minutes to brown the potato topping. Serve hot with a selection of steamed vegetables.

Quick Vegetable Curry
Serves 4
Calories per serving: 247
Grams saturated fat per serving: 0.8
Milligrams cholesterol per serving: 0
Preparation time: 40 minutes

30ml (2 tbsp) oil
5 cloves garlic, finely chopped
2 medium onions, finely chopped
5ml (1 tsp) Rechard or tandoori paste (more if a hotter dish is desired)
10ml (2 tsp) freshly ground black pepper
5ml (1 tsp) turmeric
5ml (1 tsp) crushed cumin
455g (1 lb) potatoes, peeled and cubed
225g (8oz) carrots, peeled and sliced
1 medium cauliflower, trimmed and chopped
500ml (1 pint) vegetable stock or water
15ml (1 tbsp) brown sugar
10ml (2 tsp) garam masala

Heat the oil in a large pan over a medium heat. Add the garlic and onion and sauté until tender, about 5 minutes. Now add the spicy paste, pepper, turmeric and cumin and continue the sauté, stirring constantly.

When the spices are well blended, add the prepared vegetables and stir until they are well coated with the sauté mixture. Add the stock, cover the pan and leave over a medium heat for 15 minutes, stirring occasionally.

Add the brown sugar and garam masala, stir well and leave the curry over a low heat for a further 5–10 minutes – until the vegetables are tender and you are ready to serve. This is good by itself or over a portion of hot rice.

Light & Easy Stir-Fry
Serves 4
Calories per serving: 192
Grams saturated fat per serving: 0.5
Milligrams cholesterol per serving: 0
Preparation time: 30 minutes

15ml (1 tbsp) oil
3 cloves garlic, finely chopped
1 small onion, finely chopped
455g (1 lb) courgettes, sliced
3 sticks celery, chopped
10ml (2 tsp) freshly ground black pepper
5ml (1 tsp) Rechard or tandoori paste (optional)
140ml (5 fl.oz) apple or grape juice
1 × 455g (16 oz) tin kidney beans, partly drained

Heat the oil in a saucepan over a medium heat. Add the garlic and onion and sauté until tender, about 5 minutes.

Now add the courgette and celery and continue the sauté, adding the pepper and paste after 5 minutes. Stir frequently and add the fruit juice as soon as the mixture begins to look a little dry. Now add the kidney beans, stir well and leave the mixture to simmer, covered, over a low heat for 5–10 minutes. Serve hot over rice or beside a selection of steamed vegetables or a slice of vegetable loaf.

SAUCES, DIPS & SPREADS

Rich & Easy Gravy
Serves 4
Calories per serving: 76
Grams saturated fat per serving: 0.7
Milligrams cholesterol per serving: 0
Preparation time: 10 minutes

15ml (1 tbsp) oil
3 cloves garlic, finely chopped
1 small onion, finely chopped
15ml (1 tbsp) gravy powder (e.g. Bisto)
285ml (10 fl.oz) soya milk
10ml (2 tsp) freshly ground black pepper

Heat the oil in a small saucepan over a medium heat. Add the garlic and onion and sauté until tender.

Mix the gravy powder to a cream consistency with a little cold water and add to the sauté, stirring constantly. Gradually add the soya milk, stirring well after each addition. Add water to the gravy at this stage if a thinner gravy is desired.

Add the pepper (and any variation ingredients) and leave the gravy to bubble gently for 2–3 minutes. Serve immediately.

Variations:
- Add 140ml (5 fl.oz) fruit juice to the gravy instead of additional water.

- Add fresh, chopped herbs at the same time as the pepper and leave to simmer for slightly longer. Some tasty herbs to try are marjoram, thyme, rosemary or tarragon.

- Let the garlic and onion sauté to a crispy, brown stage to add a deeper flavour to the gravy. Or add additonal sautéd onions to the prepared gravy.

Creative White Sauce
Serves 4
Calories per serving: 73
Grams saturated fat per serving: 0.6
Milligrams cholesterol per serving: 0
Preparation time: 15 minutes

15ml (1 tbsp) oil or margarine
15ml (1 tbsp) cornflour
425ml (15 fl.oz) soya milk

Heat the oil or margarine in a saucepan over a medium heat. Sprinkle the cornflour over the oil and stir constantly to make a thick paste, or roux. Keep the paste over the heat and gradually add the soya milk, stirring well after each addition to make a smooth sauce.

This makes a very plain white sauce. For added flavour, colour or texture, try one or more of the following variations:

Variations:
- Add finely chopped garlic and onion to the heated oil and sauté for 3–5 minutes before adding the cornflour. Continue as directed.

- Stir one or more of the following dry ingredients in with the cornflour before sprinkling it over the hot oil:
    (a) chilli powder – for added bite
    (b) nutritional yeast flakes – for a cheesy flavour
    (c) turmeric – for a lovely yellow colour
    (d) mustard powder or paste – for a subtle tang
    (e) freshly ground black pepper

(f) brown sugar – when using as part of a pudding or sweet dish

(g) fresh or dried herbs – see the next recipe!

• Stir some carob or chocolate powder or pieces into the hot sauce (along with some sugar?) to make a rich sauce for cakes or pies.

Perfect Parsley Sauce
Serves 4
Calories per serving: 93
Grams saturated fat per serving: 0.6
Milligrams cholesterol per serving: 0
Preparation time: 15 minutes

1 recipe of *Creative White Sauce* (see page 130)
10ml (2 tsp) ground coriander
200ml (7 fl.oz) vegetable stock
1 bunch fresh parsley, finely chopped

Make the White Sauce as directed, stirring the coriander into the cornflour and adding the vegetable stock as additional liquid to make a thinner sauce. Leave the sauce over a low heat for 5 minute, stirring frequently, before adding the chopped parsley. Stir well and bring back to a low simmer, then serve immediately.

Cheesy Tofu Dip
Serves 4
Calories per serving: 103
Grams saturated fat per serving: 1.2
Milligrams cholesterol per serving: 0
Preparation time: 15 minutes

140g (5 oz) plain, firm tofu
30ml (2 tbsp) olive oil
60ml (2 fl.oz) soya milk
5ml (1 tsp) freshly ground black pepper
5ml (1 tsp) mustard powder
30ml (2 tbsp) nutritional yeast flakes
15ml (1 tbsp) cider vinegar
pinch of salt

Measure all the ingredients together in a blender and purée to a smooth, even consistency. Adjust the pepper, mustard and salt to taste. Pour the spread into a jar, seal and keep in a cool place for up to 3 days.

Speedy Applesauce
Serves 4
Calories per serving: 300

Grams saturated fat per serving: 0.2
Milligrams cholesterol per serving: 0
Preparation time: 45 minutes

1350g (3 lbs) cooking apples, washed and chopped
juice of ½ lemon
115g (4 oz) brown sugar
5ml (1 tsp) ground cinnamon
2.5ml (½ tsp) ground cloves
2.5ml (½ tsp) ground nutmeg

Do not discard the apple core, peel, etc., but turn the entire chopped apple into a large enamel or glass saucepan and place over a low heat. Add the lemon juice, cover the pan and leave to cook for 15–20 minutes, stirring often.

When the apple has soften and reduced to a rough pulp, run the mass through a seive or hand-mouli and discard the skin and seeds at this stage. Turn the sauce back into the pan and add the remaining ingredients.

Stir well and cook over a low heat for a further 10 minutes, stirring often. Ladle the sauce into clean jars and keep in a cool place for 1 week. Serve hot or cold with any meal.

Sweet Orange Sauce
Serves 4
Calories per serving: 65
Grams saturated fat per serving:.4
Milligrams cholesterol per serving: 0
Preparation time: 15 minutes

15ml (1 tbsp) oil or margarine
15ml (1 tbsp) brown sugar
15ml (1 tbsp) cornflour
juice and zest of 1 orange
140ml (5 fl.oz) water

Heat the oil and brown sugar together in a small saucepan over a medium heat. Stir the cornflour into a little cold water to make a smooth paste. Add this paste to the hot oil and sugar and stir constantly to make a thick paste.

Gradually add the orange juice, zest and water, stirring well after each addition to make a smooth, light sauce. Add more juice or water if desired to thin the sauce.

Serve hot or cold over puddings, rice, sweet potatoes or carrots.

Creamy Guacamole
Serves 4
Calories per serving: 211
Grams saturated fat per serving: 2.8
Milligrams cholesterol per serving: 0
Preparation time: 15 minutes

2 ripe avocados
2 medium tomatoes, peeled and finely chopped
2 cloves garlic, crushed
2.5ml (½ tsp) chilli powder
140g (5 oz) silken tofu
60ml (2 fl.oz) soya milk
salt to taste

Slice the avocados in half, remove the pips and scoop the flesh into a mixing bowl. Add the remaining ingredients and blend well, using first a fork then a wire whisk. An electric blender may be used if a completely smooth consistency is desired. Serve at once on toast, with pitta or as an accompaniment to salad.

Rich Tomato Sauce
Makes 285ml (10 fl.oz)
Serves 4
Calories per serving: 192
Grams saturated fat per serving: 0.4
Milligrams cholesterol per serving: 0
Preparation time: 30 minutes

140ml (5 fl.oz) water
140ml (5 fl.oz) cider vinegar
60ml (2 fl.oz) soy sauce
4 large prunes, dates, figs or other dried fruit, finely chopped
210g (7 ½ oz) tomato purée
1.25ml (¼ tsp) ground cloves
5ml (1 tsp) ground coriander
5ml (1 tsp) chilli powder
15ml (1 tbsp) oil
3 cloves garlic, finely chopped
1 medium onion, finely chopped
15g (½ oz) fresh parsley, finely chopped

Mix the water, vinegar, soy sauce and dried fruit together in a jug and leave to one side.

Measure the tomato purée into a small saucepan. Add the spices and stir well, then add the liquid with the softened fruit. Stir well.

Simmer the mixture over a low heat for 10 minutes, keeping it covered except for one or two stirs. Meanwhile, heat the oil in a small pan and sauté the garlic and onion until tender. Add the sauté to the mixture in the saucepan and stir well. If a very smooth sauce is desired, run the sauce through a mouli or blender at this point.

Add the chopped parsley to the sauce, stir well and bring back to a low simmer.

Serve this sauce hot over pasta, rice, vegetable loaf, steamed vegetables or as the sauce for barbecue or baked beans.

Tofu Cinnamon Cream
Makes 285ml (10 fl.oz)
Serves 4
Calories per serving: 95
Grams saturated fat per serving: 0.7
Milligrams cholesterol per serving: 0
Preparation time: 10 minutes

285g (10 oz) plain tofu
140ml (5 fl.oz) soya milk concentrate
15ml (1 tbsp) malt extract or golden syrup
10ml (2 tsp) ground cinnamon

Purée all the ingredients together in a blender.

If a thinner cream is preferred, add a little cold water. Serve chilled over pies, puddings, cakes and fruit salads.

Quick Thick Catsup
Makes 285ml (10 fl.oz)
Serves 4
Calories per serving: 35
Grams saturated fat per serving: 0.1
Milligrams cholesterol per serving: 0
Preparation time: 10 minutes

200ml (7 oz) tomato purée
15ml (1 tbsp) soy sauce
60ml (4 tbsp) cider vinegar
10ml (2 tsp) molasses
2 cloves garlic, crushed
2.5ml (½ tsp) chilli powder
5ml (1 tsp) basil, fresh or dried

Mix all the ingredients together in a bowl. Stir well and allow to stand for 30–60 minutes before serving, if possible. This catsup will keep in a cool place for 2 days.

Spicy Peanut Sauce
Serves 4
Calories per serving: 40
Grams saturated fat per serving: 0.4
Milligrams cholesterol per serving: 0
Preparation time: 20 minutes

15ml (1 tbsp) unsalted, crunchy peanut butter
3 cloves garlic, finely chopped
15ml (1 tbsp) soy sauce
juice of 1 lemon
140ml (5 fl.oz) water
pinch of chilli powder

Heat the peanut butter in a small saucepan and place over a medium flame. Add the chopped garlic and stir often.

When the garlic begins to soften, add the soy sauce. Stir well then add the lemon juice. Again, stir well and gradually add the water. When a smooth sauce made, add the chilli powder.

Reduce the heat and keep covered for 5–10 minutes. Serve hot or cold with any rice or vegetable dish.

Refreshing Fennel Sauce
Serves 8
Calories per serving: 30
Grams saturated fat per serving: 0
Milligrams cholesterol per serving: 0
Preparation time: 10 minutes

1 large sweet fennel, chopped
1 large green eating apple, cored and quartered
juice of 1 lemon
10ml (2 tsp) ground coriander

Place all the ingredients together in a food processor and purée to a fine, smooth consistency.

Serve chilled with raw vegetables, in soups or as a dressing to a salad.

Buttery Lentil Pâté
Serves 8
Calories per serving: 99
Grams saturated fat per serving: 0.3
Milligrams cholesterol per serving: 0
Preparation time: 45 minutes, plus chilling time

225g (8 oz) dried red lentils, washed and drained

550ml (1 pint) water
pinch of salt
5ml (1 tsp) turmeric
115g (4 oz) porridge oats (*or* 50g (2 oz) porridge oats and 50g (2oz) rice flakes)
5ml (1 tsp) freshly ground black pepper
5ml (1 tsp) ground ginger

Measure the lentils into the water with the salt and turmeric and bring to a soft boil over a medium heat. Cover, reduce the heat and simmer for 30 minutes, stirring often.

Add the remaining ingredients and simmer for another 5–10 minutes.

Remove from the heat, stir very well and spoon into a serving dish, pressing down as you fill the dish. Allow the paté to cool, then chill or serve immediately on bread or crackers or as an accompaniment to salad.

Tangy Tofu Dip
Serves 4
Calories per serving: 108
Grams saturated fat per serving: 0.6
Milligrams cholesterol per serving: 0
Preparation time: 15 minutes

455g (1 lb) peas, cooked and drained
285g (10 oz) tofu
1 small onion, very finely chopped
15ml (1 tbsp) fresh mint, finely chopped
5ml (1 tsp) paprika

Measure the peas and tofu into a blender and purée to a smooth, even consistency. Now turn the purée into a mixing bowl and add the remaining ingredients. Blend the mixture very well and then chill or serve immediately on toast, in sandwiches or as a dip for crudites or crackers.

Cooling Apple & Onion Sauce
Serves 4
Calories per serving: 85
Grams saturated fat per serving: 0.6
Milligrams cholesterol per serving: 0
Preparation time: 15 minutes, plus 1 hour for chilling

285g (10 oz) tofu

60ml (2 fl.oz) soya milk
1 green eating apple, cored and quartered
2–3 spring onions, very finely sliced
1 small piece of cinnamon *or* star anise

Place the tofu, soya milk and apple into a blender and purée to a smooth consistency. Turn the mixture into a serving bowl and stir in the onion and spice. Chill the sauce for 1 hour before serving on salads, soups or baked potatoes.

DESSERTS, DRINKS & DELICACIES

Lime & Lemonade with Orange Cubes
Serves 4
Calories per serving: 78
Grams saturated fat per serving: 0
Milligrams cholesterol per serving: 0
Preparation time: 2 hours

270ml (½ pint) orange juice
1 orange
6 lemons
2 limes
1 litre (2 pints) water
2 sprigs fresh mint

Pour the orange juice into an ice cube tray and freeze. Wash and slice the orange, lemons and limes into a deep bowl. Boil the water and pour over the lemons and limes. Allow to cool. When tepid, add the clean mint. Stir well, allow to cool further and add the frozen orange cubes just before serving.

Spice & Citrus Brew
Serves 4
Calories per serving: 22
Grams saturated fat per serving: 0
Milligrams cholesterol per serving: 0
Preparation time: 10 minutes

1 litre (2 pints) boiling water
4 slices lemon
4 slices orange
2 whole cloves
1 small piece cinnamon
2 whole allspice

Boil the water and use a little to warm a tea pot that has not been used for normal tea. Add the citrus slices and spices to the pot. Pour the boiling water over, stir, cover and allow to steep for 5 minutes. This is a very refreshing drink which also stimulates your digestion.

Sweet Almond Milk
Serves 4
Calories per serving: 167
Grams saturated fat per serving: 1.4
Milligrams cholesterol per serving: 0
Preparation time: 45 minutes, plus overnight soaking time

115g (4 oz) whole sweet almonds
850ml (1.5 pints) very cold water
pinch of ground coriander, to garnish

Measure the almonds into a mixing bowl and cover them with tepid water. Leave them to soak overnight, or for 8–12 hours. Alternatively, pour boiling water over them and leave to soak for 20 minutes.

Drain and rinse the soaked almonds and remove their skins.

Put the peeled almonds in a food processor with the very cold water. Purée to a very fine, very smooth consistency.

Strain the milk through cheesecloth or a paper coffee filter or a fine seive into a jug. Allow 10–15 minutes for the milk to finish filtering. Serve this pure white milk immediately in pretty glasses. Sprinkle a little ground coriander over each glassful if desired. Use the almond pulp in baking if you wish.

Baked Fruit Compote
Serves 4
Calories per serving: 231
Grams saturated fat per serving: 0.2
Milligrams cholesterol per serving: 0
Preparation time: 45 minutes

2 grapefruit, peeled and sectioned
2 oranges, peeled and sectioned
1 eating apple, finely chopped
2 bananas, peeled and sliced
55g (2 oz) raisins
Sauce:
285ml (10 fl.oz) red wine
6 whole cloves
1 small piece cinnamon

Pre-heat the oven to 170°C / 325°F / Gas Mark 3.

Mix the fruits together in a shallow casserole dish.

Prepare the sauce by simply mixing the wine and spices together in a jug. Pour the sauce over the fruit and allow to soak for 10 minutes. Stir again.

Cover the casserole dish and bake the compote for 20 minutes.

Serve immediately, pouring a little extra sauce over each serving.

Soya & Orange Rice Pudding
Serves 4
Calories per serving: 201
Grams saturated fat per serving: 1
Milligrams cholesterol per serving: 0
Preparation time: 1 hour and 30 minutes

140ml (5 fl.oz) fresh orange juice
zest of 1 orange
55g (2 oz) raisins
225g (8 oz) pudding rice
425ml (15 fl.oz) soya milk concentrate
5ml (1 tsp) ground cinnamon
15ml (1 tbsp) margarine

Pre-heat the oven to 160°C / 300°F / Gas Mark 2 and lightly oil a casserole dish.

Measure the orange juice, zest and raisins into a small bowl, stir them together and leave to one side.

Wash and drain the rice. Mix the rice, soya milk and cinnamon together in a bowl and pour this mixture into the casserole. Cover the casserole and bake the pudding for 30 minutes.

Remove the pudding from the oven, add the orange and raisin mixture and stir well. Drop tiny pieces of margarine over the top of the pudding. Cover the casserole and bake a further 30 minutes.

Uncover the pudding and bake for a final 10 minutes at 180°C / 350°C / Gas Mark 4.

Spoon the pudding into serving dishes and serve immediately *or* cover, allow to cool, and chill before serving.

Almond Nibbles
Makes 24 biscuits
Calories per 4 biscuits: 184
Grams saturated fat per 4 biscuits: 1.5
Milligrams cholesterol per 4 biscuits: 0
Preparation time: 30 minutes

225g (8 oz) flour

25g (1 oz) flakes almonds
10ml (2 tsp) egg replacer
5ml (1 tsp) baking powder
55g (2 oz) margarine
5ml (1 tsp) natural almond essence
140ml (5 fl.oz) soya milk

Pre-heat the oven to 180°C / 350°F / Gas Mark 4.

Measure the flour, flaked almonds, egg replacer and baking powder into a mixing bowl and stir well.

Cut the margarine into the dry mixture until an even consistency is reached.

Add the almond essence and the soya milk and work the dough to an evenly moist paste. Use a spoon or your hands.

Roll the dough into approximately 24 walnut-sized balls and arrange these on a baking tray. Then press the balls of dough flat using the bottom of a glass tumbler. Dip the glass in water to prevent the dough sticking.

Bake for 12–15 minutes. Cool on wire racks.

Slice & Serve Brunch Bars
Makes 1 dozen
Calories per bar: 168
Grams saturated fat per bar: 0.2
Milligrams cholesterol per bar: 0
Preparation time: 40 minutes

225g (8 oz) whole wheat flour
55g (2 oz) rolled oats
55g (2 oz) sugar
10ml (2 tsp) egg replacer
5ml (1 tsp) baking powder
5ml (1 tsp) ground cinnamon *or* allspice
15ml (1 tbsp) oil
55g (2 oz) raisins
1 × 285g (10 oz) tin pineapple chunks, undrained
5ml (1 tsp) natural vanilla essence
140ml (5 fl.oz) water

Pre-heat the oven to 160°C / 300°F / Gas Mark 3 and lightly oil a 20cm (8-inch) cake tin.

Mix the first six ingredients together in a mixing bowl.

Add the oil and work evenly into the dry mix. Now add the raisins, pineapple chunks (including their juice), vanilla essence and water to the dry mix and stir very well.

Spoon the batter into the cake tin, spread evenly to the edges and bake for 25 minutes. Allow to cool, then slice and serve.

Unfrosted Cherry & Carob Cake
Serves 8
Calories per serving: 233
Grams saturated fat per serving: 1.3
Milligrams cholesterol per serving: 0
Preparation time: 45 minutes

225g (8 oz) whole wheat flour
15ml (1 tbsp) egg replacer
5ml (1 tsp) baking powder
55g (2 oz) carob powder
85ml (3 fl.oz) oil or margarine
1 × 375g (14 oz) tin red or black cherries, undrained
285ml (10 fl.oz) water

Pre-heat the oven to 170°C / 325°F / Gas Mark 3 and lightly oil a deep, 20cm (8-inch) cake tin.

Measure the first four ingredients into a mixing bowl and stir well.

Work the oil or margarine into the dry mix to an even, crumbly consistency.

Now add the cherries, their liquid and the water and blend well to make a light batter.

Turn the batter into the cake tin and bake for 25–30 minutes. Cool for 10 minutes in the tin, then remove and cool on a wire rack before serving.

Mint & Gooseberry Ice Cream
Serves 4
Calories per serving: 152
Grams saturated fat per serving: 0.9
Milligrams cholesterol per serving: 0
Preparation time: 1 hour and 10 minutes

225g (8 oz) fresh gooseberries (or seedless grapes if preferred)
15ml (1 tbsp) fresh mint, chopped
285ml (10 fl.oz) soya milk concentrate
45ml (3 tbsp) sugar
285g (10 oz) firm tofu

Measure all the ingredients together into a blender and purée to a smooth, even consistency.

Pour the purée into four serving bowls and place in the freezer for at least one hour. Serve immediately you remove the ice creams from the freezer.

Fresh Dates Filled with Spiced Cream
Serves 8
Calories per serving: 280
Grams saturated fat per serving: 1.1
Milligrams cholesterol per serving: 0
Preparation time: 30 minutes

455g (1 lb) fresh dates, washed and drained
225g (8 oz) firm tofu
140ml (5 fl.oz) soya milk concentrate
7.5ml (1½ tsp) ground coriander
115g (4 oz) walnut halves

Slice each date in half lengthwise and remove the pit.

Purée the tofu, soya milk and coriander together until very smooth. Add more milk if necessary to make a thick, creamy filling. Spoon a little of this filling into each half date and press a walnut half onto each filled date. Arrange on a plate and chill until ready to serve, or serve immediately.

Fruit & Carrot Pudding
Serves 8
Calories per serving: 258
Grams saturated fat per serving: 0.7
Milligrams cholesterol per serving: 0
Preparation time: 1 hour

225g (8 oz) carrots, peeled and grated
115g (4 oz) mixed dried fruit
30ml (2 tbsp) brown sugar
30ml (2 tbsp) oil
500ml (1 pint) water
285g (10 oz) whole wheat flour
115g (4 oz) oat bran
15ml (1 tbsp) egg replacer
5ml (1 tsp) baking powder
5ml (1 tsp) ground cinnamon
5ml (1 tsp) ground allspice
2.5ml (½ tsp) ground nutmeg

Pre-heat the oven to 180°C / 350°F / Gas Mark 4 and lightly oila 23cm (9-inch) cake tin.

Mix the first five ingredients together in a mixing bowl and put to one side.

Mix the remaining ingredients together in a separate mixing bowl.

Then stir the two mixture together until just blended. Turn into the cake tin and bake for 20 minutes. Reduce the oven heat to 170°C / 325°F / Gas Mark 3 and bake for a further 25 minutes. Leave to cool in the cake tin for 10 minutes before serving. Serve with a generous helping of Sweet Orange Sauce (page 132) or Tofu Cinnamon Cream (page 134).

Carob & Almond Tea Cake
Serves 8
Calories per serving: 370
Grams saturated fat per serving: 2
Milligrams cholesterol per serving: 0
Preparation time: 1 hour

225g (8 oz) flour
15ml (1 tbsp) egg replacer
5ml (1 tsp) baking powder
115g (4 oz) sugar
115g (4 oz) oil or margarine
55g (2 oz) flaked almonds
100g (3½ oz) carob flakes
5ml (1 tsp) almond essense
285ml (10 fl.oz) water

Pre-heat the oven to 180°C / 350°F / Gas Mark 4 and lightly oil a 20cm (8-inch) cake tin.

Measure the first four ingredients into a mixing bowl and stir well. Add the oil and work to an even consistency. Now add the almonds and carob flakes. (Note: the carob flakes may be made by grating a carob bar.)

Add the essense and water and stir briskly until the ingredients are well blended. Turn the batter into the cake tin and bake for 15 minutes. Reduce the heat to 160°C / 300°F / Gas Mark 2 and bake for a further 30 minutes. Let the cake cool in the tin for 10 minutes, then turn onto a wire rack to cool before serving.

Pistachio Cake
Serves 8
Calories per serving: 390
Grams saturated fat per serving: 1.8
Milligrams cholesterol per serving: 0
Preparation time: 1 hour and 10 minutes

285g (10 oz) flour
115g (4 oz) rolled oats
15ml (1 tbsp) egg replacer

5ml (1 tsp) baking powder
115g (4 oz) sugar
10ml (2 tsp) ground coriander
60ml (2 fl.oz) oil
115g (4 oz) mixed dried fruit, finely chopped
85g (3 oz) pistachio kernals, finely chopped
425ml (15 fl.oz) water

Pre-heat the oven to 180°C / 350°C / Gas Mark 4 and lightly oil a 23cm (9-inch) cake tin.

Measure the first six ingredients together into a large mixing bowl and stir well. Add the oil and work it in to an even consistency. Now add the fruit and nuts and stir the whole mixture very well.

Finally, add the liquid to the dry mixture and blend to an even batter. Turn the batter into the cake tin and bake for 15 minutes. Reduce the heat and bake at 160°C / 300°F / Gas Mark 2 for a further 40 minutes. Leave to cool in the tin for 10 minutes, then turn onto a wire rack to cool completely before serving.

Avocado & Almond Milkshake

Serves 4
Calories per serving: 168
Grams saturated fat per serving: 1.8
Milligrams cholesterol per serving: 0
Preparation time: 15 minutes

1 large, ripe avocado
850ml (1½ pints) soya milk, chilled
10ml (2 tsp) sugar (optional)
10ml (2 tsp) ground almonds
flaked almonds to garnish

Slice the avocado in half, remove the stone and scoop the flesh out into a food processor. Add the cold milk, sugar and ground almonds and purée to a smooth, even consistency. Pour the mixture into four tumblers (you may chill these beforehand!) and garnish with the flaked almonds. Serve immediately. This drink has a very thick consistency and so may be eaten with a spoon or a straw.

Family Fruit & Nut Cake

Serves 8
Calories per serving: 268
Grams saturated fat per serving: 1
Milligrams cholesterol per serving: 0
Preparation time: 1 hour

115g (4 oz) raisins or currants
55g (2 oz) brown sugar
30ml (2 tbsp) oil
285ml (10 fl.oz) apple juice
225g (8 oz) whole wheat flour
55g (2 oz) rolled oats
10ml (2 tsp) egg replacer
5ml (1 tsp) baking powder
5ml (1 tsp) ground ginger
55g (2 oz) citrus peel
55g (2 oz) flaked almonds

Pre-heat the oven to 190°C / 375°F / Gas Mark 5 and lightly oil a 23cm (9-inch) cake tin.

Measure the first four ingredients together in a mixing bowl and stir well. Leave to one side to soak.

Mix the remaining ingredients together in a large mixing bowl and stir well. Stir the raisin mixture into the dry mixture to make a thick batter. Turn the batter into the cake tin and bake for 40 minutes. Let the cake cool in the tin for 10 minutes before turning it onto a wire rack to cool completely. Serve as it is or with Sweet Orange Sauce (page 132).

Spicy Kisses
Makes 24 kisses
Calories per 4 kisses: 216
Grams saturated fat per 4 kisses: 1.2
Milligrams cholesterol per 4 kisses: 0
Preparation time: 20 minutes

55g (2 oz) margarine
115g (4 oz) icing sugar
15ml (1 tbsp) soya milk
225g (8 oz) whole wheat flour
5ml (1 tsp) caraway seed
5ml (1 tsp) ground cumin
2.5ml (½ tsp) ground cloves

Pre-heat the oven to 190°C / 375°F / Gas Mark 5.

Measure the margarine, sugar and soya milk into a small mixing bowl and blend well to a smooth, even consistency. Mix the dry ingredients together and gradually add to the sugar mixture, stirring after each addition.

Roll the dough into a cylinder the size of a tin and slice into 24 rounds. Arrange these on baking trays and bake the kisses for 12 minutes. Cool on a wire rack before serving.

Peach Cocktail
Serves 4
Calories per serving: 132
Grams saturated fat per serving: 0.3
Milligrams cholesterol per serving: 0
Preparation time: 15 minutes, plus chilling time

4 ripe peaches
500ml (1 pint) apple juice
2.5ml (½ tsp) ground cloves
230ml (8 fl.oz) soya milk concentrate

Peel the peaches by plunging them into boiling water for 1 minute, then remove them and quickly peel the skin away. Slice the peaches in half and remove the pips. Place the fruit into a blender with the apple juice and cloves and purée to an even consistency.

Divide the purée into four large tumblers. Pour 60ml (2 fl.oz) of soya milk concentrate into each serving and stir the milk briefly into the purée. Serve at once or chill for 1 hour before serving.

Rum & Banana Milkshake
Serves 4
Calories per serving: 245
Grams saturated fat per serving: 0.7
Milligrams cholesterol per serving: 0
Preparation time: 10 minutes

1 litre (2 pints) soya milk, chilled
4 very ripe bananas, peeled
2.5ml (½ tsp) ground nutmeg
120ml (4 fl.oz) rum

Purée the soya milk, bananas and nutmeg together in a blender. Divide the mixture between four large tumblers and pour 30ml (1 fl.oz) of rum into each serving. Stir briskly and serve at once.

THE NEW RULES FOR NO-CHOLESTEROL COOKING

Over the last few years, a growing awareness of how diet can affect your health has meant that certain cooking methods have gained in popularity, while others have had to take the blame for contributing to ill health. Here are just a few cooking methods which can make a beneficial difference to your health:

STEAMING

This method is used primarily for vegetables (although you may wish to try steaming grains such as rice, millet or couscous). The vegetables are prepared in the standard way – washing, trimming and cutting into manageable sized pieces. Then, instead of dropping them into boiling water, the vegetables are placed in the top of a double boiler or in a Universal Steamer (see below) with a little boiling water in the pan below. In this way the water never touches the vegetables and so more of the vitamin and mineral content is retained in the food, instead of seeping into the boiling water. In addition, the colour and texture of steamed vegetables is improved with less colour being lost and none of the 'limp' look so common to boiled vegetables. Steaming is as quick as, and sometimes quicker than, boiling vegetables and does not involve any additional preparation time or techniques.

THE NEW SAUTE

The recipes included here use a standard sauté technique but, if you would like to further reduce the amount of fat you consume, try this Instead of oil, use approximately 60ml (2 fl.oz) of liquid and heat until it bubbles in the pan over a medium heat. Then add the food to be sautéed and continue in the usual way. Virtually any liquid may be used – plain water, dilute yeast extract, tomato juice or any fruit juice are all successful. It is important to have the heat high enough to maintain a brisk bubbling of the liquid and also important to stir the food frequently as it sautés. This ensures that the food acquires the same texture and flavour so familiar to a sauté.

MARINADES

This is an ancient method of preserving food in a tasty and nutritious sauce, one that usually includes some vinegar. The marinades included here allow you to make, say, a large salad and keep it over two or three days without loss of flavour, texture or nutritional value. In fact, some people find the flavour of their marinades improves with keeping. Certainly, it has been difficult to keep the marinades we have made for longer than one day – they get eaten too quickly! Always use an enamel or glass pan when cooking the marinade, and store in a glass or plastic container, as aluminium or iron can taint the marinade.

COOKING BROWN RICE

450g (1 lb) of raw brown rice makes approximately 6 cupfuls of cooked rice (the rice trebles in bulk). This is usually enough to serve 6–8 people when a sauce or savoury accompanies the rice. Therefore, as an approximate guide, use 55g (2 oz) dried rice per serving.

Method:

Measure the rice into a mixing bowl and cover with cold water. Now wash the rice by swirling your hand through it and exerting a scrubbing motion. Drain the water and repeat this process three times until the water is fairly clear. Drain the rice and tip into an iron pot.

When cooking rice, the ratio of water to rice is generally 2:1.

Cover the clean rice in the pan with twice its volume in water. Cover the pan and place over a high flame. Bring the water to the boil, then reduce the flame as much as possible and leave to simmer for approximately 50 minutes or until the water is completely absorbed. Keep the pan covered while it cooks, only lifting the lid at the end of the cooking time to check that the rice is finished.

Don't stir the rice at this point, or it may become gummy. If it is still too firm at the end of 50 minutes, boil the kettle and add a little boiling water to the rice. Cover again and cook for another 10 minutes.

Brown rice takes longer to cook than white rice because it is a whole grain. However, it is more nutritious than white, refined rice and has 10 times the flavour.

COOKING BEANS

Most beans double in bulk and approximately quadruple in weight once they are cooked.

Method:

Measure the beans into a mixing bowl and pick them over to remove any stones or unwanted pieces of bean.

Cover the beans with cold water and wash them very well by

swirling your hand through them and exerting a scrubbing motion. Pour the water away and repeat this process three times, or until the water is clear. Drain the beans.

Cover the beans with water and leave them to soak overnight or all day while you are at work. Soaking the beans helps to prevent the flatulence that some people suffer from eating beans.

Drain the beans and throw the water away. Tip the beans into an iron pot and cover them with water. Bring them to the boil and simmer with the pan partially covered for 1–3 hours, depending on the type of bean you are cooking. The beans must remain covered in water and they must cook until they are easily squashed between your tongue and the top of your mouth. If they are under-cooked you will get a stomach ache.

Alternatively, some beans may be pressure cooked. Cover the beans with water, cover the cooker and bring up to pressure. Cook at pressure for 20–40 minutes, depending on the type of bean you are cooking. (Please refer to the leaflet accompanying your pressure cooker.)

In both methods, adding a teaspoon of salt or a strip of Kombu to the water will help to soften the beans.

Red lentils and split peas do not require soaking or pressure cooking. They *do* require washing. The red lentils are especially quick to cook and are therefore very useful for a quick, nutritious meal.

Here is a table of approximate cooking times for a selection of beans:

- Chickpeas: Take 30 minutes in the pressure cooker; 3 hours in the pot.

- Kidney Beans: Take 30 minutes in the pressure cooker; 1½ hours in the pot.

- Butter Beans: Take 30 minutes in the pressure cooker; 1½ hours in the pot.

- Soybeans: Take 40 minutes in the pressure cooker; at least 3 hours in the pot.

- Black-eyed Beans: Take 20 minutes in the pressure cooker; 1 hour in the pot.

- Lentils & Split Peas: Take 20 minutes in the pressure cooker; 1 hour in the pot.

ESSENTIAL UTENSILS

Some of the labour-saving kitchen equipment on the market really does put an end to the 'slave' part of leaning over the kitchen stove, while other equipment is all the better for being very traditional. Here is a list of our preferences:

IRON POTS & PANS

If you keep these well oiled to prevent rust, they will add to the iron in your diet every time you cook with them. Aluminium is to be avoided because you actually get some of that in your cooking as well – but this time it's *not* good for you. Enamel or glass pots and pans are very good, too, as they are neutral – neither adding to nor tainting the food in any way.

PRESSURE COOKER

A real time saver when you cook beans (see list in previous chapter). Buy one that is stainless steel, not aluminium.

FOOD PROCESSOR

Apart from the noise, these are as good as having your own kitchen maid. They make *very* short work of shredding, slicing, grating and, of course, blending and puréeing. If I really can't face the noise, or if I'm not in a hurry, then I chop and slice in the normal way, with pleasure.

MOULI

This is a hand-turned sieve, with a sloping, perforated blade, that rests on a bowl or pan. Use it to turn soups and jams and sauces into a smooth potage or purée.

UNIVERSAL STEAMER

A perforated metal basket that adjusts to fit into almost any size pan. Place your vegetables in the basket, a bit of water under the basket, cover the pan, place over the heat and steam away.

WOK

Though not specified in these recipes, a wok is the ideal pan for cooking a stir-fry or sauté. It is a bowl-shaped iron pan (again, *not* aluminium) which distributes the heat so effectively that very little oil is necessary to cook your vegetables to perfection. Just the pan to make a low- or no-cholesterol dish.

A NEW WORLD OF FOOD

Some of the ingredients listed in the recipes may be new to you but most of them are, in fact, very common to groups of people in other parts of the world or to people who follow diets that are different from what we call traditional. All of these foods are readily available in supermarkets or in the increasingly common whole-food or healthfood shops. Here are introductions to just a few foods included in these recipes:

- *Arami* – is a seaweed with a very curly, lacy texture. It is delicious and not at all fishy! 55g (2 oz) will feed 4 people.

- *Bulghur* – is a whole grain, famous in Middle Eastern cooking. Most supermarkets have it, though they may market it as cracked wheat. If you don't find it, try *couscous* or *pourgouri* instead, both of which are also popular as well as similar in texture, flavour and cooking method to bulghur. It is handy because it is generally very quick and simple to prepare and is also versatile – just add a few vegetables and you have a meal!

- *Cider vinegar* – a natural food with possible health benefits attributed to it. It is easy to find in either supermarkets or health food shops, where it may even be purchased in organic form. Use as much as you like, more than these recipes call for if that suits your taste.

- *Dried fruits* – dried prunes, figs, dates, currants and raisins are included in these recipes. All of them are available in supermarkets and healthfood shops. We recommend that you try to find sun-dried varieties that are not coated in sugar or mineral oil – more and more shops are stocking fruits of this sort. Dried fruits are naturally sweet and rich in minerals. Most need a quick wash before they are used.

- *Egg replacer* – a useful product for those people who want to bake light cakes and quick breads while still reducing their consumption of cholesterol-rich eggs. The most widely distributed egg replacer is 'Ener-G', produced by General Design Ltd, PO Box 38E, Worcester Park, Surrey, tel. 01-337 9366. This packet has a number of useful recipes on it. Two more egg replacers (egg white and whole egg) are also made by G. F. Dietary Group of Companies Ltd, 494–496

Honeypot Lane, Stanmore, Middx, HA7 1HJ. These are also sold in some healthfood shops (Boots, for instance) and they also sell mail order (phone them for details).

- *Frozen foods* – most of the vegetables called for in these recipes may be purchased in frozen form. Peas, carrots, corn, beans, Brussels sprouts and many others are easy to find in any supermarket or frozen food centre. By all means use these foods if you like as they are very convenient and make meal preparation exceptionally quick. However, fresh food is always richer in nutrients than frozen or tinned food and we will always recommend that you use fresh food when possible.

- *Herbs and spices* – in their fresh form many herbs and spices are rich in vitamins and minerals. Fresh parsley is an excellent example of a nutrient-rich fresh herb. In their dried form, some of the nutrients are lost, while the flavours tend to become more concentrated. We have listed specific amounts of most of the herbs and spices included, with occasional instructions to use them 'to taste'. In fact, you should feel free to explore the very wide range of herbs and spices available and to use them according to your preference. They will make little effect on the nutritional outcome of your meal, but may greatly affect your enjoyment of it!

- *Kombu* – is another seaweed. This one is used to thicken soups and stews, soften beans while cooking, and to add a very subtle, buttery flavour to broths and sauces. It is not listed in the recipes but is highly recommended for the flavour, texture and nutritional bonus it brings to a dish.

- *Margarine* – most of the recipes call for oil. Some call for margarine, however, or on occasion, you may wish to substitute margarine for oil. In these cases use a low-fat, non-dairy margarine.

- *Molasses* – this is a by-product of sugar production so it is very sweet. However, it is also rich in the B vitamins, iron and other minerals. It is included in a few recipes to add nutritional value, flavour and sweetness. You may reduce the amounts called for if you wish.

- *Nutritional yeast flakes* – in these recipes, we are thinking specifically of Engevita Nutritional Yeast Flakes, by Marigold Foods. However, there are brands of similar product available from both supermarkets and healthfood shops. Yeast products are rich in the B group of vitamins as well as a number of trace minerals. These yeast flakes add a very subtle flavour to your food and a cheese-like texture and appearance.

- *Oat bran* – available from supermarkets and healthfood shops. It should be stored in an airtight container in a cool place. Oat bran, and indeed all of the oat foods are inexpensive and very nutritious. Oats are one of the foods most important in a cholesterol control diet as they are very high in soluble fibre, a substance which helps to reduce cholesterol in your blood.

- *Pasta* – always popular and easy to find. But check the label to make sure the pasta you buy is made without eggs, as eggs are very high in cholesterol.

- *Rechard or tandoori paste* – some dishes need a little extra bite to make them scrumptious and these two spicy pastes are given as perfect examples of how to achieve this. Try your own personal favourite, if you prefer, but avoid those with a great deal of oil or with animal fats included.

- *Rice* – most recipes simply call for 'rice' and you must decide whether you wish to use a white or brown variety. When possible, however, we recommend brown rice as it is very nutritious, though it does take longer to cook than white rice, so you may have to alter your cooking schedule somewhat. An alternative is to use basmati rice, which is very tasty, aromatic and quick to cook. Brown, white or basmati rice is available at all supermarkets and healthfood stores.

- *Soya milk* – is made from the soybean. It is easy to find and a really tasty, healthy alternative to cow's milk. The recipes call for two types: plain soya milk, which is a standard dilution resembling cow's milk, and soya milk concentrate which resembles cream and may be used diluted or undiluted (the recipe will specify if it is to be diluted).

- *Soya mince* – also called TVP, this is yet another soybean product made to resemble the look and texture of mince beef. It is a high-protein food which is quick and versatile to cook.

- *Soy sauce* – yet another soybean product which adds depth to savoury dishes. If you are in a whole-food shop, Tamari and Shoyu are natural forms of soy sauce.

- *Tempeh* – also a soybean product (what a wonderful plant!). This is a block of fermented beans which you buy frozen from a whole food shop. Don't pull a face at the look of it until you've tried the recipe. Delicious! It is rich in an abundance of vitamins and minerals and can easily substitute for the meat in your sandwich or on your breakfast plate.

- *Tinned foods* – the tinned foods in these recipes are included to help keep the preparation of meals as quick and easy as possible. Many manufacturers currently market low-salt versions of their tinned products because public interest in health has increased over the last few years and we recommend that you select these in preference to the high-salt versions. All supermarkets and healthfood shops have a selection for you to choose from.

The precise weight of the tinned food may vary from brand to brand. Therefore you may use the weights listed in the recipes as approximations and purchase the size tin closest to that recommended.

- *Tofu* – this is often called 'bean curd' because it is made from soybeans. The beans are made into milk and the milk into tofu, in a process similar to making cheese. Tofu is widely available in both supermarkets and healthfood shops. It comes either soft or firm and is usually packed in water (some varieties are dried). Use the soft variety instead of yogurt, the firm variety instead of cheese. Most supermarkets stock a 'silken' variety – which is a soft tofu. Some of these recipes call for a firm tofu which you are certain to find in a healthfood shop. There are a great many brand names and you may try them all until you find the brand you are happiest with. Every manufacturer makes a recognizably different tofu, so if you don't like the first type you try, move on to another!

  Tofu is very low in fat, contains no cholesterol and is high in protein and minerals. It is a light, versatile food that, though bland by itself, may be prepared as a vehicle for other flavours.

- *Tostadas* – these are made from corn (maize) in a similar way to the Indian pappadam. They are low in calories and fats with a distinct flavour and texture. Most large supermarkets and some healthfood shops stock these. Taco shells are the same product, but simply folded!

- *TVP* – made from soybeans and is processed into a high protein, low-fat food made to resemble the texture of some meat products. It is highly versatile as it comes in mince and chunk form, various 'meaty' flavours (beef, chicken, bacon) as well as plain, and will conform to the other flavours and textures you want from your meal. Most supermarkets and all healthfood shops sell TVP products.

- *VegeBurger mix* – this is a meat-free burger mix sold in a foil packet. It is an excellent all-natural basis for many traditional dishes, as well as some that you haven't thought of yet. Available in supermarkets and healthfood shops. Prepare it using the eggless technique.

- *Yeast extract* – there are many varieties on the market now and it is easy to pick one that is low in salt. Apart from the ever-famous Marmite, there is Barmene, Tastex and Natex. Or try one of the vegetable extracts, such a Vecon.

NO TIME TO COOK?
HERE'S A WEEK'S WORTH
OF FAST-FOOD MENUS...

Let's be honest with each other and agree that, no matter how good one's intentions, there simply are times when it's too much fuss, bother and hassle to delve into any cookery book and experiment with new recipes. And if you work during the day, it just won't be practical for you to specially prepare something for lunch at your workplace. Most people, rightly or wrongly, depend on easy access to fast food to keep them going during their busy days. But 'fast food' doesn't *have* to mean 'junk food'. The seven day menus which follow have been especially designed for busy people... they use easily available foodstuffs, which keep food preparation times right down to an absolute minimum. And, as you can see, they're all low in saturated fat and cholesterol – just to show you what can be done to reduce your cholesterol intake before trying the no-cholesterol recipes in the main part of this book.

MONDAY

Breakfast
Glass of orange juice
1 serving breakfast cereal with low-fat milk or soya milk
1 bowlful stewed mixed fruit
Cup of coffee (with low-fat milk or soya milk)

Lunch
Baked potato filled with ½ tin baked beans
1 apple
Cup of tea (with low-fat milk or Soya milk)

Dinner
A Starter of tomato soup
followed by
2 slices of cheese and tomato pizza beside a large mixed salad with low-cal French dressing
with a dessert of
1 bowlful stewed figs

Calories: 2023

Total fat (grams): 25
Saturated fat (grams): 9
Cholesterol (miligrams): 39

It's very, very important to start your day with a good breakfast- a burnt slice of toast and a quick coffee 'fix' just isn't good enough! If you eat a good breakfast, the feeling of fullness will stay with you until lunchtime so you'll not be tempted to 'snack-out' with a chocolate bar for elevenses. All the week's breakfasts (apart from Sunday Brunch) are very quick to prepare, because time is usually very short first thing in the morning. You can choose your own favourite breakfast cereal, although you should avoid those few which contain large amounts of fat (read the label). Alternatively, it only takes 3–5 minutes to make a delicious bowl of porridge oats, and oats do have a good effect on cholesterol levels (make it with water, not cream, and pour a little low-fat milk or soya milk on top if you want to). Today's breakfast includes a bowl of stewed mixed fruit – you can buy packets of dried mixed fruit at all healthfood shops. Cheap, delicious and nutritious, stewed mixed fruit should be soaked overnight in cold water (just cover it in a bowl) and it will be ready to eat the next morning.

Tea and coffee have been included in the week's menus because so many people like to drink these beverages, although there is some evidence that they may modestly increase blood cholesterol levels. If you don't mind giving them up, try substituting a herbal tea instead (there are many varieties to choose from, some much nicer than others).

Lunch (baked potato with baked beans) can either be prepared at home (using a microwave to speed things up if you've got one) or can be bought from many snack bars and fast food outlets. Baked beans, in particular, contain soluble fibre which is known to be able to lower cholesterol levels.

Dinner today is equally easy – tomato soup comes straight out of a tin or packet, and the ubiquitous pizza can be bought anywhere and everywhere, as can the mixed salad (but you may like to prepare your own). Alternatively, if you don't want to eat at home, you can simply order 2 slices of pizza with side salad (but avoid the creamy dressing). You should be watchful that the amount of cheese on your pizza is not excessive, and avoid 'deep pan' pizzas which really pile on the fat and the calories. If you choose not to have any cheese at all on your pizza, ask for a 'Marinara' pizza (this is made without cheese, but with a delicious tomato, herbs and and garlic topping). To finish, a bowl of stewed figs (prepared in the same way as the breakfast mixed fruit) will be delicious and very satisfying, but if you're eating out, you may just want to ask for a fruit salad (avoiding those lashings of cream).

TUESDAY

Breakfast
Glass of orange juice
1 serving breakfast cereal with low-fat milk or soya milk
1 banana
Cup of coffee (with low-fat milk or soya milk)

Lunch
1 serving vegetable soup with 1 slice wholewheat toast
(buttered or margarine)
1 cup of tea (with low-fat milk or soya milk)
1 ounce dried pumpkin seeds

Dinner
A starter of half a grapefruit
1 serving of pasta (e.g. spaghetti, fusilli or pasta shells) with Napoli
tomato sauce
with a dessert of
1 serving lemon sorbet

Calories: 1716
Total fat (grams): 41
Saturated fat (grams): 11
Cholesterol (miligrams): 30

Lunch today (vegetable soup) can come out of a tin or from a take-away, but just check there are not excessive amounts of fat in it (a very greasy taste is a warning sign, as is a dollop of cream floating in it!) A handful of pumpkin seeds (mixed with a handful of raisins if you wish) makes a nutritious and satisfying snack at any time of the day when you feel you need a little bit extra sustenance. Don't have more than an ounce or so, though, because many types of nuts and seeds contain large amounts of fat.

Dinner tonight can be equally easy at home or in a restaurant – pasta with basic, beautiful Italian tomato sauce is one of the all-time classic dishes, easy and quick to prepare and very satisfying. If you simply can't face it without a sprinkling of parmesan, go ahead (just a teaspoon!) because its flavour is so strong you need very little indeed. Lemon sorbet is a water ice (i.e. made without animal fat) and can be served straight out of the freezer (just check the label when you buy it to ensure there aren't any other fatty ingredients).

WEDNESDAY

Breakfast
Glass of orange juice

1 serving breakfast cereal with low-fat milk or soya milk
2 slices toasted granary bread with Jam & butter or
margarine
Cup of coffee (with low-fat milk or soya milk)

Lunch
1 pitta stuffed with hummus and mixed salad
1 fresh banana
1 cup of tea (with low-fat milk or soya milk)

Dinner
A starter of 2 falafels with freshly squeezed lemon juice
followed by
Indian dal with plain boiled rice and Indian chutney or pickles
with a dessert of
1 slice of apple pie

Calories: 1996
Total fat (grams): 64
Saturated fat (grams): 21
Cholesterol (miligrams): 61

Today's menu has a Middle Eastern and Indian flavour to it. Lunch consists of a piece of pitta bread stuffed with a chickpea spread, called hummus, and salad. You can buy it from almost every fast-food kebab house, and it's usually very good value for money. Alternatively, you can buy the pitta bread, the hummus (tinned or fresh) and the salad from most healthfood shops or delicatessens.

Dinner, too, starts off in a Middle Eastern way – falafels are little round chickpea patties, bought from kebab houses or 'delis'. The main course is rice with dal, which again can be made at home or can easily be obtained from any Indian restaurant. Rice and dal is a staple Indian dish, essentially low in fat (sadly unlike much other Westernized Indian restaurant cooking). Indian restaurants and take-aways will often have several types of dal on offer – it is usually best to insist on 'plain dal' which is not only cheaper but also comes without a huge lake of floating oil which often ruins fancier and more expensive versions. Chutneys and pickles are, of course, one of the star attractions of Indian cooking, and most good restaurants and 'delis' offer a mouth-watering selection.

THURSDAY

Breakfast
Glass of orange juice
1 serving breakfast cereal with low-fat milk or soya milk
Half a grapefruit

No Time to Cook?

Cup of coffee (with low-fat milk or soya milk)

Lunch
Mixed bean salad (kidney beans, sweetcorn, potato salad) with low-cal
French dressing
1 cup of tea
1 ounce dried pumpkin seeds

Dinner
A starter of minestrone soup
followed by
2 vegetable burgers with peas, carrots, new potatoes and
gravy
with a dessert of
1 serving fruit salad in its own juice topped with chopped almonds

Calories: 1875
Total fat (grams): 42
Saturated fat (grams): 8
Cholesterol (miligrams): 108

For lunch, the mixed bean salad can usually be found in the salad bar
of most pizza and hamburger restaurants (good hunting ground for
many low-cholesterol meals), or can be prepared at home and taken in
to work in a plastic container.

For dinner, vegetable burgers can be bought from all healthfood
stores and most supermarkets and take just a few minutes to heat and
serve. The accompanying vegetables can be steamed or microwaved,
and the gravy is good, old-fashioned made-up gravy (but just check the
label to make sure no animal fat has been added).

FRIDAY

Breakfast
Glass of orange juice
1 serving breakfast cereal with low-fat milk or soya milk
1 serving fresh pineapple
Cup of coffee (with low-fat milk or soya milk)

Lunch
1 serving of ratatouille with 1 slice granary bread and
butter or margarine
1 cup of tea (with low-fat milk or soya milk)

Dinner
A starter of avocado vinaigrette (half an avocado with vinaigrette
dressing)

followed by Chinese stir-fry (bean-sprouts, bamboo shoots,
water-chestnuts, tofu, broccoli, mushrooms, garlic)
served with brown rice
with a dessert of
oriental fruit (lychees and guavas)

Calories: 1518
Total fat (grams): 86
Saturated fat (grams): 16
Cholesterol (miligrams): 29

Lunch today consists of Ratatouille, which is a gorgeous Mediterranean
dish (eaten hot or cold) made from french beans, courgettes, peppers,
carrots, onion and tomato, and can be bought from any 'deli' or tinned
from every supermarket.

Dinner starts with half an avocado and vinaigrette dressing –
avocado is one of the few fruit or vegetables to contain appreciable
amounts of saturated fat, so go easily here and, if in any doubt, just
substitute it for any one of the recipes in this book. The Chinese stir-fry
is best made in a real Chinese wok – they are specially designed to
enable a small amount of oil to go a long way in this style of cooking.
All the ingredients can easily be bought (fresh or tinned) from any
supermarket, as can the sweet. If you're eating out in a Chinese restaurant, make sure you choose dishes which haven't been fried in large
amounts of pork fat.

SATURDAY

Breakfast
Glass of orange juice
1 serving breakfast cereal with low-fat milk or soya milk
Cup of coffee (with low-fat milk or soya milk)

Lunch
1 bowlful lentil soup with
1 large salad sandwich
1 cup of tea (with low-fat milk or soya milk)
1 ounce dried pumpkin seeds with 1 ounce raisins

Dinner
A starter of fresh honeydew melon
1 generous serving of pasta (e.g. spaghetti, fusilli or pasta shells) with
pesto (basil) sauce
with a dessert of
fresh fruit salad

No Time to Cook?

Calories: 1583
Total fat (grams): 50
Saturated fat (grams): 9
Cholesterol (miligrams): 33

Saturdays tend to be 'action days', so the menu today is very quick and easy – lunch consists of no more than opening a tin of soup and throwing together a tasty salad sandwich.

Dinner is equally quick – but very classy! Pasta with pesto sauce is served at almost all Italian restaurants, and the basic pesto sauce can be bought in jars in supermarkets, health food shops and 'delis'. Pesto sauce is itself quite rich (containing pine nuts, basil and olive oil) but it has such an intense flavour that you hardly need to do any more than show it to the pasta to obtain a beautiful, spectacular aroma. A great choice for eating out, and just as good if you're intending to curl up at home in front of the video, with a glass of chianti!

SUNDAY

Brunch
Glass of orange juice
1 serving breakfast cereal with low-fat milk or soya milk
½ tin baked beans over 1 slice wholewheat toast
with 2 vegetable burgers and grilled tomato garnish
2 slices toast with butter or margarine and jam or marmalade
1 serving stewed rhubarb with a sprinkling of sugar
Cup of coffee (with low-fat milk or soya milk)

Dinner
A starter of fresh honeydew melon
followed by 2 slices cheese and tomato pizza with mixed
salad and low-cal French dressing
with a dessert of
fresh cherries, peaches or other seasonal fruit
Cup of tea (with low-fat milk or soya milk)

Calories: 1870
Total fat (grams): 37
Saturated fat (grams): 9
Cholesterol (miligrams): 40

Sunday should be relaxed and indulgent – forget about an early-riser breakfast, and concentrate on a long, delicious brunch which is a traditional-style feast for family and friends. There are many different kinds of vegetable burgers available in supermarkets and healthfood shops – do check the label to make sure the one you choose doesn't contain large amounts of fat (most don't). Also, try something new – there are several new vegetable sausages in the shops now, which are equally tasty and low in fat (grill them, don't fry).

Sunday's dinner is simple and no-fuss – a take-away pizza with salad (or a sit-down in a restaurant if you prefer). See the notes about pizza under 'Monday'.

PART THREE:

THE CHOLESTEROL COUNTER

HOW TO USE THE
CHOLESTEROL COUNTER

Using the counter is simplicity itself. Make sure you carry it with you when you're eating out – it'll be your guide as you navigate through restaurant menus. And remember to take it to the supermarket when you're shopping, because it works just as well there, too. The main golden rule to remember is:

the lowest number is best

The food is arranged in alphabetical order, so you should be able to find what you want immediately – for example, to look up 'marmalade', look under the Ms, to look up 'Yorkshire pudding', look under the Ys. Some foods, shown below, are gathered together under a main heading, because it makes better sense to keep them all together – this allows you to look at similar foods within a group and see how their ratings compare. The main food groups are:

Alcohol
Beans and Pulses
Beef
Biscuits
Bread
Breakfast Cereals
Cakes
Carbonated Drinks
Cereals and Grains
Cheese
Chicken
Chocolate
Eggs
Fat
Fish and Shellfish
Flour
Ham
Lamb
Margarine
Milk

Nut and Seed Butters
Nuts
Oil
Pies
Pork
Potatoes
Puddings
Rice
Salads
Salad Dressings
Sandwiches
Sauces
Sausages
Seeds and Seed Products
Soup
Spices
Sweets
Turkey
Veal

A NOTE ABOUT THE FOODS

We have tried to include a good selection of the common and not-so-common (especially ethnic) foods that people eat, and we've also tried to make this book as easy to use as possible.

In some cases, it simply has not been possible to obtain reliable information for some kinds of food. We have, however, included information for many different kinds of 'raw' food, which will allow you to calculate your own ratings for a recipe or dish which is not included here. Where a dish has been analysed (for example, Wiener Schnitzel) it should be understood that there are many individual ways of preparing it, each involving differing amounts of fat and cholesterol, and therefore our figures can only be an approximate guide. For the sake of clarity, figures have been rounded to the nearest whole number.

SETTING YOUR LIMITS

Each food has three figures next to it: the total grams of fat contained in the serving; the amount of saturated fat in grams; and the amount of cholesterol in milligrams. What maximum limits should you set for your intake of these three substances? It goes without saying that you should always take professional advice on this, since your medical advisor knows your own health, history and circumstances. The guidelines that follow are generalisations and may not be appropriate for everyone.

TOTAL FAT

Reducing your total fat consumption will help you to lose weight if you need to, and – providing you also reduce your saturated fat consumption – will also help you to lower blood cholesterol levels. The following table gives you a range of limits, together with comments on likely effects.

MAXIMUM TOTAL DAILY FAT INTAKE (g)	% OF DAY'S CALORIES (assumes 2000 cal per day)	COMMENT
30 g	13.5%	The lowest suggested limit – lower not advised
40 g	18%	Maintains weight loss
50 g	22.5%	Many experts feel this is an appropriate level for adults. Gradual weight loss still occurs[60]
65 g	30%	Government's recommendation for adults.
90 g	40%	Average adult intake

SATURATED FAT

The amount of cholesterol in your blood doesn't just depend on the amount of cholesterol in your diet. You see, the problem with simply measuring the amount of cholesterol you eat in your food is that it only tells you part of the story. In fact, the level of cholesterol in your body depends on both the amount of cholesterol and the amount of saturated fat you eat! It's a complicated relationship, but of the two, the amount of saturated fat you consume probably affects your cholesterol level more dramatically than the amount of cholesterol you eat! And, with a few exceptions, food which is high in cholesterol will also be high in saturated fat. The golden rule here is:

choose the lowest saturated fat figure you can find – then check that the cholesterol is low, too

Official government guidelines suggest that no more than 10 per cent of our total dietary energy (calories) should come from saturated fat. For a person consuming 2000 calories a day, this means a maximum of 22 g of saturated fat a day. Less is better – and zero is possible!

CHOLESTEROL

Finally, you should check to ensure that the food you choose is low in (or free of) cholesterol. Official government guidelines suggest that we should not exceed today's average cholesterol consumption, which is about 245 milligrams per day. After checking to make sure that your food is the lowest it can be in saturated fat, also make sure that it's low (or free of) cholesterol. The golden rule here is:

choose food which is the lowest in cholesterol – zero is possible!

THE FOODS

	Total fat (g)	Saturated fat (g)	Cholesterol (mg)
ALCOHOL			
Beer			
Bitter and Stout, ½ Pint (285ml)	0	0	0
Lager, ½ Pint (285ml)	0	0	0
Bloody Mary			
1 Glass	0	0	0
Champagne			
1 Glass	0	0	0
Cider			
½ Pint (285ml)	0	0	0
Creme de Menthe, 36% vol			
1 Glass	0	0	0
Daiquiri			
1 Glass	0	0	0
1 Tin	0	0	0
Fortified Wines (Port, Sherry)			
1 Glass	0	0	0
Gin and Tonic			
1 Glass	0	0	0
Gin Fizz			
1 Glass	0	0	0
Liqueur			
Coffee with Cream, 17% vol, 1 Measure	7	5	7
Coffee, 26.5% vol, 1 Measure	0	0	0
Coffee, 31.5% vol, 1 Measure	0	0	0
Manhattan Cocktail			
1 Glass	0	0	0
Martini Cocktail			
1 Glass	0	0	0
Pina Colada			
1 Glass	3	1	0
1 Tin	17	15	05
Spirits (Brandy, Gin, Rum, Vodka, Whisky)			
1 Measure	0	0	0
Whisky and Soda			
1 Glass	0	0	0

	Total fat (g)	Saturated fat (g)	Cholesterol (mg)
Wine			
Dessert, Dry, 1 Glass	0	0	0
Dessert, Sweet, 1 Glass	0	0	0
Table, All, 1 Glass	0	0	0
Alfalfa Seeds			
Sprouted, Fresh, 1 Cup (33g)	0	0	0
Almonds			
Dried, 1 Cup Kernels (142g)	74	7	0
Dry Roasted, 1 Cup Kernels (138g)	71	7	0
Apple Juice			
Frozen Concentrate, Diluted, 1 Glass	0	0	0
Frozen Concentrate, Undiluted,			
6 Fl.oz Container (211g)	1	0	0
Tinned or Bottled, 1 Glass	0	0	0
Apples			
Dried, Stewed, 1 Cup (280g)	0	0	0
Dried, Uncooked, 1 Cup (86g)	0	0	0
Frozen Rings, 1 Cup (206g)	1	0	0
Raw, with Skin, 1 Fruit	1	0	0
Raw, without Skin, 1 Fruit	0	0	0
Tinned, 1 Cup (204g)	1	0	0
Applesauce			
Tinned, 1 Cup (255g)	1	0	0
Apricot Nectar			
Tinned or Bottled, 1 Glass (251g)	0	0	0
Apricots			
Dried, Stewed, 1 Cup (270g)	0	0	0
Dried, Uncooked, 1 Cup (130g)	1	0	0
Frozen, 1 Cup (242g)	0	0	0
Fresh, 3 Fruits	0	0	0
Tinned, 1 Cup (248g)	0	0	0
Arrowroot			
Boiled, 1 Piece (12g)	0	0	0
Fresh, 1 Piece (12g)	0	0	0
Artichokes			
Globe, Boiled, 1 Med Artichoke (120g)	0	0	0
Globe, Boiled, ½ Cup Hearts (84g)	0	0	0
Jerusalem, Boiled, 1 Cup Slices (150g)	0	0	0
Asparagus			
Boiled, 4 Spears (60g)	0	0	0
Tinned, Drained Solids, 1 Tin (248g)	2	0	0

	Total fat (g)	Saturated fat (g)	Cholesterol (mg)
Tinned, Solids and Liquid, 1 Tin (411g)	1	0	0
Aubergine			
Boiled or Baked, 1 Cup Cubes (96g)	0	0	0
Fried in Butter, 1 Cup Cubes (96g) and 1 oz Butter	23	14	62
Fried in Margarine, 1 Cup, Cubes (96g) and 1 oz Margarine	23	4	0
Fried in Oil, 1 Cup Cubes (96g) and 2 Tablespoons Oil	27	2	0
Avocado Dip – See Guacamole			
Avocado and Prawn Cocktail			
1 Fruit, Prawns (64g) and Dressing	54	8	127
Avocado Vinaigrette			
1 Fruit and Vinaigrette with Olive Oil	39	6	0
Avocados			
Fresh, 1 Fruit	31	5	0
Bacon			
Cured, Tinned, 3.5oz (100g)	72	23	89
Long Back, Grilled, 2 Slices (46.5g)	4	1	27
Long Back, Raw, 2 Slices (56.7g)	4	1	28
Streaky, Grilled, Shallow-fried or Roasted, 3 Medium Slices (19g)	9	3	16
Streaky, Raw, 3 Medium Slices (68g)	39	15	46
Top Back, Grilled or Roasted,3 Raw Slices (34g)	13	4	36
Top Back, Raw, 3 Slices (68g)	25	9	47
Bacon Substitute, Meatless			
1 Strip (8g)	2	0	0
1 Cup (144g)	43	7	0
Bagels			
Plain, 1 Bagel	1	0	0
Baked Beans			
See under Beans			
Baked Potato			
Also see under Potato			
1 Medium	0	0	0
1 Medium with ½ Tin (220g) Baked Beans	1	0	0
1 Medium with 1 Pat Butter	4	3	11
1 Medium with ½ Cup Lo-fat Cottage Cheese	2	1	10
1 Medium with 1 Pat Butter and 55g Cheddar	23	15	71

	Total fat (g)	Saturated fat (g)	Cholesterol (mg)
Baking Powder			
1 tbsp (9.5g)	0	0	0
Balsam-pear			
Boiled, 1 Cup (58g)	0	0	0
Raw, ½ Cup (24g)	0	0	0
Bamboo Shoots			
Boiled, 1 Cup Slices (120g)	0	0	0
Tinned, 1 Tin (262g)	1	0	0
Fresh, 1 Cup Slices (151g)	1	0	0
Bananas			
Dehydrated or Banana Flakes,			
1 tbsp (6.2g)	0	0	0
1 Cup (100g)	2	1	0
Fresh, 1 Fruit	1	0	0
Barley, Pearl, Pot or Scotch			
1 Cup (200g)	2	0	0
BEANS AND PULSES			
Aduki Beans			
1 Cup Boiled (230g)	0	0	0
1 Cup Tinned (296g)	0	0	0
Yokan, 3 Slices (43g)	0	0	0
Baked Beans			
Home Recipe with Pork, 1 Cup (253g)	13	5	13
Tinned, Plain or Vegetarian, 1 Cup (254g)	1	0	0
Tinned, with Beef, 1 Cup (266g)	9	5	59
Tinned, with Pork, 1 Cup (253g)	4	2	18
Tinned, with Sausages, 1 Cup (257g)	17	6	15
2 Slices Buttered Toast and 1 Tin (440g) Beans	12	6	22
2 Slices Toast with Margarine and			
1 Tin (440g) Beans	11	1	0
Beansprouts			
Stir-Fried, 1 Cup (124g)	0	0	0
Tinned, 1 Cup (125g)	0	0	0
Mixed, Fresh, ½ Cup (52g)	0	0	0
12oz Package (340g)	1	0	0
Bengal Gram – See Chickpeas			
Black Beans			
Boiled, 1 Cup (172g)	1	0	0
Black-eyed Beans			
Boiled, 1 Cup (171g)	1	0	0
Borlotti Beans			
Boiled, 1 Cup (169g)	1	0	0

	Total fat (g)	Saturated fat (g)	Cholesterol (mg)
British Field Beans			
Boiled, 1 Cup (177g)	1	0	0
Tinned, 1 Cup (262g)	1	0	0
Broadbeans			
Boiled, 1 Cup (170g)	1	0	0
Tinned, 1 Cup (256g)	1	0	0
Butter Beans			
Boiled, 1 Cup (188g)	1	0	0
Tinned, 1 Cup (241g)	0	0	0
Cannellini Beans			
Boiled, 1 Cup (179g)	1	0	0
Chickpeas			
Boiled, 1 Cup (164g)	4	0	0
Hummus, Home Recipe, 1 Cup (246g)	21	3	0
Tinned, 1 Cup (240g)	3	0	0
Dwarf Beans			
Boiled, 1 Cup (182g)	1	0	0
Flageolet Beans			
Boiled, 1 Cup (177g)	1	0	0
Tinned, 1 Cup (260g)	1	0	0
French Beans			
Boiled, 1 Cup (177g)	1	0	0
Ful Medames			
Boiled, 1 Cup (87g)	0	0	0
Garbanzo Beans – See Chickpeas			
Gram – See Chickpeas			
Haricot Beans			
Boiled, 1 Cup (182g)	1	0	0
Sprouted, Fresh, 1 Cup (104g)	1	0	0
Tinned, 1 Cup (262g)	1	0	0
Kidney Beans			
Boiled, 1 Cup (177g)	1	0	0
Sprouted, Fresh, 1 Cup (184g)	1	0	0
Tinned, 1 Cup (256g)	1	0	0
Lentils			
Boiled, 1 Cup (198g)	1	0	0
Dhal, Home Recipe, 1 Cup (210g)	15	2	0
Sprouted, Fresh, 1 Cup (77g)	0	0	0
Sprouted, Stir-fried, 3½oz (100g)	1	0	0
Lima Beans			
Boiled, 1 Cup (170g)	1	0	0
Tinned, 1 Cup (248g)	1	0	0

	Total fat (g)	Saturated fat (g)	Cholesterol (mg)
Mixed White Beans			
Boiled, 1 Cup (179g)	1	0	0
Tinned, 1 Cup (262g)	1	0	0
Mung Beans			
Boiled, 1 Cup (202g)	1	0	0
Sprouted, Boiled, 1 Cup (124g)	0	0	0
Sprouted, Fresh, 1 Cup (100g)	0	0	0
Sprouted, Stir-fried, 1 Cup (124g)	0	0	0
Sprouted, Tinned, 1 Cup (125g)	0	0	0
Navy Beans			
Boiled, 1 Cup (172g)	10	1	0
Pigeon Peas			
Boiled, 1 Cup (168g)	1	0	0
Pinto Beans			
Boiled, 1 Cup (171g)	1	0	0
Tinned, 1 Cup (240g)	1	0	0
Red Gram – See Pigeon Peas			
Refried Beans			
Tinned, 1 Cup (253g)	3	1	0
Runner Beans			
Boiled, 1 Cup (125g)	0	0	0
Tinned, 1 Cup (135g)	0	0	0
Soybeans			
Boiled, 1 Cup (172g)	15	2	0
Dry Roasted, 1 Cup (172g)	37	5	0
Roasted, 1 Cup (172g)	44	6	0
Sprouted, Fresh, ½ Cup (35g)	2	0	0
Sprouted, Steamed, 1 Cup (94g)	4	1	0
Sprouted, Stir-fried, 3½oz (100g)	7	1	0
Urd Beans			
Boiled, 1 Cup (180g)	1	0	0
Winged Beans			
Boiled, 1 Cup (62g)	0	0	0
Yardlong Beans			
Boiled, 1 Cup Slices (104g)	0	0	0
Yellow Snap Beans			
Boiled, 1 Cup (177g)	2	1	0

	Total fat (g)	Saturated fat (g)	Cholesterol (mg)
BEEF			
Also see under Luncheon Meat; Steak			
Carcass: Whole			
Choice Cuts, Lean and Fat, Raw,			
1 lb (453.6g)	110	46	336
Composite of Trimmed Cuts			
Lean and Fat, Cooked, 3oz (85g)	23	10	77
Lean and Fat, Raw, 1 lb (453.6g)	107	46	318
Lean, Cooked, 3oz (85g)	9	3	77
Lean, Raw, 1 lb (453.6g)	29	11	272
Fat Trimmed from Retail Cuts			
Cooked, 3oz (85g)	60	25	81
Raw, 4oz (113g)	80	35	112
Good Cuts, Lean and Fat, Raw,			
1 lb (453.6g)	104	44	336
Carcass: Parts			
Arm Pot Roast			
Lean and Fat, Braised, 3oz (85g)	22	9	84
Lean and Fat, Raw, 1 lb (453.6g)	90	38	313
Lean, Braised, 3oz (85g)	9	3	86
Lean, Raw, 1 lb (453.6g)	23	9	272
Blade Roast			
Lean and Fat, Braised, 3oz (85g)	26	11	88
Lean and Fat, Raw, 1 lb (453.6g)	107	46	331
Lean, Braised, 3oz (85g)	13	5	90
Lean, Raw, 1 lb (453.6g)	41	16	295
Brain			
Shallow-fried, 3oz (85g)	14	3	1696
Simmered, 3oz (85g)	11	3	1746
Raw, 1 lb (452g)	42	10	7560
Brisket			
Flat Half			
Lean and Fat, Braised, 3oz (85g)	30	12	78
Lean and Fat, Raw, 1 lb (453.6g)	144	61	345
Lean, Braised, 3oz (85g)	14	5	77
Lean, Raw, 1 lb (453.6g)	44	17	290
Lean and Fat, Braised, 3oz (85g)	25	10	81
Lean and Fat, Raw, 1 lb (453.6g)	111	47	322
Lean, Braised, 3oz (85g)	7	3	81
Point Half			
Lean, Raw, 1 lb (453.6g)	22	7	268

	Total fat (g)	Saturated fat (g)	Cholesterol (mg)
Whole			
Lean and Fat, Braised, 3oz (85g)	28	11	79
Lean and Fat, Raw, 1 lb (453.6g)	128	54	336
Lean, Braised, 3oz (85g)	11	4	79
Lean, Raw, 1 lb (453.6g)	33	11	277
Calf			
Heart, Braised, 1 Cup Chopped (145g)	13	7	397
Liver, Fried, 3oz Slice (85g)	11	3	372
Sweetbreads, Braised, 3oz (85g)	3	1	396
Sweetbreads, Raw, 3½oz (100g)	2	1	250
Tongue, Braised, 1 Slice (20g)	1	1	20
Tongue, Raw, 3½oz (100g)	5	3	70
Chuck			
Blade			
Lean and Fat, Braised, 3oz (85g)	26	11	88
Lean and Fat, Raw, 1 lb (453.6g)	107	46	331
Lean, Braised, 3oz (85g)	13	5	90
Lean, Raw, 1 lb (453.6g)	41	16	295
Roast			
Lean and Fat, Braised, 3oz (85g)	22	9	84
Lean and Fat, Raw, 1 lb (453.6g)	90	38	313
Lean, Braised, 3oz (85g)	9	3	86
Lean, Raw, 1 lb (453.6g)	23	9	272
Corned Beef			
Brisket, Cooked, 3oz (85g)	16	5	83
Brisket, Raw, 1 lb (453.6g)	68	22	245
Dripping			
1 tbsp (12.8g)	13	6	14
1 Cup (205g)	205	102	224
Flank			
Lean and Fat, Braised, 3oz (85g)	13	6	61
Lean and Fat, Grilled, 3oz (85g)	14	6	60
Lean and Fat, Raw, 1 lb (453.6g)	57	26	236
Lean, Braised, 3oz (85g)	12	5	60
Lean, Grilled, 3oz (85g)	13	5	60
Lean, Raw, 1 lb (453.6g)	43	18	227
✗ **Kidneys**			
Simmered, 3oz (85g)	3	1	329
Raw 1 lb (452g)	14	4	1288
✗ **Liver**			
Braised, 3oz (85g)	4	2	331
Shallow-fried, 3oz (85g)	7	2	410

	Total fat (g)	Saturated fat (g)	Cholesterol (mg)
Raw, 1 lb (452g)	17	7	1600
Mince			
Lean			
Baked, Medium, 3oz (85g)	16	6	66
Baked, Well Done, 3oz (85g)	16	6	84
Grilled, Medium, 3oz (85g)	16	6	74
Grilled, Well Done, 3oz (85g)	15	6	86
Shallow-fried, Medium, 3oz (85g)	16	6	71
Shallow-fried, Well Done, 3oz (85g)	15	6	81
Raw, 4oz (113g)	23	9	85
Raw, 1 lb (452g)	93	38	340
Regular			
Baked, Medium, 3oz (85g)	18	7	74
Baked, Well Done, 3oz (85g)	18	7	92
Grilled, Medium, 3oz (85g)	18	7	77
Grilled, Well Done, 3oz (85g)	17	7	86
Shallow-fried, Medium, 3oz (85g)	19	8	76
Shallow-fried, Well Done, 3oz (85g)	16	6	83
Raw, 4oz (113g)	30	12	96
Raw, 1 lb (452g)	120	49	384
Porterhouse Steak			
Lean and Fat, Grilled, 3oz (85g)	18	8	71
Lean and Fat, Raw, 1 lb (453.6g)	106	45	318
Lean, Grilled, 3oz (85g)	9	4	68
Lean, Raw, 1 lb (453.6g)	36	14	272
Rib			
Large End			
Lean and Fat, Grilled, 3oz (85g)	28	12	74
Lean and Fat, Roasted, 3oz (85g)	26	11	72
Lean and Fat, Raw, 1 lb (453.6g)	142	62	331
Lean, Grilled, 3oz (85g)	12	5	70
Lean, Roasted, 3oz (85g)	12	5	69
Lean, Raw, 1 lb (453.6g)	43	19	268
Small End			
Lean and Fat, Grilled, 3oz (85g)	21	9	71
Lean and Fat, Roasted, 3oz (85g)	25	11	72
Lean and Fat, Raw, 1 lb (453.6g)	118	51	318
Lean, Grilled, 3oz (85g)	10	4	68
Lean, Roasted, 3oz (85g)	12	5	68
Lean, Raw, 1 lb (453.6g)	37	15	268
Whole			
Lean and Fat, Grilled, 3oz (85g)	26	11	73

	Total fat (g)	Saturated fat (g)	Cholesterol (mg)
Lean and Fat, Roasted, 3oz (85g)	27	11	72
Lean and Fat, Raw, 1 lb (453.6g)	132	57	327
Lean, Grilled, 3oz (85g)	11	5	70
Lean, Roasted, 3oz (85g)	12	5	69
Lean, Raw, 1 lb (453.6g)	41	17	268
Roast Beef			
Also see under individual cuts			
Frozen Dinner, with Potatoes, Peas and Corn, 1 Serving (100g)	3	2	50
Home Recipe, 1 Portion	26	11	72
Tinned, 3½oz (100g)	13	5	80
Round			
Bottom Round			
Lean and Fat, Braised, 3oz (85g)	13	5	82
Lean and Fat, Raw, 1 lb (453.6g)	71	29	295
Lean, Braised, 3oz (85g)	8	3	82
Lean, Raw, 1 lb (453.6g)	28	10	268
Eye of Round			
Lean and Fat, Roasted, 3oz (85g)	12	5	62
Lean and Fat, Raw, 1 lb (453.6g)	57	24	272
Lean, Roasted, 3oz (85g)	6	2	59
Lean, Raw, 1 lb (453.6g)	19	7	245
Full Cut			
Choice, Lean and Fat, Grilled 3oz (85g)	16	6	71
Choice, Lean and Fat, Raw, 1 lb (453.6g)	80	34	299
Choice, Lean, Grilled, 3oz (85g)	7	3	70
Choice, Lean, Raw, 1 lb (453.6g)	22	8	263
Tip Round			
Lean and Fat, Roasted, 3oz (85g)	13	5	71
Lean and Fat, Raw, 1 lb (453.6g)	62	26	295
Lean, Roasted, 3oz (85g)	6	2	69
Lean, Raw, 1 lb (453.6g)	20	7	272
Top Round			
Lean and Fat, Grilled, 3oz (85g)	8	3	72
Lean and Fat, Raw, 1 lb (453.6g)	40	17	272
Lean, Grilled, 3oz (85g)	5	2	71
Lean, Raw, 1 lb (453.6g)	18	7	259
Rump Steak			
Lean and Fat, Grilled, 3oz (85g)	15	6	77
Lean and Fat, Raw, 1 lb (453.6g)	92	39	313

	Total fat (g)	Saturated fat (g)	Cholesterol (mg)
Shank Crosscuts			
Lean and Fat, Simmered, 3oz (85g)	10	4	67
Lean and Fat, Raw, 1 lb (453.6g)	35	14	195
Lean, Simmered, 3oz (85g)	5	2	66
Lean, Raw, 1 lb (453.6g)	18	6	177
Sirloin			
Lean and Fat, Grilled, 3oz (85g)	15	6	77
Lean and Fat, Raw, 1 lb (453.6g)	92	39	313
Lean, Grilled, 3oz (85g)	7	3	76
Lean, Raw, 1 lb (453.6g)	23	8	277
Steaks – See under individual cuts			
Suet			
1oz (28.35g)	27	15	19
4oz (113g)	106	59	77
Sweetbreads			
Calf, Braised, 3oz (85g)	3	1	396
Calf, Raw, 3½oz (100g)	2	1	250
Braised, 3oz (85g)	21	7	250
Raw, 4oz (113g)	23	8	252
Raw, 1 lb (452g)	92	32	1008
T-bone Steak			
Lean and Fat, Grilled, 3oz (85g)	21	9	71
Lean and Fat, Raw, 1 lb (453.6g)	119	51	322
Lean, Grilled, 3oz (85g)	9	4	68
Lean, Raw, 1 lb (453.6g)	36	15	272
Tenderloin			
Lean and Fat, Grilled, 3oz (85g)	15	6	72
Lean and Fat, Roasted, 3oz (85g)	19	8	74
Lean and Fat, Raw, 1 lb (453.6g)	82	35	313
Lean, Grilled, 3oz (85g)	8	3	71
Lean, Roasted, 3oz (85g)	10	4	73
Lean, Raw, 1 lb (453.6g)	30	12	281
Thymus – See Sweetbreads			
Tongue			
Calf, Braised, 1 Slice (20g)	1	1	20
Calf, Raw, 3½oz (100g)	5	3	70
Potted or Devilled, 3½oz (100g)	23	10	110
Simmered, 3oz (85g)	18	8	91
Smoked, 3½oz (100g)	29	14	68
Whole, Tinned or Pickled, 3½oz (100g)	20	9	90
Raw, 4oz (113g)	18	8	98

	Total fat (g)	Saturated fat (g)	Cholesterol (mg)
Raw, 1 lb (452g)	73	31	392
Top Loin			
Lean and Fat, Grilled, 3oz (85g)	16	7	67
Lean and Fat, Raw, 1 lb (453.6g)	104	45	313
Lean, Grilled, 3oz (85g)	8	3	65
Lean, Raw, 1 lb (453.6g)	29	12	268
Tripe			
Pickled, 3½oz (100g)	1	1	68
Raw, 4oz (113g)	5	2	107
Raw, 1 lb (452g)	18	9	428
Wedge-bone Sirloin			
Lean and Fat, Grilled, 3oz (85g)	15	6	77
Lean and Fat, Raw, 1 lb (453.6g)	92	39	313
Lean, Grilled, 3oz (85g)	7	3	76
Lean, Raw, 1 lb (453.6g)	23	8	277
Beef: Dishes			
Beef and Vegetable Stew			
Tinned, 15oz Tin (425g)	13	4	60
With Lean Chuck, 1 Cup (245g)	11	5	64
Beef Broth and Tomato Juice			
Tinned, 5½ Fl.oz Tin (168g)	0	0	0
Beef Bourguignonne			
Home Recipe, 1 Portion	32	13	112
Beef Burger			
Grilled, 3oz (85g)	17	7	80
Beef Pie			
Commercial, Frozen, 3½oz (100g)	10	3	18
Home Recipe, Baked, 1 Piece			
(⅓ Pie) (210g)	31	8	44
Bolognaise Sauce			
With Mince, Home Recipe,			
1 Cup	33	9	75
Carpaccio			
(Thin-sliced Beef with Olive Oil Sauce)			
Home Recipe, 1 Portion	15	2	12
Chilli Con Carne			
With Mince, Home Recipe, 1 Cup	8	3	133
Lasagne			
With Mince, Home Recipe,			
1 Portion	21	9	79
Meatloaf			
Home Recipe, 1 Serving (100g)	13	6	65

	Total fat (g)	Saturated fat (g)	Cholesterol (mg)
Moussaka			
With Mince, Home Recipe, 1 Serving (225g)	30	11	90
Roast Beef			
Frozen Dinner with Potatoes, Peas and Corn, 3½oz (100g)	3	2	50
Home Recipe, 1 Portion	26	11	72
Tinned, 3½oz (100g)	13	5	80
Roast Beef Sandwich			
1 Sandwich (139g)	14	4	52
Shepherd's Pie			
With Mince, Home Recipe, 1 Portion	24	9	77
Steak and Kidney Pie			
Home Recipe, 1 Portion	30	22	378
Steak au Poivre			
Home Recipe, 1 Portion	41	22	132
Stuffed Peppers			
With Minced Beef and Breadcrumb Filling, 1 Pepper (185g)	10	5	70
Beef: Prepared Meats			
Bierwurst			
1 Slice (23g)	7	3	14
Bologna			
1 Slice (28.35g)	8	3	16
Chipolatas			
Cooked, 3 Sausages	27	13	236
Corned Beef			
Jellied Loaf, 2 Slices (56.7g)	4	2	27
Tinned, 1 Slice (21g)	3	1	18
Tinned, with Potato, 15½oz Tin (439g)	50	24	145
Dried Beef			
1oz (28.35g)	1	1	12
Smoked, Creamed, 1 Cup (245g)	25	14	98
Frankfurter			
1 Frankfurter (57g)	16	7	35
Ham and Beef Bologna			
1 Slice (28.35g)	4	2	20
Jellied Beef Luncheon Meat			
2 Slices (56.7g)	2	1	19
Pastrami			
2 Slices (56.7g)	17	6	53

	Total fat (g)	Saturated fat (g)	Cholesterol (mg)
Pickled Tongue			
3½oz (100g)	20	9	90
Pickled Tripe			
3½oz (100g)	1	1	68
Potted Beef			
5½oz Tin (156g)	30	14	122
1 Cup (225g)	43	20	176
Potted Tongue			
3½oz (100g)	23	10	110
Pressed Beef			
Loaf, 2 Slices (56.7g)	15	6	36
Salami			
Smoked, 1 Slice (23g)	5	2	15
Sausage			
Grilled, 1 Sausage (68g)	21	7	48
Meat, Raw, 1 lb (454g)	107	53	948
Smoked, Cooked, 1 Sausage (43g)	12	5	29
Smoked Beef			
Dried, Creamed, 1 Cup (245g)	25	14	98
Smoked Chopped Beef			
2 Slices (56.7g)	3	1	26
Smoked Tongue			
3½oz (100g)	29	14	68
Thin-sliced Beef			
5 Slices (21g)	1	0	9
Beer – See under Alcohol			
Beetroot Greens			
Boiled, 1 Cup (144g)	0	0	0
Fresh, 1 Cup, 1-inch Pieces (38g)	0	0	0
Beetroot			
Boiled, 2 Medium Beetroot (100g)	0	0	0
Harvard, Tinned,			
1 Cup Slices (246g)	0	0	0
Pickled, Tinned,			
1 Cup Slices (227g)	0	0	0
Raw, 2 Medium Beetroot (163g)	0	0	0
Tinned, 1 Cup (246g)	0	0	0
Bilberries			
Frozen, 1 Cup Thawed (230g)	0	0	0
Fresh, 1 Cup (145g)	1	0	0
Tinned, 1 Cup (256g)	1	0	0

	Total fat (g)	Saturated fat (g)	Cholesterol (mg)

BISCUITS

Also see under Crackers

Assorted Biscuits

4 Biscuits (35g)	7	1	14

Brownies

Commercial, with Egg, Water and Nuts, 1 Brownie (20g)	4	1	9
Commercial, with Nuts and Chocolate Icing, 1 Brownie (24½g)	5	2	10
Home Recipe, with Nuts and Butter, 1 Brownie (20g)	6	2	22
Home Recipe, with Nuts and Vegetable Shortening, 1 Brownie (20g)	6	1	17

Butter Biscuits

Thin, Rich, 4 Biscuits (50g)	9	4	38

Cheese Biscuits

10 Round Biscuits (34.4g)	7	3	11

Cheese Sandwich Type

4 Sandwiches (28g)	7	2	5

Chocolate Biscuits

4 Biscuits (50g)	8	2	19

Chocolate Chip

Commercial, 4 Biscuits (42g)	9	3	16
Home Recipe, made with Butter, 4 Biscuits (40g)	11	5	39
Home Recipe, made with Vegetable Shortening, 4 Biscuits (40g)	12	3	20

Coconut Biscuits

4 Biscuits (36g)	9	3	39

Digestive Biscuits

Chocolate Coated, 1 Biscuit (13g)	3	1	0
Chocolate Coated, 4 Biscuits (50g)	12	4	0
Plain, 1 Biscuit (14.2g)	1	0	0
Plain, 4 Biscuits (56.8g)	5	1	0
Plain, 1 Cup Crumbs (85g)	8	2	0

Fig Bars

4 Biscuits (56g)	3	1	22

Ginger Biscuits

4 Biscuits (28g)	2	1	11

Ladyfingers

4 Ladyfingers (44g)	3	1	157

	Total fat (g)	Saturated fat (g)	Cholesterol (mg)
Macaroons			
2 Biscuits (38g)	9	6	41
Marshmallows			
4 Biscuits covered with Coconut (72g)	10	6	55
4 Biscuits covered with Chocolate (52g)	7	4	40
Oatmeal			
With Raisins, 4 Biscuits (52g)	8	2	20
Peanut Biscuits			
4 Biscuits (50g)	10	2	19
Raisin			
4 Biscuits (71g)	4	1	28
Rich Tea Biscuits			
4 Biscuits (50g)	12	3	1
Sandwich Type Biscuits			
4 Biscuits (3^1/$_8$×1^1/$_4$ inch) (60g)	14	4	23
4 Biscuits (1^3/$_4$ inch diameter) (40g)	9	2	16
Shortbread			
4 Biscuits (30g)	7	2	12
Sugar Wafers			
4 Biscuits (3½×1×½ inch) (38g)	7	2	15
4 Biscuits (2½×¾×¼inch) (14g)	3	1	5
Vanilla Wafers			
4 Regular, 1¾ inch diameter (16g)	3	1	6
Vienna Biscuits			
Home Recipe, made with Butter, 4 Biscuits (32g)	5	3	24
Home Recipe, made with Vegetable Shortening, 4 Biscuits (32g)	5	1	12
Water Biscuits			
10 Biscuits (28.4g)	3	1	0
1 Cup Crumbs (70g)	8	2	0
Whole wheat Biscuits			
3½oz (100g)	14	3	0
Bitter Melon – See Balsam-pear			
Blackberries			
Fresh, 1 Cup (144g)	1	0	0
Frozen, 1 Cup (151g)	1	0	0
Tinned, 1 Cup (256g)	1	0	0
Juice, Tinned, 1 Cup (100g)	1	0	0
Blancmange			
1 Cup (255g)	10	6	36

	Total fat (g)	Saturated fat (g)	Cholesterol (mg)
Borage			
Boiled, 3½oz (100g)	1	0	0
Fresh, 1 Cup, 1-inch Pieces (89g)	1	0	0
Bran			
100% Wheat Bran, 1 Cup (66g)	3	1	0
Corn Bran, 1 Cup (36g)	1	0	0
Rice Bran, 1 tbsp (13.6g)	14	3	0
Rice Bran, 1 Cup (218g)	218	43	0
Brazilnuts			
1oz (6–8 Kernels) (28.4g)	19	5	0
1 Cup (32 Kernels) (140g)	93	23	0
BREAD			
Bagels			
Plain, 1 Bagel	1	0	0
Breadcrumbs			
Dry, 1 Cup (100g)	5	1	5
Breadstuffing Mix			
Dry, 1 Cup Crumbs (70g)	3	1	3
Dry, 1 Cup Cubes (30g)	1	0	1
With Water, Table Fat and Egg, 1 Cup (200g)	26	13	132
With Water and Table Fat, 1 Cup (140g)	31	16	90
Crisp Bread			
4 Pieces (28.35g)	3	1	6
Croissant			
With Butter, 1 Croissant	25	14	216
Crumpet			
With Butter, 1 Crumpet	6	2	13
Dough			
Frozen, Unraised, 1 Loaf or 24 Rolls (680g)	34	8	34
1 Roll (28g)	1	0	1
French or Vienna			
Fresh, 1 Slice (35g)	1	0	1
Toasted, 3 Slices (100g)	4	1	4
Granary			
1 Slice (25g)	1	0	1
Italian			
1 Slice (30g)	0	0	0
Pumpernickel			
1 Slice (32g)	0	0	0

	Total fat (g)	Saturated fat (g)	Cholesterol (mg)
Raisin			
1 Slice (25g)	1	0	1
Raisin Rolls and Buns 2 Buns (100g)	3	1	3
Home Recipe, Made with Milk,			
1 Roll (35g)	3	1	12
Rolls and Buns			
Commercial, Brown and Serve,			
1 Roll (26g)	2	1	2
Hard Crust, 1 Roll (25g)	1	0	1
Soft, 1 Roll (28g)	2	0	2
Sweet, 2 Buns (100g)	9	2	9
Rusk			
Hard Crisp Bread or Toast,			
1 Rusk (9g)	1	0	1
13 Rusks (113g)	10	3	10
Rye			
Crispbread, Wholegrain,			
10 Wafers (65g)	1	0	1
8oz Package (227g)	3	0	2
Pumpernickel, 1 Slice (32g)	0	0	0
Salt-rising			
1 Slice (24g)	1	0	1
Sourdough			
1 Slice (24g)	1	0	1
Sticks			
Vienna Bread Type,			
1 Stick (35g)	1	0	1
White Bread			
1 Slice (23g)	1	0	1
Wholewheat Bread			
1 Slice (28g)	1	0	1
Breadfruit			
1 Cup (220g)	1	0	0
BREAKFAST CEREALS			
40% Bran Flakes			
1 Cup (39g)	1	0	0
100% Wheat Bran			
1 Cup (66g)	3	1	0
All-Bran			
1 Cup (35.4g)	1	0	0

	Total fat (g)	Saturated fat (g)	Cholesterol (mg)
Bran Buds			
1 Cup (84g)	2	0	0
Cheerios			
1 Cup (42.6g)	3	0	0
Cocoa Krispies			
1 Cup (36g)	1	0	0
Corn Bran			
1 Cup (36g)	1	0	0
Corn Flakes			
1 Cup (36g)	0	0	0
Honey and Nut, 1 Cup (56g)	3	3	0
Cream of Rice			
Cooked with Water, 1 Cup (244g)	0	0	0
Cream Of Wheat			
Cooked with Water, 1 Cup (241g)	1	0	0
Crispy Rice			
1 Cup (28g)	0	0	0
Crispy Wheats 'N Raisins			
1 Cup (43g)	1	1	0
Farina			
Cooked with Water, 1 Cup (233g)	0	0	0
Frosted Rice Krispies			
1 Cup (28.4g)	0	0	0
Grape-Nuts			
1oz (28.4g)	0	0	0
1 Cup (113.4g)	0	0	0
Grape-Nuts Flakes			
1 Cup (40g)	0	0	0
Kellogg's 40% Bran Flakes			
1 Cup (39g)	1	0	0
Most			
1 Cup (52g)	1	0	0
Muesli			
Homemade, (Oats, Wheat Germ),			
1 Cup (122g)	33	6	0
Toasted, 1 Cup (113g)	20	13	0
Oat Flakes			
Fortified, (Oat With Other Grains),			
1 Cup (48g)	1	1	0
Oats			
With Apple and Cinnamon,			
1 Cup (104g)	20	16	1

	Total fat (g)	Saturated fat (g)	Cholesterol (mg)
With Raisins and Dates, 1 Cup (110g)	20	14	1
Instant, Prepared with Water, 1 Cup (100g)	1	0	0
Rolled or Porridge, Dry, 1 Cup (81g)	5	1	0
Porridge			
Made with Whole Milk, 1 Cup (220g)	17	9	50
Made with Skimmed Milk, 1 Cup (220g)	6	1	6
Made with ½ Skimmed Milk, ½ Water, 1 Cup (220g)	5	1	3
✳ Made with Water, 1 Cup (234g)	2	0	0
Puffed Rice			
1 Cup (14g)	0	0	0
Puffed Wheat			
1 Cup (12g)	0	0	0
Raisin Bran			
1 Cup (36.9g)	1	0	0
Rice Krispies			
1 Cup (28.4g)	0	0	0
Shredded Wheat			
Large Biscuit, 2 Biscuits (37.8g)	0	0	0
Small Biscuit, 1 Cup (40.8g)	1	0	0
Special K			
1 Cup (28.4g)	0	0	0
Sugar Frosted Flakes			
1 Cup (35g)	0	0	0
Sugar Smacks			
1 Cup (28.4g)	1	0	0
Sugar Frosted Wheat Biscuits			
4 Biscuits (31.0g)	0	0	0
Team			
1 Cup (42g)	1	0	0
Toasted Wheat Germ			
1 Cup (113g)	12	2	0
Weetabix			
2 Biscuits (38g)	1	0	0
Wheaties			
1 Cup (28.4g)	1	0	0
Broccoli			
Boiled, 1 Cup Chopped (170g)	1	0	0
Fresh, 1 Cup Chopped (90g)	0	0	0

	Total fat (g)	Saturated fat (g)	Cholesterol (mg)
Brussels Sprouts			
Boiled, 1 Cup (155g)	1	0	0
Fresh, 1 Cup (90g)	0	0	0
Buckwheat			
Whole-grain, Steamed, 3½oz (100g)	2	0	0
Bulgur Wheat			
Steamed, 1 Cup (175g)	3	0	0
Tinned, 1 Cup (135g)	5	1	0
Burdock Root			
Boiled, 1 Cup, 1-inch Pieces (125g)	0	0	0
Fresh, 1 Cup, 1-inch Pieces (118g)	0	0	0
Burrito			
With Beans, 2 Regular (217g)	14	7	5
With Beans and Beef, 2 Regular (231g)	18	8	48
With Beans and Cheese, 2 Regular (186g)	12	7	27
With Beans, Cheese and Beef, 2 Regular (203g)	13	7	125
With Beef, 2 Regular (220g)	21	10	65
Butter Oil			
Ghee, 1 Cup (205g)	204	127	525
Ghee, 1 tbsp (12.8g)	13	8	33
Butter			
Hard, 1 Pat (5g)	4	3	11
4oz (113.4g)	92	57	248
Whipped, 1 Pat (3.8g)	3	2	8
4oz (75.6g)	61	38	166
Butterbur			
Boiled, 1 Cup (100g)	0	0	0
Tinned, 1 Cup (124g)	0	0	0
Fresh, 1 Cup (94g)	0	0	0
Cabbage			
Chinese, Boiled, 1 Cup Shredded (170g)	0	0	0
Chinese, Fresh, 1 Cup Shredded (70g)	0	0	0
Red, Boiled, 1 Cup Shredded (75g)	0	0	0
Red, Fresh, 1 Cup Shredded (70g)	0	0	0
Savoy, Boiled, 1 Cup Shredded (145g)	0	0	0
Savoy, Fresh, 1 Cup Shredded (70g)	0	0	0
Spring, Fresh, 1 Cup Shredded (70g)	0	0	0
1 Head (908g)	2	0	0
White, Boiled, 1 Cup Shredded (150g)	0	0	0
1 Head (1262g)	3	0	0

	Total fat (g)	Saturated fat (g)	Cholesterol (mg)
White, Fresh, 1 Cup Shredded (70g)	0	0	0
1 Head (908g)	2	0	0

CAKES

See also under Icing

Angelfood

	Total fat (g)	Saturated fat (g)	Cholesterol (mg)
Made from Mix with Water, 1 Portion (80g)	0	0	0
Home Recipe, 1 Portion (90g)	0	0	0

Brownies

	Total fat (g)	Saturated fat (g)	Cholesterol (mg)
Home Recipe, with Nuts and Butter, 1 Brownie (20g)	6	2	22
Home Recipe, with Nuts and Vegetable Shortening, 1 Brownie (20g)	6	1	17

Caramel Cake

	Total fat (g)	Saturated fat (g)	Cholesterol (mg)
Cake and Icing made with Butter, 1 Portion (158g)	21	11	147
Cake made with Vegetable Shortening, Icing made with Butter, 1 Portion (158g)	23	7	102
Uniced, Cake made with Butter, 1 Portion (108g)	17	9	124
Uniced, Cake made with Vegetable Shortening, 1 Portion (108g)	19	5	84

Chocolate Cake

	Total fat (g)	Saturated fat (g)	Cholesterol (mg)
Cake and Choc Icing made with Butter, 1 Small Cake (44g)	7	4	29
Cake made with Vegetable Shortening, Choc Icing made with Butter, 1 Small Cake (44g)	7	3	21
Cake and White Icing made with Butter, 1 Small Cake (44g)	6	3	30
Cake made with Vegetable Shortening, White Icing made with Butter, 1 Small Cake (44g)	6	2	21
Malt, Cake made with Eggs, Icing made with Butter, 1 Portion (132g)	12	4	72

Cottage Pudding

	Total fat (g)	Saturated fat (g)	Cholesterol (mg)
Made with Butter, No Sauce, 1 Portion (73g)	8	4	59
Made with Butter, with Sauce, 1 Portion (99g)	8	4	58
Made with Vegetable Shortening, No Sauce, 1 Portion (73g)	8	2	44

	Total fat (g)	Saturated fat (g)	Cholesterol (mg)
Made with Vegetable Shortening, with Sauce, 1 Portion with Sauce (99g)	9	3	44
Fruitcake			
Light, made with Butter, 1 Portion (43g)	7	2	11
Light, made with Vegetable Shortening, 1 Portion (43g)	7	2	3
Rich, made with Butter, 1 Portion (43g)	6	2	28
Rich, made with Vegetable Shortening, 1 Portion (43g)	7	1	19
Genoa			
Made with Butter, 1 Portion (85g)	10	5	68
Made with Vegetable Shortening, 1 Portion (85g)	11	3	46
Gingerbread			
Baked from Mix, 1 Portion (71g)	5	1	1
Made with Butter, 1 Portion (132g)	13	7	87
Made with Vegetable Shortening, 1 Portion (132g)	14	4	57
Honey Spice Cake			
Made with Eggs, Caramel Icing made with Butter, 1 Portion (154g)	17	5	90
Madeira Cake			
Made with Butter, 1 Portion (83g)	12	7	33
Made with Vegetable Shortening, 1 Portion (83g)	13	4	2
Marble Cake			
Made with Eggs, with Boiled White Icing, 1 Portion (131g)	11	3	67
Mocha Cake			
Made with Eggs and Milk, 1 Portion (54g)	5	1	33
Plain Cake			
Cake and Icing made with Butter, 1 Portion (123g)	15	8	42
Made with Butter, with Coconut Icing, 1 Portion (122g)	15	9	33
Made with Egg Whites, Choc Icing made with Butter, 1 Portion (143g)	15	6	3
Made with Vegetable Shortening, Icing made with Butter, 1 Portion (123g)	16	5	10
Made with Vegetable Shortening, with Coconut Icing, 1 Portion (122g)	16	6	2

	Total fat (g)	Saturated fat (g)	Cholesterol (mg)
Pound Cake			
Made with Butter, 1 Portion (62g)	11	5	118
Made with Vegetable Shortening, 1 Portion (62g)	12	3	95
Rock Cakes			
1 Cake (55g)	9	3	22
Sponge Cake			
1 Portion (65g)	4	1	161
Layered with Cream, made with Butter, 1 Portion (103g)	9	4	104
Layered with Cream, made with Vegetable Shortening, 1 Portion (103g)	10	3	89
Vanilla Cake			
Cake and Choc Icing made with Butter, 1 Portion (139g)	18	10	97
Cake and Icing made with Butter, 1 Portion (137g)	15	8	99
Cake made with Butter, No Icing, 1 Portion (97g)	12	6	90
Made with Vegetable Shortening, Choc Icing made with Butter, 1 Portion (139g)	19	7	69
Made with Vegetable Shortening, White Icing made with Butter, 1 Portion (137g)	16	5	71
Made with Vegetable Shortening, 1 Portion (97g)	14	4	63
Calabash			
White-flowered Gourd, Boiled, 1 Cup, 1-inch Cubes (146g)	0	0	0
Cape-gooseberries			
Fresh, 1 Cup (140g)	1	0	0
Carambola			
Fresh, 1 Fruit (127g)	0	0	0
CARBONATED DRINKS			
Club Soda			
12 Fl.oz Tin (355g)	0	0	0
Cola			
12 Fl.oz Tin (370g)	0	0	0
Cream Soda			
12 Fl.oz Tin (371g)	0	0	0
Ginger Ale			
12 Fl.oz Tin (366g)	0	0	0

	Total fat (g)	Saturated fat (g)	Cholesterol (mg)
Lemonade			
12 Fl.oz Tin (368g)	0	0	0
Lemon-lime Soda			
12 Fl.oz Tin (368g)	0	0	0
Low Calorie Cola			
12 Fl.oz Tin (355g)	0	0	0
Low Calorie Drinks			
12 Fl.oz Tin (355g)	0	0	0
Orange			
12 Fl.oz Tin (372g)	0	0	0
Root Beer			
12 Fl.oz Tin (370g)	0	0	0
Tonic Water			
12 Fl.oz (366g)	0	0	0
Cardoon			
Boiled, 3½oz (100g)	0	0	0
Fresh, 1 Cup Shredded (178g)	0	0	0
Carissa			
Fresh, 1 Fruit (20g)	0	0	0
Carrot Juice			
1 Cup (224g)	0	0	0
Carrots			
Boiled, 1 Cup Slices (150g)	0	0	0
Fresh, 1 Cup Shredded (110g)	0	0	0
Tinned, 1 Cup Slices (200g)	1	0	0
Cashew Nuts			
Dry Roasted, 1 Cup (137g)	64	13	0
Cassava			
3½oz (100g)	0	0	0
Cauliflower Cheese			
1 Portion (225g)	18	10	38
Cauliflower			
Boiled, 1 Cup, 1-inch Pieces (125g)	0	0	0
Fresh, 1 Cup, 1-inch Pieces (120g)	0	0	0
Celeriac			
Boiled, 3½oz (100g)	0	0	0
Fresh, 1 Cup (156g)	1	0	0
Celery			
Boiled, 1 Cup Diced (150g)	0	0	0
Fresh, 1 Cup Diced (120g)	0	0	0

	Total fat (g)	Saturated fat (g)	Cholesterol (mg)

CEREALS AND GRAINS

	Total fat (g)	Saturated fat (g)	Cholesterol (mg)
100% Wheat Bran			
1 Cup (66g)	3	1	0
Corn Bran			
1 Cup (36g)	1	0	0
Plain Oats			
1oz (28.4g)	6	4	0
1 Cup (104g)	22	15	1
Toasted Wheat Germ			
1oz (28.4g)	3	1	0
1 Cup (113g)	12	2	0
Whole Wheat			
Cooked with Water, 1 Cup (242g)	1	1	0
Dry, 1 Cup (94g)	2	0	0
1/3 Cup (31gm)	1	0	0
Chard, Swiss, Boiled			
1 Cup Chopped (175g)	0	0	0
Chard, Swiss, Fresh			
1 Cup Chopped (48g)	0	0	0
Charlotte Russe, with Lady Fingers, Whipped			
Cream Filling 1 Serving (114g)	17	8	225
Chayote – See under Custard Marrow			

CHEESE

	Total fat (g)	Saturated fat (g)	Cholesterol (mg)
Blue			
1oz (28g)	8	5	21
Brie			
1oz (28g)	8	5	28
Camembert			
1oz (28g)	7	4	20
Caraway			
1oz (28g)	8	5	26
Cheddar			
1oz (28g)	9	6	29
1 Cup, Shredded (113g)	37	24	119
Cheshire			
1oz (28g)	9	6	29
Cottage			
Creamed, 1 Cup (210g)	10	6	31

	Total fat (g)	Saturated fat (g)	Cholesterol (mg)
Creamed, with Fruit, 1 Cup (226g)	8	5	25
Low Fat, 1% Fat, 1 Cup (226g)	2	2	10
Low Fat, 2% Fat, 1 Cup (226g)	4	3	19
Cream Cheese			
1oz (28g)	10	6	31
Curd Cheese			
Uncreamed, Dry, 1 Cup (145g)	1	0	10
Edam			
1oz (28g)	8	5	25
Emmental			
1oz (28g)	8	5	26
Feta			
1oz (28g)	6	4	25
Fontina			
1oz (28g)	9	5	33
Gjetost			
1oz (28g)	8	5	26
Gouda			
1oz (28g)	8	5	32
Gruyère			
1oz (28g)	9	5	31
Limburger			
1oz (28g)	8	5	25
Mozzarella			
Part Skimmed Milk, 1oz (28g)	5	3	16
Whole Milk, 1oz (28g)	6	4	22
Muenster			
1oz (28g)	8	5	27
Neufchatel			
1oz (28g)	7	4	21
Parmesan			
Grated, 1 tbsp (5g)	2	1	4
1oz (28g)	8	5	22
Processed Cheese			
Pasteurized, 1oz (28g)	9	6	26
Pasteurized, Swiss, 1oz (28g)	7	5	24
Port De Salut			
1oz (28g)	8	5	34
Provolone			
1oz (28g)	8	5	19
Ricotta			
Part Skimmed Milk, 1 Cup (246g)	20	12	76

	Total fat (g)	Saturated fat (g)	Cholesterol (mg)
Whole Milk, 1 Cup (246g)	32	20	125
Romano			
1oz (28g)	8	5	29
Roquefort			
1oz (28g)	9	5	25
Swiss			
1oz (28g)	8	5	26
Tilsit			
Whole Milk, 1oz (28g)	7	5	29
Cheese and Tomato Sandwich			
1 Sandwich (100g)	25	15	71
Cheeseburger			
1 Regular	16	7	41
1 Double-decker	28	13	110
Cheeseburger			
With Ham or Bacon and Condiments,			
1 Burger with Ham	48	21	122
1 Burger with Bacon	37	16	112
Cheese Cake			
With Fruit Topping, 1 Portion			
(1/6 of Cake)	21	12	55
Cheese Fondue			
3½oz (100g)	18	9	224
Cheese Pudding			
1 Serving (140g)	15	8	182
Cheese Sauce			
Prepared with Milk, 1 Cup (279.2g)	17	9	53
Cheese Soufflé			
1 Portion (110g)	19	10	204
Cheese Spread			
Pasteurized Processed, 1oz (28g)	6	4	16
Cheese Straws			
Made with Lard, 10 Pieces (60g)	18	8	32
Made with Vegetable Shortening,			
10 Pieces (60g)	18	6	19
Cherries			
Acerola, Juice, 1 Cup (242g)	1	0	0
Frozen, Thawed, 1 Cup (259g)	0	0	0
Maraschino, Bottled, 3½oz (100g)	0	0	0
Fresh, 10 Fruits (68g)	1	0	0
1 Cup (145g)	1	0	0

	Total fat (g)	Saturated fat (g)	Cholesterol (mg)
Tinned, 1 Cup (244g)	0	0	0
Chervil			
Fresh, 3½oz (100g)	1	0	0
Chewing Gum			
1 Piece (1.7g)	0	0	0

CHICKEN

CAPONS (WHOLE BIRDS)			
Meat and Skin and Giblets and Neck			
Roasted, 1 Chicken (1418g)	166	47	1461
Whole Bird			
Raw, 1 Chicken (2152g)	364	105	1872
Meat and Skin			
Roasted, 1 Portion (196g)	23	6	169
½ Chicken (637g)	74	21	548
Raw, 1 Portion (297g)	51	15	223
½ Chicken (964g)	165	48	723
Giblets			
Simmered, 1 Cup (145g)	8	3	629
Raw 115g	6	2	336

CHICKEN: DISHES			
Chicken and Noodles			
1 Cup (240g)	19	6	96
Chicken Casserole			
1 Cup (245g)	34	13	186
Chicken Chow Mein			
Without Noodles, Home Recipe,			
1 Cup (250g)	10	2	78
Chicken Dinner			
Frozen Fried Chicken and			
Mixed Vegetables,			
1 Serving (100g)	9	3	49
Chicken Fricassee			
1 Cup (240g)	22	7	96
Chicken Liver Pâté			
Tinned, 1 tbsp (13g)	2	1	51
1oz (28.35g)	4	1	111
Chicken Pie			
Baked, Home Recipe,			
1 Piece (232g)	31	11	72
Commercial, 1 Piece (100g)	12	3	13

	Total fat (g)	Saturated fat (g)	Cholesterol (mg)
Chicken Roll			
Light Meat, 2 Slices (56.7g)	4	1	28
Chicken Salad			
1 Portion (218g)	2	1	72
Chicken Salad Sandwich Spread			
1oz (28.35g)	4	1	9
Chicken Sandwich			
Plain, 1 Sandwich (182g)	29	9	60
With Cheese, 1 Sandwich (228g)	39	12	76
Chicken Spread			
Tinned, 1oz (28.35g)	3	1	15
Chicken Vegetable Soup			
Tinned, Ready-to-serve, 1 Cup			
(8 Fl.oz) (240g)	5	1	17
1 Tin (19oz) (539g)	11	3	38
Fried Chicken			
Breast or Wing, 2 Pieces (163g)	30	8	149
Drumstick or Thigh, 2 Pieces (148g)	27	7	165
Dinner, Frozen with Mixed Vegetables,			
1 Serving (100g)	9	3	49
Potted Chicken			
5½oz Tin (156g)	30	14	122
1 Cup (225g)	43	20	176
Roast Chicken			
1 Portion (210g)	28	8	160
1 Chicken (1072g)	140	39	1008
Roast Stuffing Mix			
With Water, Table Fat and Egg,			
1 Cup (200g)	26	13	132
With Water and Table Fat,			
1 Cup (140g)	31	16	90
Sweet and Sour Chicken			
1 Portion (130g)	18	6	61
Tinned Chicken with Broth			
1 Tin, 5oz (142g)	11	3	88
CHICKEN: FRYERS AND BROILERS: WHOLE BIRDS			
Meat and Skin and Giblets and Neck			
Fried, Floured, 1 Portion (212g)	32	9	237
1 Chicken (708g)	108	30	793
Fried, in Batter, 1 Portion (308g)	54	14	317
1 Chicken (1028g)	180	48	1059

	Total fat (g)	Saturated fat (g)	Cholesterol (mg)
Roasted, 1 Portion (205g)	27	8	219
1 Chicken (682g)	91	25	730
Stewed, 1 Portion (225g)	28	8	218
1 Chicken (751g)	93	26	729
Raw, 1 Chicken (1046g)	155	44	941
Meat and Skin			
Fried, Floured, 1 Portion (188g)	28	8	169
½ Chicken (314g)	47	13	283
Fried, in Batter, 1 Portion (280g)	49	13	244
½ Chicken (466g)	81	22	405
Roasted, 1 Portion (178g)	24	7	157
½ Chicken (299g)	41	11	263
Stewed, 1 Portion (200g)	25	7	156
½ Chicken (334g)	42	12	261
Raw, 1 Portion (276g)	42	12	207
½ Chicken (460g)	69	20	345
Meat Only			
Fried, 1 Portion (140g)	13	3	132
Roasted, 1 Portion (140g)	10	3	125
Stewed, 1 Portion (140g)	9	3	116
Raw, 1 Portion (197g)	6	2	138
½ Chicken (329g)	10	3	230
Dark Meat and Skin			
Fried, Floured, 1 Portion (110g)	19	5	101
½ Chicken (184g)	31	8	169
Fried, in Batter, 1 Portion (167g)	31	8	149
½ Chicken (278g)	52	14	247
Roasted, 1 Portion (101g)	16	4	92
½ Chicken (167g)	26	7	152
Stewed, 1 Portion (110g)	16	5	90
½ Chicken (184g)	27	8	151
Raw, 1 Portion (160g)	29	8	130
½ Chicken (266g)	49	14	216
Dark Meat Only			
Fried, 1 Portion (140g)	16	4	134
Roasted, 1 Portion (140g)	14	4	130
Stewed, 1 Portion (140g)	13	3	123
Raw, 1 Portion (109g)	5	1	87
½ Chicken (182g)	8	2	146
Light Meat and Skin			
Fried, Floured, 1 Portion (78g)	9	3	68
½ Chicken (130g)	16	4	113

	Total fat (g)	Saturated fat (g)	Cholesterol (mg)
Fried, in Batter, 1 Portion (113g)	17	5	95
½ Chicken (188g)	29	8	158
Roasted, 1 Portion (79g)	9	2	66
½ Chicken (132g)	14	4	111
Stewed, 1 Portion (90g)	9	3	67
½ Chicken (150g)	15	4	111
Raw, 1 Portion (116g)	13	4	78
½ Chicken (194g)	22	6	130
Light Meat Only			
Fried, 1 Portion (64g)	4	1	58
Roasted, 1 Portion (64g)	3	1	54
Stewed, 1 Portion (71g)	3	1	55
Raw, 1 Portion (88g)	2	0	51
½ Chicken (147g)	2	1	85

CHICKEN: FRYERS AND BROILERS: PART BIRDS
Back
Meat and Skin

	Total fat (g)	Saturated fat (g)	Cholesterol (mg)
Fried, Floured, 1 Portion (72g)	15	4	64
Fried, in Batter, 1 Portion (120g)	26	7	106
Roasted, 1 Portion (53g)	11	3	47
Stewed, 1 Portion (61g)	11	3	48
Raw, ½ Back (99g)	29	8	78
Meat Only			
Fried, 1 Portion (58g)	9	2	54
Roasted, 1 Portion (40g)	5	1	36
Stewed, 1 Portion (42g)	5	1	36
Raw, ½ Back (51g)	3	1	41

Breast
Meat and Skin

	Total fat (g)	Saturated fat (g)	Cholesterol (mg)
Fried, Floured, 1 Portion (98g)	9	2	87
Fried, in Batter, 1 Portion (140g)	19	5	119
Roasted, 1 Portion (98g)	8	2	82
Stewed, 1 Portion (110g)	8	2	83
Raw, ½ Breast (145g)	13	4	93
Meat Only			
Fried, 1 Portion (86g)	4	1	78
Roasted, 1 Portion (86g)	3	1	73
Stewed, 1 Portion (95g)	3	1	73
Raw, ½ Breast (118g)	2	0	68

	Total fat (g)	Saturated fat (g)	Cholesterol (mg)
Drumstick			
Meat and Skin			
Fried, in Batter, 1 Drumstick (72g)	11	3	62
Roasted, 1 Drumstick (52g)	6	2	47
Stewed, 1 Drumstick (57g)	6	2	47
Raw, 1 Drumstick (73g)	6	2	59
Meat Only			
Fried, 1 Drumstick (42g)	3	1	40
Roasted, 1 Drumstick (44g)	3	1	41
Stewed, 1 Drumstick (46g)	3	1	41
Fat			
From Raw Chicken, from 1 lb Ready to Cook Chicken	22	7	19
from ½ Chicken	35	11	30
Giblets			
Fried, 1 Cup (145g)	20	6	647
Simmered, 1 Cup (145g)	7	2	570
Raw, Giblets (75g)	3	1	197
Gizzard			
Simmered, 1 Cup (145g)	5	2	281
Raw, 1 Gizzard (37g)	2	0	48
Heart			
Simmered, 1 Cup (145g)	12	3	351
Raw, 1 Heart (6.1g)	1	0	8
Leg			
Meat and Skin			
Fried, Floured, 1 Leg (112g)	16	4	105
Fried, in Batter, 1 Leg (158g)	26	7	142
Roasted, 1 Leg (114g)	15	4	105
Stewed, 1 Leg (125g)	16	5	105
Raw, 1 Leg (167g)	20	6	139
Meat Only			
Fried, 1 Leg (94g)	9	2	93
Roasted, 1 Leg (95g)	8	2	89
Stewed, 1 Leg (101g)	8	2	90
Raw, 1 Leg (130g)	5	1	104
Liver			
Simmered, 1 Cup (140g)	8	3	883
Raw, 1 Liver (32g)	1	0	141
Neck			
Meat and Skin			
Fried, Floured, 1 Neck (36g)	9	2	34

	Total fat (g)	Saturated fat (g)	Cholesterol (mg)
Fried, in Batter, 1 Neck (52g)	12	3	47
Simmered, 1 Neck (38g)	7	2	27
Raw, 1 Neck (50g)	13	4	50
Meat Only			
Fried, 1 Neck (22g)	3	1	23
Simmered, 1 Neck (18g)	2	0	14
Raw, 1 Neck (20g)	2	1	17
Skin			
Fried, Floured, from ½ Chicken (56g)	24	7	41
Fried, in Batter, from ½ Chicken (190g)	55	15	141
Roasted, from ½ Chicken (56g)	23	6	47
Stewed, from ½ Chicken (72g)	24	7	45
Raw, from ½ Chicken (79g)	26	7	86
Thigh			
Meat and Skin			
Fried, Floured, 1 Thigh (62g)	9	3	60
Fried, in Batter, 1 Thigh (86g)	14	4	80
Roasted, 1 Thigh (62g)	10	3	58
Stewed, 1 Thigh (68g)	10	3	57
Raw, 1 Thigh (94g)	14	4	79
Meat Only			
Fried, 1 Thigh (52g)	5	1	53
Roasted, 1 Thigh (52g)	6	2	49
Stewed, 1 Thigh (55g)	5	2	50
Raw, 1 Thigh (69g)	3	1	57
Wing			
Meat and Skin			
Fried, Floured, 1 Wing (32g)	7	2	26
Fried, in Batter, 1 Wing (49g)	11	3	39
Roasted, 1 Wing (34g)	7	2	29
Stewed, 1 Wing (40g)	7	2	28
Raw, 1 Wing (49g)	8	2	38
Meat Only			
Fried, 1 Wing (20g)	2	1	17
Roasted, 1 Wing (21g)	2	1	18
Stewed, 1 Wing (24g)	2	1	18
Raw, 1 Wing (29g)	1	0	17
CHICKEN: ROASTER: WHOLE BIRDS			
Meat and Skin and Giblets and Neck			
Roasted, 1 Portion (235g)	31	9	221
1 Chicken (1072g)	140	39	1008
Raw, 1 Chicken (1509g)	233	67	1298

	Total fat (g)	Saturated fat (g)	Cholesterol (mg)
Meat and Skin			
Roasted, 1 Portion (210g)	28	8	160
½ Chicken (480g)	64	18	365
Raw, ½ Chicken (668g)	106	30	488
Meat Only			
Roasted, 1 Portion (140g)	9	3	105
Raw, ½ Chicken (477g)	13	3	310
Dark Meat			
Roasted, 1 Portion (140g)	12	3	105
Raw, ½ Chicken (258g)	9	2	186
Light Meat			
Roasted, 1 Portion (140g)	6	2	105
Raw, ½ Chicken (220g)	4	1	125
Giblets			
Simmered, 1 Cup (145g)	8	2	518
Raw, Giblets (113g)	6	2	267
CHICKEN: STEWING: WHOLE BIRDS			
Meat and Skin and Giblets			
Stewed, 1 Portion (202g)	36	10	206
1 Chicken (593g)	107	29	605
Meat, Skin, Giblets and Neck			
Raw, 1 Chicken (905g)	177	50	787
Meat and Skin			
Stewed, 1 Portion (178g)	34	9	141
Raw, ½ Chicken (398g)	81	23	283
Meat Only			
Stewed, 1 Portion (140g)	17	4	116
Raw, ½ Chicken (284g)	18	5	179
Dark Meat			
Stewed, 1 Portion (73g)	11	3	69
Raw, ½ Chicken (154g)	13	3	119
Light Meat			
Stewed, 1 Portion (64g)	5	1	45
Raw, ½ Chicken (130g)	6	1	61
Giblets			
Simmered,			
1 Cup (145g)	14	4	515
Raw, Giblets (81g)	8	2	194
Chicory, Fresh			
1 Head (53g)	0	0	0

	Total fat (g)	Saturated fat (g)	Cholesterol (mg)
Chilli			
Also see under Peppers; Sauces			
Chilli Con Carne, Home Recipe, 1 Cup	8	3	133
Tinned, With Beans, 1 Cup (255g)	14	6	43
Chilli Sauce, Red, Tinned, 1 Cup (245g)	2	0	0
Chips			
Also see under Potatoes			
Fried in Animal Fat, 1 Regular			
Portion (76g)	12	6	13
1 Large Portion (115g)	19	9	20
Fried in Animal Fat and Vegetable Oil,			
1 Regular Portion (76g)	12	5	11
1 Large Portion (115g)	19	8	16
Fried in Vegetable Oil, 1 Regular			
Portion (76g)	12	4	0
1 Large Portion (115g)	19	6	0
Chinese Cabbage			
Boiled, 1 Cup Shredded (170g)	0	0	0
Fresh, 1 Cup Shredded (70g)	0	0	0
Chives			
Fresh, 1 tbsp Chopped (3g)	0	0	0

CHOCOLATE

	Total fat (g)	Saturated fat (g)	Cholesterol (mg)
Also see under Sweets			
Baking Chocolate			
1oz (28g)	15	8	0
1 Cup, Grated (132g)	70	39	0
Hot Chocolate			
Made with Milk, 1 Cup Milk and 2–3			
Heaped Teaspoons Powder (266g)	9	6	32
Chocolate Bar			
Bitter, 3½oz (100g)	40	22	0
Milk, Plain, 3½oz (100g)	32	18	20
Milk, With Almonds, 3½oz (100g)	36	16	17
Milk, With Peanuts, 3½oz (100g)	38	16	13
Semisweet, 3½oz (100g)	35	20	0
Sweet, 3½oz (100g)	35	20	1
With Coconut centre, 3½oz (100g)	18	10	1
With Fudge, Peanuts and Caramel centre,			
3½oz (100g)	23	6	2
With Nougat and Caramel centre,			
3½oz (100g)	14	4	5

	Total fat (g)	Saturated fat (g)	Cholesterol (mg)
Chocolate Fudge			
Plain, 1oz (28g)	3	1	0
With Nuts, 1oz (28g)	5	1	0
Chocolate Mints			
1 Mint (35g)	4	1	0
Chocolate Shake			
1 Medium (283g)	11	7	37
Chocolate Syrup			
1 tbsp (18.8g)	0	0	0
1 Cup (300g)	4	2	0
Fudge Type, 2 tbsp (37½g)	5	3	0
1 Cup (300g)	41	23	0
Prepared with Milk, 1 Cup Milk and 1 tbsp Syrup (263g)	8	5	34
Chop Suey with Meat			
Home Recipe, 1 Cup (250g)	17	9	100
Tinned, 3½oz (100g)	3	1	12
Chow Mein			
Chicken, without Noodles, Home Recipe, 1 Cup (250g)	10	2	78
Chicken, without Noodles, Tinned, 1 Cup (250g)	0	0	8
Christmas Pudding			
1 Serving (170g)	81	9	102
Citron Peel			
Candied, 1oz (28g)	0	0	0
Citrus Fruit Drink			
1 Cup (248g)	0	0	0
Cocktails – See under Alcohol			
Cocoa			
Made with Milk, 1 Cup Milk and 2–3 Heaped Teaspoons Powder (266g)	9	6	32
Powder, 1oz Packet (3–4 Heaped tsp) (28.4g)	1	1	1
Powder, made with Water, 6 Fl.oz and 3–4 Heaped tsp (206g)	1	1	2
Coconuts			
Cream, Fresh (Liquid Expressed From Grated Meat), 1 tbsp (15g)	5	5	0
1 Cup (240g)	83	74	0

	Total fat (g)	Saturated fat (g)	Cholesterol (mg)
Cream, Tinned (Liquid Expressed From Grated Meat), 1 tbsp (19g)	3	3	0
1 Cup (296g)	53	47	0
Meat, Dried (Desiccated), 1oz (28.4g)	18	16	0
3½oz (100g)	65	57	0
Meat, Dried (Desiccated), Creamed, 1oz (28.4g)	20	17	0
3½oz (100g)	69	61	0
Meat, Dried (Desiccated), Flaked, 1oz (28.4g)	9	8	0
1 Cup (77g)	24	22	0
Meat, Dried (Desiccated), Shredded, 1oz (28.4g)	10	9	0
1 Cup (93g)	33	29	0
Meat, Dried (Desiccated), Toasted, 1oz (28.4g)	13	12	0
3½oz (100g)	47	42	0
Meat, Fresh, 1 Piece (45g)	15	13	0
1 Cup Grated (80g)	27	24	0
Milk, Frozen (Liquid Expressed from Grated Meat and Water), 1 Cup (240g)	50	44	0
Milk, Fresh, 1 Cup (240g)	57	51	0
Milk, Tinned, 1 Cup (226g)	48	43	0
Water (Liquid From Coconuts), 1 Cup (240g)	1	0	0
Coffee			
Brewed, 6 Fl.oz (177g)	0	0	0
Instant, 1 Rounded tsp Powder (1.8g)	0	0	0
6 Fl.oz Water and 1 Rounded tsp Powder (179g)	0	0	0
Instant, Cappuccino Flavour, 2 Rounded tsp Powder (14.2g)	2	2	0
6 Fl.oz Water and 2 Rounded tsp Powder (192g)	2	2	0
Instant, French Flavour, 2 Rounded tsp Powder (11½g)	3	3	0
6 Fl.oz Water and 2 Rounded tsp Powder(189g)	3	3	0
Instant, Mocha Flavour, 2 Rounded tsp Powder (11½g)	2	2	0
6 Fl.oz Water and 2 Rounded tsp Powder (188g)	2	2	0

	Total fat (g)	Saturated fat (g)	Cholesterol (mg)
Coffee Substitute			
Powder, 1 tsp (2.3g)	0	0	0
6 Fl.oz Water and 1 tsp Powder	0	0	0
Prepared with Milk, 6 Fl.oz Milk and 1 tsp Powder (185g)	6	4	24
Cola			
12 Fl.oz Tin (370g)	0	0	0
Coleslaw			
1 Cup (138g)	15	2	7
Collards			
Boiled, 1 Cup Chopped (170g)	0	0	0
Fresh, 1 Cup Chopped (186g)	0	0	0
Coriander			
Fresh, ¼ Cup (4g)	0	0	0
Corn Flakes			
1 Bowl with Milk	9	5	33
Corn Fritters			
1 Fritter (35g)	8	2	31
Corn on the Cob			
With Butter, 1 Ear (146g)	3	2	6
Cornsalad			
Fresh, 1 Cup (56g)	0	0	0
Cornbread			
Home Recipe, made with Lard, 1 Piece (93g)	6	2	69
Home Recipe, made with Vegetable Shortening, 1 Piece (93g)	6	1	65
Mix, made with Egg and Milk, 1 Piece (100g)	8	3	69
Cornmeal			
Whole Ground, Cooked, 1 Cup (122g)	5	1	0
Cornstarch			
1 tbsp (8g)	0	0	0
Courgette			
Boiled, 1 Cup (223g)	0	0	0
In Tomato Sauce, Tinned, 1 Cup (227g)	0	0	0
Fresh, 1 Cup Slices (130g)	0	0	0
Crab			
Also see under Fish/Shellfish			
Devilled, 1 Cup (240g)	23	7	245
Dressed, 1 Cup (220g)	17	9	308

	Total fat (g)	Saturated fat (g)	Cholesterol (mg)
Crab Apples			
Fresh, 1 Cup Slices (110g)	0	0	0
Crackers			
Animal, 2oz Package			
(approximately 22) (57g)	5	1	0
10 Crackers (26g)	2	1	0
Cheese, 10 Round Crackers (34.4g)	7	3	11
10 Cocktail Crackers (10.8g)	2	1	4
Cheese Sandwich Type, 1 Packet			
(6 Sandwiches) (42g)	10	3	7
1 Packet (4 Sandwiches) (28g)	7	2	5
Cream, 10 Large Crackers (50.4g)	7	2	0
10 Small Crackers (28.4g)	4	1	0
Matzos, 10 Crackers (38g)	7	2	0
Water Biscuits,			
10 Crackers (28.4g)	3	1	0
1 Cup Crumbs (70g)	8	2	0
Wholewheat, 3½oz (100g)	14	3	0
Cranberries			
Fresh, 1 Cup (110g)	0	0	0
Cranberry Juice			
Bottled, 1 Cup (253g)	0	0	0
Cranberry Sauce			
Tinned, 1 Cup (277g)	0	0	0
Cranberry-orange Relish			
Tinned, 1 Cup (275g)	0	0	0
Cream			
Coffee or Table, 1 tbsp (15g)	3	2	10
1 Cup (240g)	46	29	159
Double, 1 tbsp (15g)	4	2	13
1 Cup (239g)	60	37	209
Heavy Whipping, 1 tbsp (15g)	6	4	21
1 Cup or 2 Cups Whipped (238g)	88	55	326
Light Whipping, 1 tbsp (15g)	5	3	17
1 Cup or 2 Cups Whipped (239g)	74	46	265
Single, 1 tbsp (15g)	2	1	6
1 Cup (242g)	28	17	89
Sour, Cultured, 1 tbsp (12g)	3	2	5
1 Cup (230g)	48	30	102
Whipped, from Heavy or Light Cream,			
2 Cups Heavy (238g)	88	55	326
2 Cups Light (239g)	74	46	265

	Total fat (g)	Saturated fat (g)	Cholesterol (mg)
Whipped, Pressurized			
1 tbsp (3g)	1	0	2
1 Cup (60g)	13	8	46
Cream Puffs			
With Custard Filling, 1 Choux Pastry,			
3½ inch (130g)	18	6	187
Cream Substitute			
Nondairy, with Hydrogenated Vegetable			
Oil and Soy Protein, ½ Cup (120g)	12	2	0
Nondairy, with Lauric Acid Oil and			
Sodium Caseinate, ½ Cup (120g)	12	11	0
Nondairy, Powdered, 1 tsp (2g)	1	1	0
Creamed Coconut			
1oz (28.4g)	20	17	0
3½oz (100g)	69	61	0
Cress			
Garden, Fresh, ½ Cup (25g)	0	0	0
Crisps			
1oz Packet (28.4g)	10	3	0
Croissant			
With Butter, 1 Croissant	25	14	216
Crumpet			
With Butter, 1 Crumpet	6	2	13
Cucumber			
Fresh, 1 Cucumber, 8¼ In (301g)	0	0	0
Currants			
Black, Fresh, 1 Cup (112g)	1	0	0
Red And White, Fresh, 1 Cup (112g)	0	0	0
Zante, Dried, 1 Cup (144g)	0	0	0
Custard			
Baked, 1 Cup (265g)	15	7	278
Custard Marrow			
Boiled, 1 Cup, 1-inch Pieces (160g)	1	0	0
Fresh, 1 Cup, 1-inch Pieces (132g)	0	0	0
1 Marrow, 5¾ inch (203g)	1	0	0
Custard Tart			
1 Small Tart (85g)	25	6	51
Dandelion Greens			
Boiled, 1 Cup Chopped (105g)	1	0	0
Fresh, 1 Cup Chopped (55g)	0	0	0
Danish Pastry			
1 Pastry (75g)	18	5	48

	Total fat (g)	Saturated fat (g)	Cholesterol (mg)
Dates			
Fresh and Dried 10 Fruits (83g)	0	0	0
1 Cup Chopped (178g)	1	0	0
Dessert Topping			
Nondairy, Powder, 1½oz (42½g)	17	16	0
Nondairy, 1½oz Powder Prepared with ½ Cup Whole Milk, 1 Cup (80g)	10	9	8
Nondairy, Pressurized, 1 Cup (70g)	16	13	0
Devilled Crab			
1 Cup (240g)	23	7	245
Dhal			
Home Recipe, 1 Cup (210g)	15	2	0
Dock			
Boiled, ½ Cup Chopped (100g)	1	0	0
Fresh, ½ Cup Chopped (67g)	1	0	0
Doughnuts			
Cake Type, 1 Doughnut (58g)	11	3	35
Yeast, Glazed, 1 Doughnut (42g)	10	2	11
Yeast, Plain, 1 Doughnut (42g)	11	3	11
Dressed Crab			
1 Cup (220g)	17	9	308
Duck			
Domesticated			
Meat and Skin, Roasted,			
1 Portion (173g)	49	17	145
½ Duck (382g)	108	37	321
Meat and Skin, Raw,			
1 Portion (287g)	113	38	218
½ Duck (634g)	249	84	482
Meat Only, Roasted,			
1 Portion (100g)	11	4	89
½ Duck (221g)	25	9	197
Meat Only, Raw, 1 Portion (137g)	8	3	106
½ Duck (303g)	18	7	233
Liver, Raw, 1 Liver (44g)	2	1	227
Wild			
Meat and Skin, Raw, ½ Duck (270g)	41	14	216
Breast Meat Only, Raw, ½ Breast (83g)	4	1	64
Dumplings			
2 Dumplings (85g)	21	6	7
Eclair			
with Custard Filling and Chocolate Icing, 1 Eclair (100g)	14	4	136

	Total fat (g)	Saturated fat (g)	Cholesterol (mg)
Egg and Cheese Sandwich			
1 Sandwich (156g)	19	7	291
Egg Salad Sandwich			
1 Sandwich (153g)	24	8	264
Eggnog			
1 Cup (254g)	19	11	149
Eggnog Flavour Mix			
Powder, 2 Heaped tsp (28.4g)	0	0	3
Eggnog Flavour Mix			
Prepared with Milk,			
1 Cup Milk			
and 2 Heaped tsp Powder (272g)	8	5	33

EGGS

Chicken			
Dried Egg White			
Powder, 1 Cup sifted (107g)	0	0	0
Dried Egg Yolk			
Powder, 1 tbsp (4g)	3	1	117
1 Cup sifted (67g)	41	12	1962
Dried Whole Egg			
1 tbsp (5g)	2	1	96
1 Cup sifted (85g)	36	11	1631
Fresh Egg			
Raw, 1 Large Egg (50g)	6	2	274
White, Raw, 1 Large Egg White (33g)	0	0	0
Yolk, Raw, 1 Large Egg Yolk (17g)	6	2	272
Fried Egg			
1 Large Egg (46g)	6	2	246
Hard-boiled			
1 Large Egg (50g)	6	2	274
1 Cup,chopped (136g)	15	5	745
Omelette			
Home Recipe, 1-Egg Omelette (64g)	15	7	301
Poached Egg			
1 Large Egg (50g)	6	2	273
Raw Egg			
White and Yolk, 1 Large Egg (50g)	6	2	274
Scrambled			
1 Large Egg (64g)	7	3	248
1 Cup (220g)	24	10	854

	Total fat (g)	Saturated fat (g)	Cholesterol (mg)
Other Eggs			
Duck			
Whole, Fresh, Raw, 1 Egg (70g)	10	3	619
Goose			
Whole, Fresh, Raw, 1 Egg (144g)	19	5	1227
Quail			
Whole, Fresh, Raw, 1 Egg (9g)	1	0	76
Turkey			
Whole, Fresh, Raw, 1 Egg (79g)	9	3	737
Elderberries			
Fresh, 1 Cup (145g)	1	0	0
Endive			
Fresh, 1 Cup Chopped (50g)	0	0	0
1 Head (513g)	1	0	0
Falafel			
1 Falafel (17g)	3	0	0
3 Falafels (51g)	9	1	0
FAT			
Also see under Oils			
Beef Dripping			
1 tbsp (12.8g)	13	6	14
1 Cup (205g)	205	102	224
Butter			
Hard, 1 Pat (5g)	4	3	11
4oz (113.4g)	92	57	248
Whipped, 1 Pat (3.8g)	3	2	8
4oz (75.6g)	61	38	166
Chicken			
1 tbsp (12.8g)	13	4	11
1 Cup (205g)	205	61	174
Duck			
1 tbsp (12.8g)	13	4	13
1 Cup (205g)	205	68	205
Ghee			
Butter Oil, 1 tbsp (12.8g)	13	8	33
1 Cup (205g)	204	127	525
Goose			
1 tbsp (12.8g)	13	4	13
1 Cup (205g)	205	57	205
Lard			
1 Cup (205g)	205	80	195
1 tbsp (12.8g)	13	5	12

	Total fat (g)	Saturated fat (g)	Cholesterol (mg)
Margarine – See under Margarine			
Mutton Tallow			
1 tbsp (12.8g)	13	6	13
1 Cup (205g)	205	97	209
Shortening			
Lard and Vegetable Oil Blend,			
1 tbsp (12.8g)	13	5	7
1 Cup (205g)	205	83	115
Vegetable Only, 1 tbsp (12.8g)	13	4	0
1 Cup (205g)	205	63	0
Turkey			
1 tbsp (12.8g)	13	4	13
1 Cup (205g)	205	60	209
Fennel			
Leaves, Fresh, 3½oz (100g)	0	0	0
Figs			
Candied, 3½oz (100g)	0	0	0
Dried, Stewed, 1 Cup (259g)	1	0	0
Dried, Uncooked, 1 Cup (199g)	2	1	0
Fresh, 1 Fruit (50–65g)	0	0	0
Tinned, 1 Cup (248g)	0	0	0
Fish and Chips			
1 Portion (167g)	23	8	42
Fish Cakes			
Fried, 1 Regular Cake (60g)	5	2	25
Fish Fillet			
Battered or Breaded, Fried,			
1 Fillet (91g)	11	3	31
Fish Fingers			
1 Finger (28g)	3	1	31
2 Fingers (57g)	7	2	64
Fish Loaf			
Cooked, 1 Slice (150g)	6	2	60
1 Whole Loaf (1215g)	45	12	486
Fish Sandwich			
With Tartar Sauce,			
1 Sandwich (158g)	23	5	55
With Tartar Sauce and Cheese,			
1 Sandwich (183g)	29	8	68

	Total fat (g)	Saturated fat (g)	Cholesterol (mg)

FISH AND SHELLFISH

Abalone

Fried, 3oz (85g)	6	1	80
Raw, 3oz (85g)	1	0	72

Anchovy

Tinned in Oil, Drained Solids, 5 Anchovies (20g)	2	0	17
1 Tin (45g)	4	1	38
Raw, 3oz (85g)	4	1	51

Barracuda

Raw, 3½oz (100g)	3	1	55

Bass

Raw, 3oz (85g)	2	0	68

Bluefish

Raw, 3oz (85g)	4	1	50

Bream

Braised or Stewed, 3oz (85g)	1	0	54
Raw, 3oz (85g)	2	1	43

Brill

Poached or Grilled, 3oz (85g)	1	0	58
Raw, 3oz (85g)	1	0	41

Burbot

Raw, 3oz (85g)	1	0	51

Carp

Grilled or Baked, 3oz (85g)	6	1	71
Raw, 3oz (85g)	5	1	56

Catfish

Breaded and Fried, 3oz (85g)	11	3	69
Raw, 3oz (85g)	4	1	49

Caviar

Black and Red, Granular, 1 tbsp (16g)	3	1	94
1oz (28g)	5	1	165

Clam

Breaded and Fried, 3oz (85g)	10	2	52
20 Small Clams (188g)	21	5	115
Steamed or Boiled, 3oz (85g)	2	0	57
20 Small Clams (90g)	2	0	60
Tinned, Drained Solids, 3oz (85g)	2	0	57
1 Cup (160g)	3	0	107
Raw, 3oz (85g)	1	0	29

	Total fat (g)	Saturated fat (g)	Cholesterol (mg)
20 Small Clams (180g)	2	0	61
Cod			
Braised or Baked, 3oz (85g)	1	0	47
Dried and Salted, 3oz (85g)	2	0	129
Tinned, Solids and Liquid, 3oz (85g)	1	0	47
1 Tin (312g)	3	1	172
Raw, 3oz (85g)	1	0	37
Crab			
Blue, Steamed or Boiled, 3oz (85g)	2	0	85
Blue, Tinned, Drained Solids or Dry Pack, 3oz (85g)	1	0	76
Blue, Raw, 3oz (85g)	1	0	66
Devilled, 1 Cup (240g)	23	7	245
Dressed, 1 Cup (220g)	17	9	308
Imitation, made from Surimi (see entry in this section), 3oz (85g)	1	0	17
King, Steamed or Boiled, 3oz (85g)	1	0	45
King, Raw, 3oz (85g)	1	0	36
Crab Cakes			
1 Cake (60g)	5	1	90
Crayfish			
Steamed or Boiled, 3oz (85g)	1	0	151
Raw, 3oz (85g)	1	0	118
Cuttlefish			
Raw, 3oz (85g)	1	0	95
Drumfish			
Breaded and Fried, 3oz (85g)	11	3	71
Raw, 3oz (85g)	3	1	52
Eel			
Grilled or Roasted, 3oz (85g)	13	3	137
Raw, 3oz (85g)	10	2	107
Fish Fingers			
Heated from Frozen, 1 Finger (28g)	3	1	31
Flounder			
Poached or Grilled, 3oz (85g)	1	0	58
Raw, 3oz (85g)	1	0	41
Grouper			
Poached or Grilled, 3oz (85g)	1	0	40
Raw, 3oz (85g)	1	0	32
Haddock			
Braised or Poached, 3oz (85g)	1	0	63
Smoked, 3oz (85g)	1	0	66

	Total fat (g)	Saturated fat (g)	Cholesterol (mg)
Raw, 3oz (85g)	1	0	49
Hake			
Braised or Baked, 3oz (85g)	1	0	47
Raw, 3oz (85g)	1	0	37
Halibut			
Grilled, Poached or Baked, 3oz (85g)	3	0	35
Raw, 3oz (85g)	2	0	27
Herring			
Grilled, 3oz (85g)	10	2	66
Kippered, 1 Fillet (40g)	5	1	33
Pickled, 1 Piece (15g)	3	0	2
Raw, 3oz (85g)	8	2	51
Kippers			
Grilled, 1 Fillet (40g)	5	1	33
Langouste			
Raw, 3oz (85g)	1	0	60
Ling			
Raw, 3oz (85g)	1	0	34
Lobster			
Steamed or Boiled, 3oz (85g)	1	0	61
Raw, 3oz (85g)	1	0	81
In Newberg Sauce, 1 Cup (250g)	27	15	455
Lobster Paste			
Tinned, 1 tsp (7g)	1	0	12
3½oz (100g)	9	5	172
Lobster Salad			
½ Cup (4oz) (260g)	17	3	120
Lox			
3oz (85g)	4	1	20
Lumpfish			
Raw, 3oz (85g)	2	0	35
Mackerel			
Grilled or Poached, 3oz (85g)	15	4	64
Raw, 3oz (85g)	12	3	60
Milkfish			
Raw, 3oz (85g)	6	1	44
Monkfish			
Raw, 3oz (85g)	1	0	21
Mullet			
Grilled or Baked, 3oz (85g)	4	1	54
Raw, 3oz (85g)	3	1	42

	Total fat (g)	Saturated fat (g)	Cholesterol (mg)
Mussel			
Steamed or Boiled, 3oz (85g)	4	1	48
Raw, 3oz (85g)	2	0	24
Octopus			
Raw, 3oz (85g)	1	0	41
Oyster			
Breaded and Fried, 6 Medium			
Oysters (88g)	11	3	71
3oz (85g)	11	3	69
Steamed or Boiled, 6 Medium			
Oysters (42g)	2	1	46
3oz (85g)	4	1	93
Tinned, 3oz (85g)	2	1	47
Raw, 6 Medium Oysters (84g)	2	1	46
Perch			
Stewed, 3oz (85g)	1	0	98
Raw, 3oz (85g)	1	0	77
Pike			
Braised, 3oz (85g)	1	0	43
Raw, 3oz (85g)	1	0	33
Pike-Perch			
Raw, 3oz (85g)	1	0	73
Plaice			
Poached or Grilled, 3oz (85g)	1	0	58
Raw, 3oz (85g)	1	0	41
Pollock			
Steamed or Baked, 3oz (85g)	1	0	82
Raw, 3oz (85g)	1	0	60
Prawn			
Breaded and Fried, 3oz (85g)	10	2	151
Steamed or Boiled, 3oz (85g)	1	0	166
Raw, 3oz (85g)	2	0	129
Roe			
Mixed Species, Raw, 1oz (28g)	2	0	105
3oz (85g)	6	1	318
Sablefish			
Smoked, 3oz (85g)	17	4	54
Raw, 3oz (85g)	13	3	42
Salmon			
Chum, Tinned, Drained Solids with			
Bone, 3oz (85g)	5	1	33
1 Tin (369g)	20	6	144

	Total fat (g)	Saturated fat (g)	Cholesterol (mg)
Chum, Raw, 3oz (85g)	3	1	63
King, Smoked, 3oz (85g)	4	1	20
King, Raw, 3oz (85g)	9	2	56
Red, Tinned, Solids with Bone and Liquid, 3oz (85g)	5	1	47
1 Tin (454g)	28	7	250
Red, Raw, 3oz (85g)	3	1	44
Sockeye, Grilled or Braised, 3oz (85g)	9	2	74
Sockeye, Tinned, Drained Solids with Bone, 3oz (85g)	6	1	37
1 Tin (369g)	27	6	162
Sockeye, Raw, 3oz (85g)	7	1	53
Sardine			
Tinned in Oil, Drained Solids with Bone, 2 Sardines (24g)	3	0	34
1 Tin (92g)	11	1	131
Tinned in Tomato Sauce, Drained Solids with Bone, 1 Sardine (38g)	5	1	23
1 Tin (370g)	44	11	226
Scallop			
Breaded and Fried, 2 Large Scallops (31g)	3	1	19
Imitation, made from Surimi, 3oz (85g)	0	0	19
Raw, 2 Large Scallops (30g)	0	0	10
3oz (85g)	1	0	28
Scampi			
Breaded and Fried, 4 Scampi (30g)	4	1	53
Raw, 4 Scampi (28g)	1	0	43
Sea Bass			
Poached, Grilled or Braised, 3oz (85g)	2	1	45
Raw, 3oz (85g)	2	0	35
Sea Bream			
Poached, Grilled or Steamed, 3oz (85g)	2	0	46
Raw, 3oz (85g)	1	0	36
Sea Perch			
Poached, Grilled or Braised, 3oz (85g)	2	1	45
Raw, 3oz (85g)	2	0	35
Sea Trout			
Raw, 3oz (85g)	3	1	71
Shad			
Raw, 3oz (85g)	12	4	64
Shark			
Batter-dipped and Fried, 3oz (85g)	12	3	50

	Total fat (g)	Saturated fat (g)	Cholesterol (mg)
Raw, 3oz (85g)	4	1	43
Sheepshead			
Braised or Stewed, 3oz (85g)	1	0	54
Raw, 3oz (85g)	2	1	43
Shrimp			
Breaded and Fried, 3oz (85g)	10	2	151
Imitation, made from Surimi, 3oz (85g)	1	0	31
Steamed or Boiled, 3oz (85g)	1	0	166
Tinned, 3oz (85g)	2	0	147
Raw, 3oz (85g)	2	0	129
Shrimp Paste			
Tinned, 1 tsp (7g)	1	0	12
3½oz (100g)	9	5	172
Skate			
Poached or Grilled, 3oz (85g)	1	0	58
Raw, 3oz (85g)	1	0	41
Smelt			
Grilled, 3oz (85g)	3	1	77
Raw, 3oz (85g)	2	0	60
Sole			
Steamed or Baked, 3oz (85g)	1	0	58
Raw, 3oz (85g)	1	0	41
Sprat			
Grilled, 3oz (85g)	10	2	66
Raw, 3oz (85g)	8	2	51
Squid			
Fried, 3oz (85g)	6	2	221
Raw, 3oz (85g)	1	0	198
Sturgeon			
Baked, Grilled or Roasted, 3oz (85g)	4	1	66
Smoked, 3oz (85g)	4	1	68
Raw, 3oz (85g)	3	1	51
Sucker			
Raw, 3oz (85g)	2	0	35
Surimi			
Parts of Various Fish used to make Imitation Fish Products , 3oz (85g)	1	0	26
Swordfish			
Baked, Grilled or Poached, 3oz (85g)	4	1	43
Raw, 3oz (85g)	3	1	33
Trout			
Raw, 3oz (85g)	6	1	49

	Total fat (g)	Saturated fat (g)	Cholesterol (mg)
Poached or Braised, 3oz (85g)	4	1	62
Tuna			
Fresh, Roasted or Grilled, 3oz (85g)	5	1	42
Fresh, Raw, 3oz (85g)	4	1	32
Tinned in Oil, Drained Solids, 3oz (85g)	7	1	26
1 Tin (178g)	14	3	55
Tinned in Water, Drained Solids, 3oz (85g)	2	1	36
1 Tin (172g)	4	1	72
Tuna Salad			
3oz (85g)	8	1	11
1 Cup (205g)	19	3	27
Turbot			
Raw, 3oz (85g)	3	1	41
Whelk			
Steamed or Boiled, 3oz (85g)	1	0	111
Raw, 3oz (85g)	0	0	55
Whitebait			
Smoked, 3oz (85g)	1	0	28
Raw, 3oz (85g)	5	1	51
Whiting			
Grilled or Poached, 3oz (85g)	1	0	71
Raw, 3oz (85g)	1	0	57
Zander			
Raw, 3oz (85g)	1	0	73

FLOUR

	Total fat (g)	Saturated fat (g)	Cholesterol (mg)
Buckwheat			
Dark, 1 Cup (98g)	3	0	0
Light, 1 Cup (98g)	1	0	0
Carob			
1 Cup (103g)	1	0	0
Chestnut			
1 Cup (100g)	4	0	0
Corn Flour			
1 Cup (117g)	3	0	0
Cottonseed			
Partially Defatted, 1 Cup (94g)	6	2	0
Peanut			
Defatted, 1 Cup (60g)	0	0	0
Low Fat, 1 Cup (60g)	13	2	0
Potato			
1 Cup (179g)	1	0	0

	Total fat (g)	Saturated fat (g)	Cholesterol (mg)
Rye			
Whole-grain, Dark, 1 Cup (128g)	3	0	0
Whole-grain, Light, 1 Cup (102g)	1	0	0
Whole-grain, Medium, 1 Cup (88g)	2	0	0
Sesame			
High Fat, 1oz (28.4g)	11	2	0
Low Fat, 1oz (28.4g)	1	0	0
Partially Defatted, 1oz (28.4g)	3	1	0
Soy			
Defatted, 1 Cup (100g)	1	0	0
Full Fat, Roasted, 1 Cup (85g)	19	3	0
Low Fat, 1 Cup (88g)	6	1	0
Sunflower Seed			
Partially Defatted, 1 Cup (80g)	1	0	0
Wheat			
80–85% Extraction, 1 Cup (100g)	1	0	0
All Purpose, 1 Cup (125g)	1	0	0
Bread, 1 Cup (137g)	2	0	0
Cake, 1 Cup (118g)	1	0	0
Gluten, 45% Gluten, 1 Cup (140g)	3	0	0
Self-raising, 1 Cup (125g)	1	0	0
Whole, 1 Cup (120g)	2	0	0
Frankfurters			
Beef, Boiled or Grilled, 1 Frankfurter (57g)	16	7	35
Beef and Pork, Boiled or Grilled, 1 Frankfurter (57g)	17	6	29
Chicken, Boiled or Grilled, 1 Frankfurter (45g)	9	3	46
Mixed Meat, Boiled or Grilled, 1 Frankfurter (56g)	15	6	35
Tinned, Boiled or Grilled, 1 Frankfurter (48g)	9	4	30
Turkey, Boiled or Grilled, 1 Frankfurter (45g)	8	3	48
Fried Chicken			
2 Pieces Breast or Wing (163g)	30	8	149
2 Pieces Drumstick or Thigh (148g)	27	7	165
Fried Fish			
Battered or Breaded, 1 Fillet (91g)	11	3	31

	Total fat (g)	Saturated fat (g)	Cholesterol (mg)
Fried Rice			
1 Serving (170g)	27	3	0
Special, with Chicken and Vegetables,			
1 Serving (205g)	30	4	47
Frog Legs			
Raw, 3½oz (100g)	0	0	50
Frozen Dinners			
Fried Chicken with Mixed Vegetables,			
1 Serving (100g)	9	3	49
Roast Beef with Potatoes, Peas and Corn,			
1 Serving (100g)	3	2	50
Fruit Cake			
Rich, 1 Slice (85g)	9	3	43
Rich, Iced, 1 Slice (100g)	12	3	40
Fruit Cocktail			
Tinned, 1 Cup (248g)	0	0	0
Fruit Punch Drink			
1 Glass (247g)	0	0	0
Tinned or Bottled, 1 Glass (186g)	0	0	0
Fruit Salad			
Tinned, 1 Cup (249g)	0	0	0
Tropical, Tinned, 1 Cup (257g)	0	0	0
Fruit			
See under individual names			
Mixed, Dried, 1 Cup (255g)	1	0	0
Mixed, Frozen, 1 Cup,			
thawed (250g)	1	0	0
Mixed, Tinned, 1 Cup (255g)	0	0	0
Fuki – See under Butterbur			
Garlic			
1 Clove (3g)	0	0	0
Garlic Granules or Powder			
1 tsp (2.8g)	0	0	0
1 tbsp (8.4g)	0	0	0
Gelatin			
Dessert, made with Water, Plain,			
1 Cup (240g)	0	0	0
Dessert, made with Water and Fruit,			
1 Cup (240g)	0	0	0
Dry, 1 Envelope (7g)	0	0	0
Ghee (Butter Oil)			
1 tbsp (12.8g)	13	8	33

	Total fat (g)	Saturated fat (g)	Cholesterol (mg)
1 Cup (205g)	204	127	525
Gherkins			
1 Cup (170g)	0	0	0
Ginger Root			
Crystallized, 1oz (28g)	0	0	0
Fresh, Finely Sliced or Grated,			
1 tbsp (11g)	0	0	0
Gingerbread			
1 Piece (117g)	15	5	70
Gluten – See under Flour			
Goose			
Meat and Skin			
Roasted, 1 Portion (188g)	41	13	171
½ Goose (774g)	170	53	704
Raw, 1 Portion (320g)	108	31	256
½ Goose (1319g)	443	129	1055
Meat Only			
Roasted, 1 Portion (143g)	18	7	137
½ Goose (591g)	75	27	567
Raw, 1 Portion (185g)	13	5	155
½ Goose (766g)	55	21	643
Giblets			
Raw, 3½oz (100g)	7	2	350
Gizzard			
Raw, 3½oz (100g)	5	1	145
Liver Pâté			
Tinned, Smoked, 1 tbsp (13g)	6	2	20
1oz (28.35g)	12	4	43
Liver			
Raw, 1 Liver (94g)	4	2	484
Gooseberries			
Fresh, 1 Cup (150g)	1	0	0
Tinned, 1 Cup (252g)	1	0	0
Gourd			
White-flowered, Boiled, 1 Cup,			
1-inch Cubes (146g)	0	0	0
Granadilla			
Fresh, 1 Fruit (18g)	0	0	0
Grape Juice			
Frozen Concentrate, Diluted, 1 Cup (250g)	0	0	0
Frozen Concentrate, Undiluted,			
6 Fl.oz Container (216g)	1	0	0

	Total fat (g)	Saturated fat (g)	Cholesterol (mg)
Tinned or Bottled, 1 Cup (253g)	0	0	0
Grapefruit			
Juice, Frozen Concentrate, Diluted, 1 Cup (247g)	0	0	0
Juice, Frozen Concentrate, Undiluted, 6 Fl.oz Container (207g)	1	0	0
Fresh, 1 Cup (247g)	0	0	0
Tinned, 1 Cup (250g)	0	0	0
Peel, Candied, 1oz (28g)	0	0	0
Fresh, 1 Fruit with Juice (230g)	0	0	0
Sections, Tinned, 1 Cup (249g)	0	0	0
Grapes			
Fresh, 1 Cup (160g)	1	0	0
Tinned, 1 Cup (256g)	0	0	0
Gravy			
Au Jus			
Dehydrated, Prepared with Water, 1 Cup (246.1g)	1	0	0
Tinned, 1 Cup (238.4g)	1	0	0
1 Tin (298g)	1	0	0
Beef			
Tinned, 1 Cup (232.8g)	6	3	7
1 Tin (291g)	7	3	9
Brown			
Dehydrated, Prepared with Water, 1 Cup (260.6g)	0	0	0
Chicken			
Dehydrated, Prepared with Water, 1 Cup (259.7g)	2	1	3
Tinned, 1 Cup (238.4g)	14	3	5
1 Tin (298g)	17	4	6
Mushroom			
Dehydrated, Prepared with Water, 1 Cup (257.9g)	1	1	0
Tinned, 1 Cup (238.4g)	7	1	0
1 Tin (298g)	8	1	0
Onion			
Dehydrated, Prepared with Water, 1 Cup (8 Fl.oz) (261.4g)	1	1	0
Pork			
Dehydrated, Prepared with Water, 1 Cup (257.9g)	2	1	3

	Total fat (g)	Saturated fat (g)	Cholesterol (mg)
Turkey			
Dehydrated, Prepared with Water,			
1 Cup (261.4g)	2	1	3
Tinned, 1 Cup (238.4g)	5	2	5
1 Tin (298g)	6	2	6
Unspecified Type, Prepared with Water,			
1 Cup (261.4g)	2	1	0
Guacamole			
Home Recipe, 4 tablespoons (60g)	8	6	0
Guava			
1 Fruit (6g)	0	0	0
1 Cup Slices (244g)	2	0	0
Guava Sauce			
Cooked, 1 Cup (238g)	0	0	0
Guinea Fowl			
Meat and Skin, Raw,			
½ Guinea (345g)	22	6	255
Meat Only, Raw, ½ Guinea (264g)	7	2	166
Giblets, Raw, 3½oz (100g)	7	2	350
HAM			
Also see under Luncheon Meat; Pork			
Devilled, Tinned, 4½oz Tin (128g)	41	15	83
1 Cup (225g)	73	26	146
Ham and Cheese Sandwich			
1 Sandwich (146g)	15	6	58
Ham Croquette			
1 Croquette (65g)	10	4	46
Ham, Egg and Cheese Sandwich			
1 Sandwich (143g)	16	7	245
Ham Salad Spread			
1oz (28.35g)	4	1	11
Ham Sandwich			
1 Sandwich (140g)	12	5	43
Hamburger			
Also see under Beef Burger; Cheeseburger			
Plain, 1 Regular Patty (90g)	12	4	36
1 Large Patty (113g)	23	8	71
With Condiments and Vegetables,			
1 Regular Patty (110g)	13	4	26
1 Large Patty (218g)	27	10	86

	Total fat (g)	Saturated fat (g)	Cholesterol (mg)
Double-decker with Condiments,			
2 Regular Patties (215g)	32	12	102
2 Large Patties (259g)	41	16	142
Haws			
Scarlet, Fresh, 3½oz (100g)	1	0	0
Hazelnuts			
Dried, 1oz (28.4g)	18	1	0
1 Cup Chopped Kernels (115g)	72	5	0
Honey			
1 tbsp (21g)	0	0	0
1 Cup (339g)	0	0	0
Horseradish-tree			
Pods, Boiled, 1 Cup Slices (118g)	0	0	0
Horseradish			
Prepared, 1 tbsp (15g)	0	0	0
Hot Chocolate			
Made with Milk,			
1 Cup Milk and 2–3 Heaped			
Teaspoons Powder (266g)	9	6	32
Hot Dog			
Plain, 1 Hot Dog (98g)	17	6	29
Hot Pot			
Casserole, 1 Serving (340g)	14	6	85
Hummus			
1 Cup (246g)	21	3	0
Ice Cream Cone			
3½oz (100g)	2	1	0
Ice Cream			
French Vanilla, Soft Serve,			
1 Cup (173g)	23	14	153
Vanilla, Approximately 10% Fat,			
1 Cup (133g)	14	9	60
Vanilla, Approximately 16% Fat,			
1 Cup (148g)	24	15	88
Sundae, Caramel, 1 Sundae (155g)	9	5	25
Sundae, Hot Fudge, 1 Sundae (158g)	9	5	21
Sundae, Strawberry, 1 Sundae (153g)	8	4	21
Ice Milk			
Vanilla, 1 Cup (131g)	6	4	18
Vanilla, Softserve, 1 Cup (175g)	5	3	13
Ices			
Water, All Flavours, 1 Cup (193g)	0	0	0

	Total fat (g)	Saturated fat (g)	Cholesterol (mg)
Icing			
Chocolate Fudge, made with Butter, 1 Cup (310g)	45	19	62
Chocolate Fudge, made with Margarine, 1 Cup (310g)	45	11	0
Coconut, made from Dry Mix, 1 Cup (166g)	13	11	0
Creamy Fudge, made from Dry Mix, 1 Cup (245g)	16	5	0
Creamy Fudge, made with Butter, 1 Cup (245g)	37	17	71
Creamy Fudge, made with Margarine, 1 Cup (245g)	37	9	0
White, Boiled, 1 Cup (94g)	0	0	0
Jambul – See Java-plum			
Jams and Preserves			
1 tbsp (20g)	0	0	0
1 Jar (284g)	0	0	0
Java-plum			
Fresh, 1 Cup (135g)	0	0	0
Jellies			
Fruit, 1 tbsp (18g)	0	0	0
1 Cup (300g)	0	0	0
Jelly			
Made with Milk, 1 Serving (170g)	3	2	10
Made with Water, 1 Serving (170g)	0	0	0
Jicama			
Boiled, 3½oz (100g)	0	0	0
Junket			
Chocolate, made from Mix with Milk, 1 Cup (255g)	10	5	31
Strawberry and Raspberry, made from Mix with Milk, 1 Cup (250g)	9	5	33
Kale			
Boiled, 1 Cup Chopped (130g)	1	0	0
Fresh, 1 Cup Chopped (67g)	1	0	0
Katuray			
Fresh, 1 Cup Flowers (20g)	0	0	0
Steamed, 1 Cup Flowers (104g)	0	0	0
Kedgeree			
1 Serving (170g)	12	4	204

	Total fat (g)	Saturated fat (g)	Cholesterol (mg)
Kidney Beans			
Tinned, 1 Cup (256g)	1	0	0
Kippers			
Grilled, 1 Fillet (40g)	5	1	33
Kiwifruit			
Fresh, 1 Fruit (91g)	0	0	0
Kohlrabi			
Boiled, 1 Cup Slices (165g)	0	0	0
Kumquat			
Fresh, 1 Fruit (19g)	0	0	0
Lager – See under Alcohol			
LAMB			
Best-End			
Choice			
Fat, Raw, 3½oz (100g)	77	43	75
Lean and Fat, Raw, 3½oz (100g)	30	17	71
Lean, Grilled, 3½oz (100g)	11	6	100
Lean, Raw, 3½oz (100g)	8	5	70
Good			
Fat, Raw, 3½oz (100g)	74	41	75
Lean and Fat, Raw, 3½oz (100g)	27	15	71
Lean, Grilled, 3½oz (100g)	10	6	100
Lean, Raw, 3½oz (100g)	8	4	70
Prime			
Fat, Raw, 3½oz (100g)	84	47	75
Lean and Fat, Raw, 3½oz (100g)	41	23	71
Lean, Grilled, 3½oz (100g)	12	7	100
Lean, Raw, 3½oz (100g)	10	5	70
Chops			
Choice			
Lean and Fat, Grilled, 3⅛oz (89g)	32	18	87
Loin, Lean and Fat, Grilled, 3½oz (100g)	28	16	93
Good			
Lean and Fat, Grilled, 3½oz (100g)	32	18	98
Loin, Lean and Fat, Grilled, 3½oz (100g)	27	15	98
Prime			
Lean and Fat, Grilled, 3½oz (100g)	47	26	98
Loin, Lean and Fat, Grilled, 3½oz (100g)	37	21	98
Composite Cuts			
Choice, Raw, Lean and Fat, 3½oz (100g)	21	12	71
Good, Raw, Lean and Fat, 3½oz (100g)	19	11	71

	Total fat (g)	Saturated fat (g)	Cholesterol (mg)
Prime, Raw, Lean and Fat, 3½oz (100g)	27	15	71
Fat			
Cooked, 3½oz (100g)	76	42	75
Heart			
Braised, 1 Cup (145g)	21	13	397
Raw, 3½oz (100g)	10	6	150
Kidneys			
Raw, 3½oz (100g)	3	1	375
Leg			
Choice			
Lean and Fat, Roasted, 3½oz (100g)	20	11	104
Lean and Fat, Raw, 3½oz (100g)	16	9	71
Lean, Roasted, 3½oz (100g)	8	4	111
Lean, Raw, 3½oz (100g)	5	3	70
Good			
Lean and Fat, Roasted, 3½oz (100g)	17	10	98
Lean and Fat, Raw, 3½oz (100g)	15	8	71
Lean, Roasted, 3½oz (100g)	7	4	100
Lean, Raw, 3½oz (100g)	5	3	70
Prime			
Lean and Fat, Roasted, 3½oz (100g)	24	13	98
Lean and Fat, Raw, 3½oz (100g)	21	12	71
Lean, Roasted, 3½oz (100g)	8	4	100
Lean, Raw, 3½oz (100g)	6	3	70
Liver			
Grilled, 1.6oz Slice (45g)	6	1	197
Raw, 3½oz (100g)	4	1	300
Loin			
Choice			
Lean, Grilled, 3½oz (100g)	7	4	98
Lean, Raw, 3½oz (100g)	6	3	70
Good			
Lean, Grilled, 3½oz (100g)	7	4	100
Lean, Raw, 3½oz (100g)	6	3	70
Prime			
Lean, Grilled, 3½oz (100g)	9	5	100
Lean, Raw, 3½oz (100g)	7	4	70
Lungs, Raw, 3½oz (100g)	2	1	150
Shoulder			
Choice			
Lean and Fat, Roasted, 3½oz (100g)	29	16	104
Lean and Fat, Raw, 3½oz (100g)	24	13	71

	Total fat (g)	Saturated fat (g)	Cholesterol (mg)
Good			
Lean and Fat, Roasted, 3½oz (100g)	25	14	98
Lean and Fat, Raw, 3½oz (100g)	22	12	71
Lean, Roasted, 3½oz (100g)	10	5	100
Lean, Raw, 3½oz (100g)	7	4	70
Prime			
Lean and Fat, Roasted, 3½oz (100g)	32	18	98
Lean and Fat, Raw, 3½oz (100g)	28	16	71
Lean, Roasted, 3½oz (100g)	11	6	100
Lean, Raw, 3½oz (100g)	9	5	70
Spleen			
Raw, 3½oz (100g)	4	1	250
Sweetbreads			
Braised, 3oz (85g)	5	2	396
Raw, 3½oz (100g)	4	1	250
Tongue			
Braised, 1 Slice (20g)	4	2	20
Raw, 3½oz (100g)	15	9	70
Lamb's Lettuce			
Fresh, 1 Cup (56g)	0	0	0
Lamb's Quarters			
Boiled, 1 Cup Chopped (180g)	1	0	0
Lard			
1 tbsp (12.8g)	13	5	12
1 Cup (205g)	205	80	195
Leeks			
Boiled, 1 Leek (124g)	0	0	0
Fresh, 1 Leek (124g)	0	0	0
Lemon			
Fresh, 1 Fruit (108g)	0	0	0
Lemon Curd			
2 tbsp (45g)	6	3	68
Lemon Juice			
Fresh, 1 tbsp (15.2g)	0	0	0
1 Cup (244g)	0	0	0
Tinned or Bottled,			
1 tbsp (15.2g)	0	0	0
1 Cup (244g)	1	0	0
Lemon Peel			
Candied, 1oz (28g)	0	0	0
Fresh, 1 tbsp (6g)	0	0	0

	Total fat (g)	Saturated fat (g)	Cholesterol (mg)
Lemonade Flavour Drink			
Prepared with Water, 1 Cup Water and			
2 tbsp Powder (266g)	0	0	0
Lemonade			
Frozen Concentrate, 6 Fl.oz Tin (219g)	0	0	0
Frozen Concentrate, Diluted, 1 Cup (248g)	0	0	0
Lentils			
Also see under Beans and Pulses			
Boiled, 1 Cup (198g)	1	0	0
Fresh, 1 Cup (192g)	2	0	0
Sprouted, Fresh, 1 Cup (77g)	0	0	0
Sprouted, Stir-fried, 3½oz (100g)	1	0	0
Lettuce			
Cos or Romaine, Fresh, 1 Inner Leaf (10g)	0	0	0
Iceberg (includes Crisphead Types), Fresh,			
1 Leaf (20g)	0	0	0
Looseleaf, Fresh, 1 Leaf (10g)	0	0	0
Roundhead (includes Butterhead Types),			
Fresh, 1 Leaf (10g)	0	0	0
Lime			
Fresh, 1 Fruit (67g)	0	0	0
Juice, Fresh, 1 tbsp (15.4g)	0	0	0
1 Cup (246g)	0	0	0
Juice, Tinned or Bottled, 1 tbsp (15.4g)	0	0	0
1 Cup (246g)	1	0	0
Limeade			
Frozen Concentrate, 6 Fl.oz Tin (218g)	0	0	0
Frozen Concentrate, Diluted, 1 Cup (247g)	0	0	0
Lobster In Newberg Sauce			
1 Cup (250g)	27	15	455
Lobster Paste			
Tinned, 1 tsp (7g)	1	0	12
3½oz (100g)	9	5	172
Lobster Salad			
½ Cup (260g)	17	3	120
Loganberries			
1 Cup (147g)	1	0	0
Longans			
Dried, 3½oz (100g)	0	0	0
Fresh, 3½oz (100g)	0	0	0
Loquats			
Fresh, 1 Fruit (9.9g)	0	0	0

	Total fat (g)	Saturated fat (g)	Cholesterol (mg)
Lotus Root			
Boiled, 10 Slices (89g)	0	0	0
Fresh, 10 Slices (81g)	0	0	0
Luncheon Meat			
Beef			
Loaved, 1 Slice (28.35g)	7	3	18
Thin Sliced, 1oz (28.35g)	1	1	12
Corned Beef Loaf			
Jellied, 1 Slice (28.35g)	2	1	13
Ham			
Chopped, Pressed, 1 Slice (28.35g)	5	2	15
Chopped, Spiced, Tinned, 1 Slice (28.35g)	5	2	14
Extra Lean (5% Fat), 1 Slice (28.35g)	1	1	13
Lean (11% Fat), 1 Slice (28.35g)	3	1	16
Minced, 1 Slice (28.35g)	6	2	20
Ham Salad Spread			
1oz (28.35g)	4	1	11
Peppered Loaf			
Pork and Beef, 1 Slice (28.35g)	2	1	13
Pickle and Pimiento Loaf			
Pork, 1 Slice (28.35g)	6	2	11
Picnic Loaf			
1 Slice (28.35g)	5	2	11
Pork and Beef			
Chopped Together, 1 Slice (28.35g)	9	3	16
Pork			
Tinned, 1 Slice (28.35g)	9	3	18
Turkey Loaf			
1 Slice (28.35g)	4	1	28
Lychees			
Dried, 3½oz (100g)	1	0	0
Fresh, 1 Cup (190g)	1	0	0
Macaroni			
Boiled, 1 Cup (140g)	1	0	0
Macaroni Cheese			
Made with Butter, 1 Cup (200g)	22	12	68
Made with Margarine, 1 Cup (200g)	22	9	42
Tinned, 1 Cup (240g)	10	4	24
1 Tin (430g)	17	8	43

	Total fat (g)	Saturated fat (g)	Cholesterol (mg)
Malt Extract			
1oz (28g)	0	0	0
Malt			
Dry, 1oz (28g)	1	0	0
Malted Milk Flavour Mix			
Chocolate, 4–5 Heaped tsp (21g)	1	0	1
Chocolate, made with Milk, 1 Cup Milk and 4–5 Heaped tsp Powder (265g)	9	6	35
Natural, 3 Heaped tsp (21g)	2	1	4
Natural, made with Milk, 1 Cup Milk and 3 Heaped tsp Powder (265g)	10	6	37
Mandarin Orange			
Fresh, 1 Fruit (84g)	0	0	0
1 Cup Sections (195g)	0	0	0
Tinned, 1 Cup (249g)	0	0	0
Mange-tout – see Peas, Edible-pod			
Mango			
Fresh, 1 Fruit (207g)	1	0	0
MARGARINE			
Diet Spreads: (40% Fat)			
Corn (Hydrogenated and Regular)			
1 tsp (4.8g)	2	0	0
1 Cup (232g)	90	15	0
Soybean (Hydrogenated)			
1 tsp (4.8g)	2	0	0
1 Cup (232g)	90	15	0
Soybean and Cottonseed			
1 tsp (4.8g)	2	0	0
1 Cup (232g)	90	19	0
Soybean and Cottonseed (Hydrogenated)			
1 tsp (4.8g)	2	0	0
1 Cup (232g)	90	17	0
Soybean and Palm (Hydrogenated and Regular)			
1 tsp (4.8g)	2	1	0
1 Cup (232g)	90	23	0
Unspecified Oils			
1 tsp (4.8g)	2	0	0
1 Cup (232g)	90	18	0
Low-fat Spreads: (60% Fat)			
Soybean (Hydrogenated) and Palm (Hydrogenated)			
1 tsp (4.8g)	3	1	0
1 Cup (229g)	139	32	0

	Total fat (g)	Saturated fat (g)	Cholesterol (mg)
Soybean (Hydrogenated) and Cottonseed (Hydrogenated)			
1 tsp (4.8g)	3	1	0
1 Cup (229g)	139	28	0
Soybean (Hydrogenated) and Palm (Hydrogenated and Regular)			
1 tsp (4.8g)	3	1	0
1 Cup (229g)	139	31	0
Unspecified Oils			
1 tsp (4.8g)	3	1	0
1 Cup (229g)	139	29	0
Hard Block: (80% Fat)			
Coconut (Hydrogenated and Regular) and Safflower and Palm (Hydrogenated)			
1 tsp (4.7g)	4	3	0
1 Block (113.4g)	91	65	0
Corn and Soybean (Hydrogenated) and Cottonseed (Hydrogenated)			
1 tsp (4.7g)	4	1	0
1 Block (113.4g)	91	17	0
Corn (Hydrogenated and Regular)			
1 tsp (4.7g)	4	1	0
1 Block (113.4g)	91	16	0
Lard (Hydrogenated)			
1 tsp (4.7g)	4	2	2
1 Block (113.4g)	91	36	58
Safflower and Soybean (Hydrogenated and Regular) and Cottonseed (Hydrogenated)			
1 tsp (4.7g)	4	1	0
1 Block (113.4g)	91	16	0
Safflower and Soybean (Hydrogenated),			
1 tsp (4.7g)	4	1	0
1 Block (113.4g)	91	16	0
and Cottonseed (Hydrogenated),			
1 tsp (4.7g)	4	1	0
1 Block (113.4g)	91	15	0
Soybean (Hydrogenated and Regular)			
1 tsp (4.7g)	4	1	0
1 Block (113.4g)	91	15	0
Soybean (Hydrogenated) and Cottonseed (Hydrogenated)			
1 tsp (4.7g)	4	1	0
1 Block (113.4g)	91	18	0
Soybean (Hydrogenated) and Corn and Cottonseed (Hydrogenated)			
1 tsp (4.7g)	4	1	0

	Total fat (g)	Saturated fat (g)	Cholesterol (mg)
1 Block (113.4g)	91	23	0
Soybean (Hydrogenated) and Palm (Hydrogenated and Regular)			
1 tsp (4.7g)	4	1	0
1 Block (113.4g)	91	20	0
Sunflower and Soybean (Hydrogenated) and Cottonseed (Hydrogenated)			
1 tsp (4.7g)	4	1	0
1 Block (113.4g)	91	14	0
Unspecified Oils			
1 tsp (4.7g)	4	1	0
1 Block (113.4g)	91	18	0
Soft Tub: (80% Fat)			
Corn (Hydrogenated and Regular)			
1 tsp (4.7g)	4	1	0
1 Cup (227g)	183	32	0
Safflower and Cottonseed (Hydrogenated) and Peanut (Hydrogenated)			
1 tsp (4.7g)	4	1	0
1 Cup (227g)	183	30	0
Safflower (Hydrogenated and Regular)			
1 tsp (4.7g)	4	0	0
1 Cup (227g)	183	21	0
Soybean (Hydrogenated and Regular)			
1 tsp (4.7g)	4	1	0
1 Cup (227g)	183	31	0
Soybean (Hydrogenated) and Cottonseed (Hydrogenated)			
1 tsp (4.7g)	4	1	0
1 Cup (227g)	183	35	0
Soybean (Hydrogenated) and Cottonseed			
1 tsp (4.7g)	4	1	0
1 Cup (227g)	183	38	0
Soybean (Hydrogenated) and Palm (Hydrogenated and Regular)			
1 tsp (4.7g)	4	1	0
1 Cup (227g)	183	39	0
Soybean (Hydrogenated) and Safflower,			
1 tsp (4.7g)	4	1	0
1 Cup (227g)	183	24	0
Sunflower and Cottonseed (Hydrogenated) and Peanut (Hydrogenated)			
1 tsp (4.7g)	4	1	0
1 Cup (227g)	183	29	0
Unspecified Oils			
1 tsp (4.7g)	4	1	0
1 Cup (227g)	182	31	0

	Total fat (g)	Saturated fat (g)	Cholesterol (mg)
Marmalade			
Citrus, 3½oz (100g)	0	0	0
Marrow			
Boiled, 1 Cup Slices (180g)	1	0	0
Fresh, 1 Cup Slices (130g)	0	0	0
Marzipan			
1oz (28.4g)	8	1	0
1 Cup Firmly Packed (227g)	62	6	0
Matzos			
Crackers, 10 Crackers (33g)	6	2	0
Mayonnaise			
See also under Salad Dressing			
Imitation, made with Milk Cream,			
1 tbsp (15.0g)	1	0	7
1 Cup (240g)	12	7	103
Imitation, made with Egg and Soybean			
Oil, 1 tbsp (15.0g)	3	1	4
1 Cup (240g)	46	8	58
Imitation, made without Egg or Milk,			
made with Soybean Oil, 1 tbsp (14.0g)	7	1	0
1 Cup (225g)	107	17	0
Made with Egg and Soybean and			
Safflower Oil, 1 tbsp (13.8g)	11	1	8
1 Cup (220g)	175	19	130
Made with Egg and Soybean Oil,			
1 tbsp (13.8g)	11	2	8
1 Cup (220g)	175	26	130
Meatloaf			
Home Recipe, 3½oz (100g)	13	6	65
Melon Balls			
1 Cup (173g)	0	0	0
Melons			
Cantaloupe, Fresh, ½ Fruit (267g)	1	0	0
Casaba, Fresh, 1/10 Fruit (164g)	0	0	0
Honeydew, Fresh, 1/10 Fruit (129g)	0	0	0
MILK			
Cow's Milk			
Buttermilk			
Dried, 1 tbsp (6½g)	0	0	5
1 Cup (120g)	7	4	83

	Total fat (g)	Saturated fat (g)	Cholesterol (mg)
Fluid, Cultured, 1 Cup (245g)	2	1	9
Chocolate Milk Drink			
1% Fat, 1 Cup (250g)	3	2	7
2% Fat, 1 Cup (250g)	5	3	17
Whole Milk, 1 Cup (250g)	9	5	31
Condensed			
Tinned, 1 Fl.oz (38.2g)	3	2	13
1 Cup (306g)	27	17	104
Dry			
Skimmed, Non-fat Solids, 2oz (60g)	0	0	12
Whole, 2oz (60g)	17	11	62
Evaporated			
Skimmed, Tinned, 1 Fl.oz (31.9g)	0	0	1
1 Cup (256g)	1	0	9
Whole, Tinned, 1 Fl.oz (31½g)	2	1	9
1 Cup (252g)	19	12	74
Low Fat			
1% Fat, 1 Cup (244g)	3	2	10
2% Fat, 1 Cup (244g)	5	3	18
Malted			
Beverage, 1 Cup Milk and 2–3 tsp Powder (265g)	10	6	37
Chocolate Flavour, Beverage, 1 Cup Milk and 2–3 tsp Powder (265g)	9	6	35
Dry Powder, 2 To 3 tsp (21g)	2	1	4
Dry Powder, Chocolate, 2 To 3 tsp (21g)	1	1	1
Skimmed			
1 Cup (245g)	0	0	4
1 Cup (244g)	8	5	33
Other Milks			
Coconut Milk			
Frozen (Liquid Expressed from Grated Meat and Water), 1 Cup (240g)	50	44	0
Fresh, 1 Cup (240g)	57	51	0
Tinned, 1 Cup (226g)	48	43	0
Goat			
1 Cup (244g)	10	7	28
Human			
1 fl.oz (30.8g)	1	1	4
1 Cup (246g)	11	5	34
Sheep			
1 Cup (245g)	17	11	66

	Total fat (g)	Saturated fat (g)	Cholesterol (mg)
Soy			
1 Cup (240g)	5	1	0
Milk Shakes			
Chocolate, 10 Fl.oz (283g)	11	7	37
Strawberry, 10 Fl.oz (283g)	8	5	31
Vanilla, 10 Fl.oz (283g)	9	5	31
Milk Substitute			
Fluid made with Hydrogenated Vegetable Oils			
1 Cup (244g)	8	2	1
Fluid made with Lauric Acid Oil			
1 Cup (244g)	8	7	1
Millet			
Whole Grain, 3½oz (100g)	3	1	0
Miso			
½ Cup (138g)	8	1	0
Molasses			
1 Cup (328g)	0	0	0
Moussaka			
Home Recipe, 1 Serving (225g)	30	11	90
Mulberries			
Fresh, 1 Cup (140g)	1	0	0
Mushrooms			
Boiled, 1 Cup Pieces (156g)	1	0	0
Fresh, 1 Cup Pieces (70g)	0	0	0
Shiitake, Cooked, 4 Mushrooms (72g)	0	0	0
1 Cup Pieces (145g)	0	0	0
Shiitake, Dried, 4 Mushrooms (15g)	0	0	0
Tinned, Drained Solids,			
1 Cup Pieces (156g)	0	0	0
Mustard Greens			
Boiled, 1 Cup Chopped (140g)	0	0	0
Fresh, 1 Cup Chopped (56g)	0	0	0
Mustard			
Prepared, Brown, 3½oz (100g)	6	1	0
Prepared, Yellow, 3½oz (100g)	4	0	0
Nachos			
With Cheese, 1 Serving (113g)	19	8	18
With Cheese, Beans and Beef,			
1 Serving (255g)	31	12	21
Natal-plum			
Fresh, 1 Fruit (20g)	0	0	0

	Total fat (g)	Saturated fat (g)	Cholesterol (mg)
Natto			
Fermented Soybean Paste, 1 Cup (175g)	19	3	0
Nectarine			
Fresh, 1 Fruit (136g)	1	0	0
Noodles			
Chow Mein, Tinned, 5oz Tin (142g)	33	9	17
1 Cup (45g)	11	3	5
Egg Noodles, Cooked, 1 Cup (160g)	2	0	50

NUT AND SEED BUTTERS

	Total fat (g)	Saturated fat (g)	Cholesterol (mg)
Almond Butter			
1 tbsp (16g)	9	1	0
1 Cup (250g)	148	14	0
Cashew Butter			
1 tbsp (16g)	8	2	0
1 Cup (227g)	112	22	0
Peanut Butter			
1 tbsp (16g)	8	2	0
1 Cup (258g)	129	25	0
Sesame Seed Paste			
1 tbsp (16g)	8	1	0
1 Cup (227g)	116	16	0
Sunflower Seed Butter			
1 tbsp(16g)	8	1	0
1 Cup (227g)	108	11	0
Tahini			
From Ground Sesame Seeds,			
1 tbsp (15g)	7	1	0
1 Cup (227g)	109	15	0

NUTS

Also see under Seeds

	Total fat (g)	Saturated fat (g)	Cholesterol (mg)
Almonds			
Dried, Blanched, 1oz (26 Kernels)			
(28.4g)	15	1	0
1 Cup Kernels (145g)	76	7	0
Dried, Unblanched, 1oz (24 Kernels)			
(28.4g)	15	1	0
1 Cup Kernels (142g)	74	7	0
Dry Roasted, 1oz (28.4g)	15	1	0
1 Cup Kernels (138g)	71	7	0
Finely Ground, Full Fat, 1oz (28.4g)	15	1	0
1 Cup (65g)	34	3	0

	Total fat (g)	Saturated fat (g)	Cholesterol (mg)
Finely Ground, Partially Defatted, 1oz (28.4g)	5	0	0
1 Cup Not Packed (65g)	10	1	0
Oil Roasted, Blanched, 1oz (24 Whole Kernels) (28.4g)	16	2	0
1 Cup Whole Kernels (142g)	80	8	0
Oil Roasted, Unblanched, 1oz (22 Whole Kernels) (28.4g)	16	2	0
1 Cup Whole Kernels (157g)	91	9	0
Brazilnuts			
1oz (6–8 Kernels) (28.4g)	19	5	0
1 Cup (32 Kernels) (140g)	93	23	0
Cashew Nuts			
Dry Roasted, 1oz (28.4g)	13	3	0
1 Cup Whole and Halves (137g)	64	13	0
Oil Roasted, 1oz (28.4g)	14	3	0
1 Cup Whole and Halves (130g)	63	12	0
Chestnuts			
Boiled and Steamed, 1oz (28.4g)	0	0	0
1 Cup (145g)	2	0	0
Dried, Unpeeled, 1oz (28.4g)	1	0	0
1 Cup (100g)	4	1	0
Fresh, Unpeeled, 1oz (28.4g)	1	0	0
1 Cup (145g)	3	1	0
Roasted, 1oz (28.4g)	1	0	0
1 Cup (143g)	3	1	0
Coconuts			
Cream, Fresh (Liquid Expressed From Grated Meat), 1 tbsp (15g)	5	5	0
1 Cup (240g)	83	74	0
Cream, Tinned, 1 tbsp (19g)	3	3	0
1 Cup (296g)	53	47	0
Meat, Dried (Desiccated), 1oz (28.4g)	18	16	0
3½oz (100g)	65	57	0
Meat, Dried (Desiccated), Creamed, 1oz (28.4g)	20	17	0
3½oz (100g)	69	61	0
Meat, Dried (Desiccated), Flaked, 1oz (28.4g)	9	8	0
1 Cup (77g)	24	22	0
Meat, Dried (Desiccated), Shredded, 1oz (28.4g)	10	9	0

	Total fat (g)	Saturated fat (g)	Cholesterol (mg)
1 Cup (93g)	33	29	0
Meat, Dried (Desiccated), Toasted,			
1oz (28.4g)	13	12	0
3½oz (100g)	47	42	0
Meat, Fresh, 1 Piece (45g)	15	13	0
1 Cup Grated (80g)	27	24	0
Milk, Frozen (Liquid Expressed from Grated			
Meat and Water), 1 Cup (240g)	50	44	0
Milk, Fresh, 1 Cup (240g)	57	51	0
Milk, Tinned, 1 Cup (226g)	48	43	0
Water (Liquid From Coconuts),			
1 Cup (240g)	1	0	0
Filberts – see Hazelnuts, below			
Ginkgo Nuts			
Dried, 1oz (28.4g)	1	0	0
3½oz (100g)	2	0	0
Fresh, 1oz (28.4g)	1	0	0
3½oz (100g)	2	0	0
Tinned, 1oz (14 Medium Kernels) (28.4g)	1	0	0
1 Cup (155g)	3	1	0
Hazelnuts			
Blanched, 1oz (28.4g)	19	1	0
1 Cup Kernels (115g)	67	5	0
Dried, Unblanched, 1oz (28.4g)	18	1	0
1 Cup Chopped Kernels (115g)	72	5	0
Dry Roasted, 1oz (28.4g)	19	1	0
1 Cup Kernels (115g)	66	5	0
Oil Roasted, 1oz (28.4g)	18	1	0
1 Cup Kernels (115g)	64	5	0
Macadamia Nuts			
1oz (28.4g)	21	3	0
1 Cup (134g)	99	15	0
Oil Roasted, 1oz (10–12 Kernels) (28.4g)	22	3	0
1 Cup Whole Or Halves (134g)	103	15	0
Mixed Nuts			
Dry Roasted, 1oz (28.4g)	15	2	0
1 Cup (137g)	71	10	0
Oil Roasted, 1oz (28.4g)	16	3	0
1 Cup (142g)	80	12	0
Peanuts			
1oz (28.4g)	14	2	0
1 Cup (146g)	72	10	0

	Total fat (g)	Saturated fat (g)	Cholesterol (mg)
Oil Roasted, 1oz (28.4g)	14	2	0
1 Cup (144g)	71	10	0
Pecans			
1oz (20 Halves) (28.4g)	19	2	0
1 Cup (Halves) (108g)	73	6	0
Dry Roasted, 1oz (28.4g)	18	2	0
1 Cup (100g)	65	5	0
Oil Roasted, 1oz (15 Halves) (28.4g)	20	2	0
1 Cup (110g)	78	6	0
Pine Nuts			
1oz (28.4g)	17	3	0
3½oz (100g)	61	9	0
Pistachio Nuts			
1oz (47 Kernels) (28.4g)	14	2	0
1 Cup (128g)	62	8	0
Dry Roasted, 1oz (28.4g)	15	2	0
1 Cup (128g)	68	9	0
Soybean Kernels			
Roasted and Toasted, 1oz (95 Kernels) (28.4g)	7	1	0
1 Cup Kernels (108g)	26	3	0
Spanish Peanuts			
Oil Roasted, 1oz (28g)	14	2	0
1 Cup (147g)	72	11	0
Fresh, 1oz (28g)	14	2	0
1 Cup (146g)	72	11	0
Walnuts			
1oz (14 Halves) (28.4g)	18	2	0
1 Cup Pieces (120g)	74	7	0
Oats			
Also see under Cereals; Porridge			
Whole Grain, 1oz (28.4g)	6	4	0
1 Cup (104g)	22	15	1
Offal – See under specific heading, e.g. Beef, Pork, etc			

OIL

	Total fat (g)	Saturated fat (g)	Cholesterol (mg)
Also see under Fat; Margarine			
Almond			
1 tbsp (13.6g)	14	1	0
1 Cup (218g)	218	18	0
Apricot Kernel			
1 tbsp (13.6g)	14	1	0
1 Cup (218g)	218	14	0

	Total fat (g)	Saturated fat (g)	Cholesterol (mg)
Butter Oil			
1 tbsp (12.8g)	13	8	33
1 Cup (205g)	204	127	525
Cocoa Butter			
1 tbsp (13.6g)	14	8	0
1 Cup (218g)	218	130	0
Coconut			
1 tbsp (13.6g)	14	12	0
1 Cup (218g)	218	189	0
Corn			
1 tbsp (13.6g)	14	2	0
1 Cup (218g)	218	28	0
Cottonseed			
1 tbsp (13.6g)	14	4	0
1 Cup (218g)	218	57	0
Ghee			
1 tbsp (12.8g)	13	8	33
1 Cup (205g)	204	127	525
Grapeseed			
1 tbsp (13.6g)	14	1	0
1 Cup (218g)	218	21	0
Hazelnut			
1 tbsp (13.6g)	14	1	0
1 Cup (218g)	218	16	0
Olive			
1 tbsp (13½g)	14	2	0
1 Cup (216g)	216	29	0
Palm			
1 tbsp (13.6g)	14	7	0
1 Cup (218g)	218	108	0
Palm Kernel			
1 tbsp (13.6g)	14	11	0
1 Cup (218g)	218	178	0
Peanut			
1 tbsp (13½g)	14	2	0
1 Cup (216g)	216	37	0
Poppyseed			
1 tbsp (13.6g)	14	2	0
1 Cup (218g)	218	29	0
Rapeseed			
1 tbsp (13.6g)	14	1	0
1 Cup (218g)	218	15	0

	Total fat (g)	Saturated fat (g)	Cholesterol (mg)
Rice Bran			
1 tbsp (13.6g)	14	3	0
1 Cup (218g)	218	43	0
Safflower			
Linoleic (over 70%), 1 tbsp (13.6g)	14	1	0
1 Cup (218g)	218	20	0
Oleic (over 70%), 1 tbsp (13.6g)	14	1	0
1 Cup (218g)	218	13	0
Sesame			
1 tbsp (13.6g)	14	2	0
1 Cup (218g)	218	31	0
Soybean			
1 tbsp (13.6g)	14	2	0
1 Cup (218g)	218	31	0
Hydrogenated, 1 tbsp (13.6g)	14	2	0
1 Cup (218g)	218	33	0
Hydrogenated and Cottonseed,			
1 tbsp (13.6g)	14	2	0
1 Cup (218g)	218	39	0
Lecithin, 1 tbsp (13.6g)	14	2	0
1 Cup (218g)	218	33	0
Sunflower			
Linoleic (60% and over), 1 tbsp (13.6g)	14	1	0
1 Cup (218g)	218	23	0
Linoleic (Hydrogenated),			
1 tbsp (13.6g)	14	2	0
1 Cup (218g)	218	28	0
Walnut			
1 tbsp (13.6g)	14	1	0
1 Cup (218g)	218	20	0
Wheat Germ			
1 tbsp (13.6g)	14	3	0
1 Cup (218g)	218	41	0
Okra			
Boiled, 1 Cup Slices (160g)	0	0	0
Fresh, 1 Cup Slices (100g)	0	0	0
Olives			
Pickled, Tinned or Bottled, Black,			
3½oz (100g)	20	2	0
Pickled, Tinned or Bottled, Green,			
3½oz (100g)	13	1	0

	Total fat (g)	Saturated fat (g)	Cholesterol (mg)
Ripe, Salt-cured, Oil-coated, Greek Style, 3½oz (100g)	36	4	0
Omelette			
Home Recipe, 1-Egg Omelette (64g)	15	7	301
Onion Rings			
Breaded, Partly-fried, Frozen, Heated In Oven, 7 Rings (70g)	19	6	0
Onions			
Boiled, 1 tbsp Chopped (15g)	0	0	0
1 Cup Chopped (210g)	0	0	0
Dehydrated Flakes, 1 tbsp (5g)	0	0	0
¼ Cup (14g)	0	0	0
Fresh, 1 tbsp Chopped (10g)	0	0	0
1 Cup Chopped (160g)	0	0	0
Shallots, Fresh, 3½oz (100g)	0	0	0
Spring, Fresh, 1 tbsp Chopped (6g)	0	0	0
1 Cup Chopped (100g)	0	0	0
Orange and Grapefruit Juice			
Tinned, 1 Cup (247g)	0	0	0
Orange and Apricot Drink			
Tinned, 1 Cup (250g)	0	0	0
Orange Drink			
Tinned, 1 Cup (246g)	0	0	0
From Frozen Concentrate, 1 Cup (248g)	0	0	0
Orange Flavour Drink			
Made with Powder and Water, 1 Cup (246g)	0	0	0
Orange Juice			
From Non-frozen Concentrate, 1 Cup (249g)	1	0	0
Frozen Concentrate, Diluted, 1 Cup (249g)	0	0	0
Frozen Concentrate, Undiluted, 6 Fl.oz Container (213g)	0	0	0
Fresh, Juice From 1 Fruit (86g)	0	0	0
1 Cup (248g)	1	0	0
Tinned, 1 Cup (249g)	0	0	0
Orange Peel			
Candied, 1oz (28g)	0	0	0
Fresh, 1 tbsp (6g)	0	0	0
3½oz (100g)	0	0	0

	Total fat (g)	Saturated fat (g)	Cholesterol (mg)
Oranges			
Mandarin, Fresh, 1 Fruit (84g)	0	0	0
1 Cup Sections (195g)	0	0	0
Navels, Fresh, 1 Fruit (140g)	0	0	0
1 Cup Sections (165g)	0	0	0
Valencias, 1 Fruit (121g)	0	0	0
1 Cup Sections (180g)	1	0	0
Fresh, with Peel, 1 Fruit (159g)	1	0	0
1 Cup Chopped (170g)	1	0	0
Oyster – See under Fish/Shellfish			
Pancakes			
Home Recipe, 1 Cake,			
6-inch Diam (73g)	5	1	39
1 Cake, 4-inch Diam (27g)	2	1	14
Made From Mix, with Egg & Milk,			
1 Cake, 6-inch Diam (73g)	5	2	54
1 Cake, 4-inch Diam (27g)	2	1	20
Papayas			
Fresh, 1 Fruit (304g)	0	0	0
1 Cup Cubed Pieces (140g)	0	0	0
Parsley			
Dried, 1 tbsp (0.4g)	0	0	0
¼ Cup (1.4g)	0	0	0
Fresh, 10 Sprigs (10g)	0	0	0
½ Cup Chopped (30g)	0	0	0
Parsnips			
Boiled, 1 Parsnip (1 Cup Slices) (160g)	1	0	0
Fresh, 1 Cup Slices (133g)	0	0	0
Passion-fruit			
Juice, 1 Cup (247g)	0	0	0
Fresh, 1 Fruit (18g)	0	0	0
Pasta – See under Macaroni; Spaghetti			
Pastrami			
Turkey (Spiced and Smoked),			
2 Slices (56.7g)	4	1	31
Pastry			
Baked, made with Lard,			
1 Flan Case (180g)	60	23	56
Baked, made with Vegetable Shortening,			
1 Flan Case (180g)	60	15	0
Choux, 3oz (85g)	17	6	145
Danish, 1 Pastry (75g)	18	5	48

	Total fat (g)	Saturated fat (g)	Cholesterol (mg)
Fruit Turnover, Home Recipe,			
1 Turnover (40g)	4	1	59
made from Mix, made with Water,			
10-oz Pack (320g)	93	23	0
Unbaked, made with Lard,			
1 Recipe (194g)	60	23	56
Unbaked, made with Vegetable Shortening,			
1 Recipe (194g)	60	15	0
Pâté de Foie Gras			
Tinned, Smoked, 1 tbsp (13g)	6	2	20
1oz (28.35g)	12	4	43
Pâté			
Chicken Liver, Tinned, 1 tbsp (13g)	2	1	51
1oz (28.35g)	4	1	111
Unspecified Type, 1 tbsp (13g)	4	1	33
1oz (28.35g)	8	3	72
Peach Nectar			
Tinned, 1 Cup (249g)	0	0	0
Peaches			
Dried, Stewed, 1 Cup Halves (270g)	1	0	0
Dried, Uncooked, 1 Cup Halves (160g)	1	0	0
Frozen, Sliced, 1 Cup Slices (250g)	0	0	0
Fresh, 1 Fruit (87g)	0	0	0
1 Cup Slices (170g)	0	0	0
Tinned, 1 Cup Halves or Slices (248g)	0	0	0
Peanut Butter			
1 tbsp (16g)	8	2	0
1 Cup (258g)	129	25	0
Peanuts			
Dried, 1oz (28.4g)	14	2	0
1 Cup (146g)	72	10	0
Boiled, 1 Cup (63g)	14	2	0
Dry Roasted, 1oz (28g)	14	2	0
1 Cup (146g)	73	10	0
Oil Roasted, 1oz (28g)	14	2	0
1 Cup (144g)	71	10	0
Fresh, 1oz (28g)	14	2	0
1 Cup (146g)	72	10	0
Pear Nectar			
Tinned, 1 Cup (250g)	0	0	0
Pears			
Candied, 3½oz (100g)	1	0	0

	Total fat (g)	Saturated fat (g)	Cholesterol (mg)
Dried, Stewed, 1 Cup Halves (280g)	1	0	0
Dried, Uncooked, 1 Cup Halves (180g)	1	0	0
Fresh, 1 Fruit (166g)	1	0	0
Tinned, 1 Cup Halves (248g)	0	0	0
Peas and Carrots			
Frozen, Boiled, 1 Cup (160g)	1	0	0
Tinned, 1 Cup (255g)	1	0	0
Peas and Onions			
Frozen, Boiled, 1 Cup (180g)	0	0	0
Tinned, 1 Cup (120g)	1	0	0
Peas			
Edible pod, Boiled, 1 Cup (160g)	0	0	0
Edible pod, Frozen, Boiled, 1 Cup (160g)	1	0	0
Edible pod, Fresh, 1 Cup (145g)	0	0	0
Fresh Green, Boiled, 1 Cup (160g)	0	0	0
Fresh Green, Fresh, 1 Cup (146g)	1	0	0
Green, Tinned, 1 Cup (170g)	1	0	0
1 Tin (313g)	1	0	0
Split, Boiled, 1 Cup (196g)	1	0	0
Split, Fresh, 1 Cup (197g)	2	0	0
Sprouted, Boiled, 3½oz (100g)	1	0	0
Sprouted, Fresh, 1 Cup (120g)	1	0	0
Sweet, Wrinkled, Tinned, 1 Cup (230g)	0	0	0
Peppers			
Chilli, Red, Dried Pods, 3½oz (100g)	9	0	0
Chilli, Red and Green, Fresh, 1 Pepper (45g)	0	0	0
½ Cup Chopped (75g)	0	0	0
Chilli, Red and Green, Tinned, 1 Pepper (73g)	0	0	0
½ Cup Chopped (68g)	0	0	0
Chilli, Red Powder, 1 tsp (2g)	0	0	0
Chilli Sauce, Green, Tinned, 1 Cup (245g)	0	0	0
Chilli Sauce, Red, Tinned, 1 Cup (245g)	2	0	0
Jalapeno, Tinned, 1 Cup Chopped (136g)	1	0	0
Sweet, Red and Green, Boiled, 1 Pepper (73g)	0	0	0
Sweet, Red and Green, Freeze-dried, 1 tbsp (0.4g)	0	0	0
¼ Cup (1.6g)	0	0	0
Sweet, Red and Green, Fresh, 1 Pepper (74g)	0	0	0

	Total fat (g)	Saturated fat (g)	Cholesterol (mg)
Sweet, Red and Green, Tinned, 1 Cup Halves (140g)	0	0	0
Sweet, Stuffed with Minced Beef and Breadcrumbs, 1 Pepper (185g)	10	5	70
Persimmons			
Japanese, Dried, 1 Fruit (34g)	0	0	0
Japanese, Fresh, 1 Fruit (168g)	0	0	0
Pheasant			
Meat and Skin, Raw, 3½oz (100g)	5	2	98
½ Pheasant (400g)	37	11	284
Meat Only, Raw, ½ Pheasant (352g)	13	4	232
Breast, Meat Only, Raw, ½ Breast (182g)	6	2	106
Leg, Meat Only, Raw, 1 Leg (107g)	5	2	86
Giblets, Raw, 3½oz (100g)	5	1	350
Pickles			
Cucumber, Dill, 1 Cup Slices (155g)	0	0	0
Cucumber, Fresh, (Gherkins), 1 Cup Slices (170g)	0	0	0
Cucumber, Sour, 1 Large Pickle (135g)	0	0	0
Cucumber, Sweet, 1 Medium Pickle (35g)	0	0	0
Gherkins, 1 Cup Slices (170g)	0	0	0
Piccalilli, with Cauliflower, Onion and Mustard, Sour, 1 Cup (240g)	3	0	0
Piccalilli, with Cauliflower, Onion and Mustard, Sweet, 1 Cup (245g)	2	0	0
Relish, Finely Cut or Chopped, 1 tbsp (15g)	0	0	0
1 Cup (245g)	2	0	0
PIES			
Apple, made with Lard, 1 Slice (118g)	13	5	13
Apple, made with Vegetable Shortening, 1 Slice (118g)	13	3	0
Apple, Frozen, Baked, 1 Slice (69g)	7	2	0
Bilberry, made with Lard, 1 Slice (118g)	13	5	13
Bilberry, made with Vegetable Shortening, 1 Slice (118g)	13	3	0
Blackberry, made with Lard, 1 Slice (118g)	13	5	13
Blackberry, made with Vegetable Shortening, 1 Slice (118g)	13	3	0
Cherry, made with Lard, 1 Slice (118g)	13	5	13

	Total fat (g)	Saturated fat (g)	Cholesterol (mg)
Cherry, made with Vegetable Shortening, 1 Slice (118g)	13	4	0
Cherry, Frozen, Baked, 1 Slice (73g)	9	2	0
Coconut Custard, made with Lard, 1 Slice (114g)	14	7	123
Coconut Custard, made with Vegetable Shortening, 1 Slice (114g)	14	6	116
Coconut Custard, Frozen, Baked, 1 Slice (75g)	9	4	77
Custard, made with Lard, 1 Slice (114g)	13	5	123
Custard, made with Vegetable Shortening, 1 Slice (114g)	13	4	120
Lemon Chiffon, made with Lard, 1 Slice (81g)	10	4	144
Lemon Chiffon, made with Vegetable Shortening, 1 Slice (81g)	10	3	137
Lemon Meringue, made with Lard, 1 Slice (105g)	11	4	105
Lemon Meringue, made with Vegetable Shortening, 1 Slice (105g)	11	3	98
Mince, made with Lard, 1 Slice (118g)	14	5	13
Mince, made with Vegetable Shortening, 1 Slice (118g)	14	4	1
Peach, made with Lard, 1 Slice (118g)	13	5	13
Peach, made with Vegetable Shortening, 1 Slice (118g)	13	3	0
Pecan, made with Lard, 1 Slice (103g)	24	4	72
Pecan, made with Vegetable Shortening, 1 Slice (103g)	24	3	65
Pineapple Chiffon, made with Lard, 1 Slice (81g)	10	4	129
Pineapple Chiffon, made with Vegetable Shortening, 1 Slice (81g)	10	3	123
Pineapple Custard, made with Lard, 1 Slice (114g)	10	4	70
Pineapple Custard, made with Vegetable Shortening, 1 Slice (114g)	10	3	63
Pineapple, made with Lard, 1 Slice (118g)	13	5	13
Pineapple, made with Vegetable Shortening, 1 Slice (118g)	13	3	0
Pumpkin, made with Lard, 1 Slice (114g)	13	5	74

	Total fat (g)	Saturated fat (g)	Cholesterol (mg)
Pumpkin, made with Vegetable Shortening, 1 Slice (114g)	13	5	70
Raisin, made with Lard, 1 Slice (118g)	13	5	12
Raisin, made with Vegetable Shortening, 1 Slice (118g)	13	3	0
Rhubarb, made with Lard, 1 Slice (118g)	13	5	13
Rhubarb, made with Vegetable Shortening, 1 Slice (118g)	13	3	0
Strawberry, made with Lard, 1 Slice (93g)	7	3	7
Strawberry, made with Vegetable Shortening, 1 Slice (93g)	7	2	0
Sweet Potato, made with Lard, 1 Slice (114g)	13	6	68
Sweet Potato, made with Vegetable Shortening, 1 Slice (114g)	13	5	62
Pigeon			
Meat and Skin, Raw, 1 Pigeon (199g)	47	17	189
Meat Only, Raw, 1 Pigeon (168g)	13	3	151
Breast Meat Only, Raw, 1 Breast (101g)	5	1	91
Giblets, Raw, 3½oz (100g)	7	2	350
Pimientos			
Tinned or Bottled, 4oz Tin or Jar (113g)	1	0	0
Pineapple and Grapefruit Juice			
Tinned, 1 Cup (250g)	0	0	0
Pineapple and Orange Juice			
Tinned, 1 Cup (250g)	0	0	0
Pineapple Juice			
Frozen Concentrate, Diluted, 1 Cup (250g)	0	0	0
Frozen Concentrate, Undiluted, 6 Fl.oz Container (216g)	0	0	0
Tinned, 1 Cup (250g)	0	0	0
Pineapple			
Candied, 8oz Container (227g)	1	0	0
Frozen, Chunks, 1 Cup Chunks (245g)	0	0	0
Fresh, 1 Slice (84g)	0	0	0
1 Cup Pieces (155g)	1	0	0
Tinned, 1 Cup Chunks (250g)	0	0	0
Pistachio Nut			
Dried, 1oz (47 Kernels) (28.4g)	14	2	0
1 Cup (128g)	62	8	0

	Total fat (g)	Saturated fat (g)	Cholesterol (mg)
Pizza			
Cheese Topping, Baked from Home Recipe, 1 Slice (65g)	5	2	12
Cheese Topping, Chilled, Baked, 1 Slice (60g)	4	1	11
Cheese Topping, Frozen, Baked, 1 Slice (57g)	4	2	10
Cheese Topping, Frozen, Baked, 1 Pizza (425g)	28	10	55
4 Mini-pizzas (312g)	21	7	41
Cheese, Ham and Vegetable Topping, Baked, 1 Slice (65g)	4	1	17
Pepperoni and Cheese Topping, Baked, 1 Slice (53g)	5	2	11
Sausage Topping, No Cheese, Baked from Home Recipe, 1 Slice (67g)	6	2	13
Sausage Topping, with Cheese, Baked from Home Recipe, 1 Slice (67g)	9	2	19
Plantain			
Boiled or Stewed, 1 Cup Slices (154g)	0	0	0
Fresh, 1 Cup Slices (148g)	1	0	0
Ploughman's Lunch			
With Cheddar, French Bread, Butter and Pickle Made with 4oz (115g) Cheddar, 3 Pats Butter	52	32	153
Plums			
Fresh, 1 Fruit (66g)	0	0	0
Tinned, 1 Cup (252g)	0	0	0
Poached Egg			
1 Large Egg (50g)	6	2	273
Pomegranate			
Fresh, 1 Fruit (154g)	1	0	0
Popcorn			
Popped, Plain, 1 Cup (6g)	0	0	0
Popped, Sugar Coated, 1 Cup (35g)	1	0	0
Popped, with Butter and Salt Added, 1 Cup (9g)	2	1	4
Popped, with Coconut Oil and Salt Added, 1 Cup (9g)	2	1	0

PORK

Also see under Luncheon Meat

	Total fat (g)	Saturated fat (g)	Cholesterol (mg)
Backfat			
Raw, 1 lb (453.6g)	402	146	259
Bacon			
Cured, Tinned, 3½oz (100g)	72	23	89
Long Back, Grilled, 2 Slices (46½g)	4	1	27
Long Back, Raw, 2 Slices (56.7g)	4	1	28
Streaky, Grilled, Shallow-fried or Roasted, 3 Medium Slices (19g)	9	3	16
Streaky, Raw, 3 Medium Slices (68g)	39	15	46
Top Back, Grilled or Roasted, 3 Raw Slices (34g)	13	4	36
Top Back, Raw, 3 Slices (68g)	25	9	47
Belly Of Pork			
Raw, 1 lb (453.6g)	241	88	327
Blade			
Boneless, Lean and Fat, Roasted, 3oz (85g)	20	7	57
Boneless, Lean and Fat, Raw, 4oz (113g)	25	9	60
Brawn			
Cured, 1 Slice Or 1oz (28.35g)	5	1	23
Brains			
Braised, 3oz (85g)	8	2	2169
Raw, 4oz (113g)	10	2	2480
Bratwurst			
Cooked, 1 Link (85g)	22	8	51
Composite Cuts			
Lean and Fat, Raw, 1 lb (453.6g)	102	37	327
Lean Only, Roasted, 3oz (85g)	11	4	79
Lean Only, Raw, 1 lb (453.6g)	31	11	295
Ears			
Raw, 1 Ear (113g)	17	6	93
Simmered, 1 Ear (111g)	12	4	100
Fat			
Cooked, 1oz (28.35g)	21	8	26
3½oz (100g)	75	27	91
Raw, 1oz (28.35g)	22	8	26
3½oz (100g)	77	28	93
Gammon Steak			
Boneless, Extra Lean, 1 Slice (56.7g)	2	1	26
Gorge			
Raw, 4oz (113g)	79	29	102

	Total fat (g)	Saturated fat (g)	Cholesterol (mg)
Ham			
Also see under Ham (Main Headings)			
Boneless			
Extra Lean (5% Fat), Roasted, 3oz (85g)	5	2	45
Extra Lean (5% Fat), Unheated,			
4oz (113g)	6	2	52
Regular (11% Fat), Roasted, 3oz (85g)	8	3	50
Regular (11% Fat), Unheated,			
4oz (113g)	12	4	64
Centre Slice			
Lean and Fat, Unheated, 4oz (113g)	15	5	60
Lean Only, Raw, 4oz (113g)	9	3	79
Croquette			
1 Croquette (65g)	10	4	46
Cured			
Chopped, 1 Slice (28.35g)	5	2	14
Dry, Long Cure, Lean, 3½oz (100g)	25	9	62
Minced, 1 Slice (28.35g)	6	2	20
Devilled Ham			
Tinned, 4½oz Tin (128g)	41	15	83
1 Cup (225g)	73	26	146
Patties			
Grilled, 1 Patty (59½g)	18	7	43
Unheated, 1 Patty (65.2g)	18	7	46
Tinned			
Extra Lean (4% Fat), Roasted, 3oz (85g)	4	1	26
Extra Lean (4% Fat), Unheated,			
4oz (113g)	5	2	44
Regular (13% Fat), Roasted, 3oz (85g)	13	4	53
Regular (13% Fat), Unheated, 4oz (113g)	15	5	44
Whole			
Lean and Fat, Roasted, 3oz (85g)	14	5	53
Lean and Fat, Unheated, 4oz (113g)	21	8	64
Lean Only, Unheated, 4oz (113g)	6	2	60
Heart			
Braised, 1 Heart (129g)	7	2	285
Raw, 1 Heart (226g)	10	3	296
Jowl			
Raw, 4oz (113g)	79	29	102
Kidneys			
Braised, 3oz (85g)	4	1	408
Raw, 1 Kidney (233g)	8	2	743

	Total fat (g)	Saturated fat (g)	Cholesterol (mg)
Lard			
1 tbsp (12.8g)	13	5	12
1 Cup (205g)	205	80	195
Leaf Fat			
Raw, 1oz (28.35g)	27	13	31
4oz (113g)	106	51	124
Leg			
Fillet End			
Lean and Fat, Roasted, 3oz (85g)	15	5	81
Lean and Fat, Raw, 1 lb (453.6g)	79	28	299
Lean Only, Roasted, 3oz (85g)	9	3	82
Lean Only, Raw, 1 lb (453.6g)	24	8	277
Knuckle End			
Lean and Fat, Roasted, 3oz (85g)	19	7	78
Lean and Fat, Raw, 1 lb (453.6g)	106	38	308
Lean Only, Roasted, 3oz (85g)	9	3	78
Lean Only, Raw, 1 lb (453.6g)	26	9	272
Whole			
Lean and Fat, Roasted, 3oz (85g)	18	6	79
Lean and Fat, Raw, 1 lb (453.6g)	94	34	336
Lean Only, Roasted, 3oz (85g)	9	3	80
Lean Only, Raw, 1 lb (453.6g)	25	9	308
Liver			
Braised, 3oz (85g)	4	1	302
Cured, 1 Slice (28.35g)	7	3	49
Fried, 3oz Slice (85g)	10	3	372
Raw, 4oz (113g)	4	1	340
Luncheon Meat			
Cured, Tinned, 1 Slice (28.35g)	9	3	18
Loin Chops			
Blade			
Lean and Fat, Braised, 1 Chop (67g)	23	8	72
Lean and Fat, Grilled, 1 Chop (77g)	26	9	76
Lean and Fat, Roasted, 1 Chop (88g)	27	10	79
Lean and Fat, Shallow-fried, 1 Chop (89g)	33	12	85
Lean and Fat, Raw, 1 Chop (110g)	31	11	79
1 lb (453.6g)	130	47	327
Lean Only, Braised, 1 Chop (50g)	10	4	57
Lean Only, Grilled, 1 Chop (59g)	13	4	59
Lean Only, Roasted, 1 Chop (71g)	14	5	63
Lean Only, Shallow-fried, 1 Chop (62g)	12	4	60
Lean Only, Raw, 1 Chop (82g)	9	3	53

	Total fat (g)	Saturated fat (g)	Cholesterol (mg)
1 lb (453.6g)	50	17	290
Centre Loin			
Lean and Fat, Braised, 1 Chop (75g)	19	7	80
Lean and Fat, Grilled, 1 Chop (87g)	19	7	84
Lean and Fat, Roasted, 1 Chop (88g)	19	7	80
Lean and Fat, Shallow-fried, 1 Chop (89g)	27	10	92
Lean and Fat, Raw, 1 Chop (124g)	27	10	87
1 lb (453.6g)	99	36	318
Lean Only, Braised, 1 Chop (61g)	8	3	68
Lean Only, Grilled, 1 Chop (72g)	8	3	71
Lean Only, Roasted, 1 Chop (75g)	10	3	68
Lean Only, Shallow-fried, 1 Chop (67g)	11	4	72
Lean Only, Raw, 1 Chop (98g)	7	2	62
1 lb (453.6g)	32	11	286
Fore Loin			
Lean and Fat, Braised, 1 Chop (67g)	18	7	64
Lean and Fat, Grilled, 1 Chop (77g)	20	7	72
Lean and Fat, Roasted, 1 Chop (79g)	19	7	64
Lean and Fat, Shallow-fried, 1 Chop (89g)	29	11	74
Lean and Fat, Raw, 1 Chop (112g)	26	10	72
1 lb (453.6g)	106	38	290
Lean Only, Braised, 1 Chop (53g)	8	3	51
Lean Only, Grilled, 1 Chop (63g)	9	3	59
Lean Only, Roasted, 1 Chop (66g)	9	3	52
Lean Only, Shallow-fried, 1 Chop (62g)	10	3	50
Lean Only, Raw, 1 Chop (86g)	7	2	47
1 lb (453.6g)	34	12	250
Hind Loin			
Lean and Fat, Braised, 1 Chop (71g)	18	7	75
Lean and Fat, Grilled, 1 Chop (84g)	21	8	82
Lean and Fat, Roasted, 1 Chop (84g)	17	6	76
Lean and Fat, Raw, 1 Chop (119g)	27	10	83
1 lb (453.6g)	101	37	318
Lean Only, Braised, 1 Chop (57g)	7	3	63
Lean Only, Grilled, 1 Chop (68g)	9	3	67
Lean Only, Roasted, 1 Chop (74g)	10	3	67
Lean Only, Raw, 1 Chop (92g)	6	2	58
1 lb (453.6g)	31	11	286
Tenderloin			
Lean Only, Raw, 4oz (113g)	3	1	72
Lean Only, Roasted, 3oz (85g)	4	1	79

	Total fat (g)	Saturated fat (g)	Cholesterol (mg)
Top Loin			
Lean and Fat, Braised, 1 Chop (70g)	20	7	67
Lean and Fat, Grilled, 1 Chop (82g)	24	9	76
Lean and Fat, Roasted, 1 Chop (83g)	21	8	68
Lean and Fat, Shallow-fried, 1 Chop (89g)	29	10	72
Lean and Fat, Raw, 1 Chop (118g)	30	11	77
1 lb (453.6g)	116	42	295
Lean Only, Braised, 1 Chop (53g)	8	3	51
Lean Only, Grilled, 1 Chop (64g)	10	3	60
Lean Only, Roasted, 1 Chop (68g)	9	3	54
Lean Only, Shallow-fried, 1 Chop (61g)	9	3	49
Lean Only, Raw, 1 Chop (88g)	7	2	48
1 lb (453.6g)	34	12	250
Whole Loin			
Lean and Fat, Braised, 1 Chop (71g)	20	7	72
Lean and Fat, Grilled, 1 Chop (82g)	22	8	77
Lean and Fat, Roasted, 1 Chop (82g)	20	7	74
Lean and Fat, Raw, 1 Chop (119g)	29	10	81
1 lb (453.6g)	110	40	308
Lean Only, Braised, 1 Chop (55g)	8	3	58
Lean Only, Grilled, 1 Chop (66g)	10	4	63
Lean Only, Roasted, 1 Chop (69g)	10	3	62
Lean Only, Raw, 1 Chop (91g)	7	2	55
1 lb (453.6g)	34	12	272
Lungs			
Braised, 3oz (85g)	3	1	329
Raw, 3½oz (98g)	3	1	314
Pancreas			
Braised, 3oz (85g)	9	3	268
Raw, 4oz (113g)	15	5	218
Pork Pie			
¼ Medium Pie (170g)	72	27	206
Pork Pie Filling			
Raw, 8oz (227g)	60	22	175
Pork Scratchings			
Simmered, 3oz (85g)	24	9	122
Raw, 1oz (28.35g)	7	2	45
Salami			
Dry or Hard, 1 Slice (10g)	3	1	8
1 Package, Net Weight 4oz (113g)	38	13	89
Salt Pork			
Raw, 8oz (227g)	183	67	195

	Total fat (g)	Saturated fat (g)	Cholesterol (mg)
Sausage (Pork)			
Also see under Sausages (Main Headings)			
Brawn			
Cured, 1 Slice Or 1oz (28.35g)	5	1	23
Bratwurst			
Cooked, 1 Link (85g)	22	8	51
Italian Sausage			
Grilled, 1 Link (67g)	17	6	52
1 Link (83g)	21	8	65
Raw, 1 Link (91g)	29	10	69
1 Link (113g)	35	13	86
Liver Sausage			
1 Slice (28.35g)	8	3	45
Polish Sausage			
1oz (28.35g)	8	3	20
1 Sausage (227g)	65	23	159
Salami			
Dry or Hard, 1 Slice (10g)	3	1	8
1 Package, Net Weight 4oz (113g)	38	13	89
Sausage Meat			
Cooked, 1 Patty (27g)	8	3	22
1 Link (13g)	4	1	11
Raw, 1 Patty (57g)	23	8	39
1 Link (28g)	11	4	19
Sausage Roll			
1 Sausage Roll (55g)	18	7	17
Sausages			
Tinned, Drained Solids, 1 Sausage (12g)	4	1	11
Tinned, Solids and Liquid, 8oz Tin (approx 16 Sausages) (227g)	87	31	152
Smoked Link Sausage			
Grilled, 1 Link (68g)	22	8	46
1 Little Link (16g)	5	2	11
Shoulder			
Arm Picnic			
Lean and Fat, Roasted, 3oz (85g)	18	7	49
Lean Only, Roasted, 3oz (85g)	6	2	41
Blade			
Lean and Fat, Braised, 1 Steak (160g)	46	17	178
Lean and Fat, Grilled, 1 Steak (185g)	53	19	191
Lean and Fat, Roasted, 1 Steak (185g)	47	17	180

	Total fat (g)	Saturated fat (g)	Cholesterol (mg)
Lean and Fat, Raw, 1 Steak (264g)	62	22	193
1 lb (453.6g)	106	38	331
Lean Only, Braised, 1 Steak (130g)	23	8	151
Lean Only, Grilled, 1 Steak (151g)	28	10	159
Lean Only, Roasted, 1 Steak (158g)	27	9	155
Lean Only, Raw, 1 Steak (210g)	20	7	143
1 lb (453.6g)	42	15	308
Picnic Shoulder			
Lean and Fat, Braised, 3oz (85g)	22	8	93
Lean and Fat, Roasted, 3oz (85g)	22	8	80
Lean and Fat, Raw, 1 lb (453.6g)	101	36	327
Lean Only, Braised, 3oz (85g)	10	4	97
Lean Only, Roasted, 3oz (85g)	11	4	81
Lean Only, Raw, 1 lb (453.6g)	28	10	295
Whole			
Lean and Fat, Roasted, 3oz (85g)	22	8	82
Lean and Fat, Raw, 1 lb (453.6g)	104	37	327
Lean Only, Roasted, 3oz (85g)	13	4	83
Lean Only, Raw, 1 lb (453.6g)	36	12	304
Spareribs			
Lean and Fat, Braised, 3oz (85g)	26	10	103
Lean and Fat, Raw, 1 lb (453.6g)	107	42	354
In Barbeque Sauce, 1 Serving (350g)	35	12	121
Spleen			
Braised, 3oz (85g)	3	1	428
Raw, 4oz (113g)	3	1	410
Stomach			
Raw, 4oz (113g)	11	4	218
Tail			
Raw, 4oz (113g)	38	13	110
Simmered, 3oz (85g)	30	11	110
Tongue			
Braised, 3oz (85g)	16	6	124
Raw, 4oz (113g)	19	7	114
Trotters			
Pickled, 3oz (100g)	16	6	92
1 lb (453.6g)	73	25	417
Simmered, ½ Trotter (71g)	9	3	71
Raw, ½ Trotter (95g)	18	6	101
Porridge			
Made with ½ Milk ½ Water, 1 Serving (235g)	5	1	3

	Total fat (g)	Saturated fat (g)	Cholesterol (mg)
Made with Skimmed Milk,			
1 Serving (235g)	6	1	6
Made with Water, 1 Serving (235g)	5	1	0
Made with Whole Milk,			
1 Serving (235g)	17	9	50
Potato Crisps			
1oz Packet (28.4g)	10	3	0
Potato Pancakes			
Home-prepared, 1 Pancake (76g)	13	3	94
Potato Salad			
1 Cup (250g)	21	4	170
Potato Sticks			
1oz Packet (28.4g)	10	3	0

POTATOES

Au Gratin			
Home-prepared using Butter,			
1 Cup (245g)	19	12	56
Home-prepared using Margarine,			
1 Cup (245g)	19	9	37
Baked			
Flesh, 1 Medium Potato (156g)	0	0	0
Flesh and Skin, 1 Medium Potato (202g)	0	0	0
Skin, Skin from 1 Potato (58g)	0	0	0
With Baked Beans, 1 Medium with			
½ Tin (220g) Baked Beans	1	0	0
With Butter, 1 Medium with 1 Pat Butter	4	3	11
With Cottage Cheese, 1 Medium with			
½ Cup Low Fat Cottage Cheese	2	1	10
With Grated Cheese, 1 Medium with			
1 Pat Butter, 55g Cheddar	23	15	71
With Sour Cream and Chives,			
1 Medium Potato with 2 tbsp			
Sour Cream (302g)	22	10	23
Boiled			
Skin and Flesh, 1 Medium Potato (136g)	0	0	0
Chips			
Frozen, Heated in Oven, 1 Cup (50g)	9	4	0
Frozen, Fried in Animal Fat and Vegetable			
Oil, 1 Cup (57g)	9	4	7
Frozen, Fried in Vegetable Oil,			
1 Cup (57g)	9	3	0

	Total fat (g)	Saturated fat (g)	Cholesterol (mg)
Crisps			
1oz Packet (28.4g)	10	3	0
Hash Brown			
Frozen, Plain, 3½oz (100g)	12	4	3
Frozen, with Butter Sauce, 3½oz (100g)	9	3	23
Home Recipe, 1 Cup (156g)	22	9	0
Mashed			
Dehydrated Flakes without Milk, Dry Form, 1 Cup (200g)	1	0	0
Dehydrated Flakes without Milk, made with Whole Milk and Butter, 1 Cup (210g)	12	7	29
Dehydrated Flakes, without Milk, made with Whole Milk and Margarine, 1 Cup (210g)	12	3	8
Dehydrated Flakes with Milk, Dry Form, 1 Cup (200g)	2	1	4
Dehydrated Flakes with Milk, made with Water and Margarine, 1 Cup (210g)	5	1	4
Home Recipe, made with Whole Milk, 1 Cup (210g)	1	1	4
Home Recipe, made with Whole Milk and Butter, 1 Cup (210g)	9	6	25
Home Recipe, made with Whole Milk and Margarine, 1 Cup (210g)	9	2	4
Microwaved			
Flesh Only, 1 Medium Potato (156g)	0	0	0
Flesh and Skin, 1 Medium Potato (202g)	0	0	0
Skin Only, Skin from 1 Potato (58g)	0	0	0
O'Brien (milk, onions, peppers, bread crumbs, butter)			
Frozen, Prepared, 3½oz (100g)	13	3	23
Home Recipe, 1 Cup (194g)	3	2	8
Salad			
1 Cup (285g)	17	3	171
Scalloped			
Home Recipe, made with Butter, 1 Cup (245g)	9	6	29
Home Recipe, made with Margarine, 1 Cup (245g)	9	3	15
Tinned			
Drained Solids, 1 Cup (180g)	0	0	0
Solids and Liquid, 1 Cup Whole (300g)	1	0	0
1 Tin (454g)	1	0	0

	Total fat (g)	Saturated fat (g)	Cholesterol (mg)
Uncooked			
Flesh, 1 Medium Potato (112g)	0	0	0
Skin, Skin from 1 Potato (38g)	0	0	0
Potted Meat			
Variety of Meats, 5½oz Tin (156g)	30	14	122
1 Cup (225g)	43	20	176
Poultry – See under specific name of bird			
Pretzels			
1 Pretzel (16g)	1	0	0
1 Cup (106g)	5	1	0
Prickly Pear			
Fresh, 1 Fruit (103g)	1	0	0
Prune Juice			
Tinned, 1 Cup (256g)	0	0	0
Prunes			
Dried, Stewed, 1 Cup, without Pits (238g)	1	0	0
Dried, Uncooked, 1 Cup, without Pits (161g)	1	0	0
Tinned, 1 Cup (234g)	1	0	0

PUDDINGS

	Total fat (g)	Saturated fat (g)	Cholesterol (mg)
Blancmange			
Home Recipe, 1 Cup (255g)	10	6	36
Bread and Butter Pudding			
1 Serving (170g)	29	7	170
Bread Pudding			
With Raisins, 1 Cup (265g)	16	8	180
Chocolate Pudding			
With Milk and Starch Base Mix, Cooked, 1 Cup (260g)	8	4	31
Home Recipe, 1 Cup (260g)	12	7	29
Christmas Pudding, 1 Serving (170g)	81	9	102
Cream Pudding, 1 Cup (165g)	8	4	160
Custard Dessert			
Made with Milk and Vegetable-gum Base Mix, Cooked, 3½oz (100g)	4	2	12
Instant Pudding			
Made with Milk and Starch Base Mix, without Cooking, 1 Cup (260g)	7	4	29
Rice Pudding			
With Raisins, 1 Cup (265g)	8	5	29

	Total fat (g)	Saturated fat (g)	Cholesterol (mg)
Sponge Pudding			
1 Serving (115g)	19	7	92
Suet Pudding			
1 Serving (85g)	15	9	3
Tapioca Dessert			
1 Cup (165g)	8	4	160
Trifle, 1 Serving (285g)	17	8	143
Turnover			
Home Recipe, 1 Turnover (40g)	4	1	59
Vanilla Pudding			
Home Recipe, 1 Cup (255g)	10	6	36
Pumpkin			
Boiled, 1 Cup Mashed (245g)	0	0	0
Fresh, 1 Cup, 1-inch Cubes (116g)	0	0	0
Tinned, 1 Cup (245g)	1	0	0
Flowers, Boiled, 1 Cup (134g)	0	0	0
Flowers, Fresh, 1 Cup (33g)	0	0	0
Purslane			
Boiled, 1 Cup (115g)	0	0	0
Fresh, 1 Cup (43g)	0	0	0
Quail			
Meat and Skin, Raw, 1 Quail (109g)	13	4	83
Meat Only, Raw, 1 Quail (92g)	4	1	64
Breast, Meat Only, Raw, 1 Breast (56g)	2	1	33
Giblets, Raw, 3½oz (100g)	6	2	350
Quiche Lorraine			
Home Recipe, 1 Slice (115g)	32	14	150
Quince			
Fresh, 1 Fruit (92g)	0	0	0
Rabbit			
Domesticated, Flesh Only, Stewed,			
1 Cup Chopped (140g)	14	6	127
Domesticated, Flesh Only, Raw,			
3½oz (100g)	8	3	65
Wild, Flesh Only, Raw, 3½oz (100g)	5	2	65
Radish Seeds			
Sprouted, Fresh, 1 Cup (38g)	1	0	0
Radishes			
Oriental, Boiled, 1 Cup Slices (147g)	0	0	0
Oriental, Dried, 1 Cup (116g)	1	0	0
Oriental, Fresh, 1 Radish,			
7-inch Long (338g)	0	0	0

	Total fat (g)	Saturated fat (g)	Cholesterol (mg)
Fresh, 10 Radishes (45g)	0	0	0
White Icicle, Fresh, 1 Radish (100g)	0	0	0
Raisins			
Golden Seedless, 1 Cup Packed (165g)	1	0	0
Seeded, 1 Cup Packed (165g)	1	0	0
Seedless, 1 Cup Packed (165g)	1	0	0
Raspberries			
Frozen, 1 Cup (250g)	0	0	0
Fresh, 1 Cup (123g)	1	0	0
Tinned, 1 Cup (256g)	0	0	0
Rhubarb			
Cooked, 1 Cup (240g)	0	0	0

RICE

	Total fat (g)	Saturated fat (g)	Cholesterol (mg)
Basmati			
Cooked, 1 Cup, Hot (175g)	0	0	0
Bran			
3½oz (100g)	16	3	0
Bran Polish			
1 Cup (105g)	13	2	0
Brown			
Cooked, 1 Cup, Hot (195g)	1	0	0
Raw, 1 Cup (185g)	4	0	0
Rice Pudding			
With Raisins, 1 Cup (265g)	8	5	29
White			
Glutinous, (Mochi Gomi), Raw, 3½oz (100g)	1	0	0
Polished, Cooked, 1 Cup, Hot (205g)	0	0	0
Polished, Raw, 1 Cup (185g)	1	0	0
Pre-cooked Instant, Dry, 1 Cup (95g)	0	0	0
Wild			
Raw, 1 Cup (160g)	1	0	0
Roast Beef			
Home Recipe, 1 Portion	26	11	72
Roast Chicken			
Home Recipe, 1 Portion (235g)	31	9	221
Roast Leg of Lamb			
Home Recipe, 3½oz (100g)	24	13	98
Roast Shoulder of Lamb			
Home Recipe, 3½oz (100g)	32	18	98

	Total fat (g)	Saturated fat (g)	Cholesterol (mg)
Rock Cakes			
1 Cake (55g)	9	3	22
Rolls – See under Bread			
Roselle			
Fresh, 1 Cup (57g)	0	0	0
Rusk			
Hard Crisp Bread or Toast,			
1 Rusk (9g)	1	0	1
13 Rusks (113g)	10	3	10
Rye Crispbread			
Wholegrain, 10 Wafers (65g)	1	0	1
8oz Package (227g)	3	0	2
Rye			
Wholegrain, 3½oz (100g)	2	0	0
SALADS			
Chef's Salad			
(Mixed Vegetables with Turkey, Ham and Cheese, without Dressing)			
1½ Cups (326g)	16	8	139
Coleslaw			
1 Cup (138g)	15	2	7
Fruit Salad			
1 Cup (249g)	0	0	0
Lobster Salad			
½ Cup (260g)	17	3	120
Mixed Salad			
Without Dressing,			
1½ Cups (207g)	0	0	0
With Cheese and Egg, without Dressing			
1½ Cups (217g)	6	3	98
With Chicken, without Dressing			
1½ Cups (218g)	2	1	72
With Pasta and Seafood, without Dressing			
1½ Cups (417g)	21	3	50
With Shrimp, without Dressing			
1½ Cups (236g)	2	1	180
Potato Salad			
1 Cup (285g)	17	3	171
Tuna Salad			
3oz (85g)	8	1	11
1 Cup (205g)	19	3	27

	Total fat (g)	Saturated fat (g)	Cholesterol (mg)

SALAD DRESSING

Blue Cheese

Low-fat, 1 Calorie/tsp, 1 tbsp (15g)	0	0	0
1 Cup (245g)	3	3	0
Low-fat, 5 Calories/tsp, 1 tbsp (16g)	1	1	0
1 Cup (255g)	15	8	0
Regular, 3½oz (100g)	52	10	17

French Dressing

Commercial, Regular, 1 tbsp (15.6g)	6	2	9
1 Cup (250g)	103	24	145
Low-fat, 1 Calorie/tsp, 3½oz (100g)	0	0	0
Low-fat, 5 Calories/tsp, 1 tbsp (16.3g)	1	0	1
1 Cup (260g)	15	2	16
Home Recipe, 1 tbsp (14.0g)	10	2	0
1 Cup (220g)	154	28	0

Italian Dressing

Low-fat, 2 Calories/tsp, 1 tbsp (15.0g)	2	0	1
1 Cup (240g)	24	3	14
Regular, 1 tbsp (14.7g)	7	1	0
1 Cup (235g)	114	17	0

Mayonnaise

Imitation, made with Milk Cream, 1 tbsp (15.0g)	1	0	7
1 Cup (240g)	12	7	103
Imitation, made with Egg and Soybean Oil, 1 tbsp (15.0g)	3	1	4
1 Cup (240g)	46	8	58
Imitation, made without Egg or Milk, made with Soybean Oil, 1 tbsp (14.0g)	7	1	0
1 Cup (225g)	107	17	0
Made with Egg and Soybean and Safflower Oil, 1 tbsp (13.8g)	11	1	8
1 Cup (220g)	175	19	130
Made with Egg and Soybean Oil, 1 tbsp (13.8g)	11	2	8
1 Cup (220g)	175	26	130

Roquefort Dressing

Low-fat, 1 Calorie/tsp, 1 tbsp (15g)	0	0	0
1 Cup (245g)	3	3	0
Low-fat, 5 Calories/tsp, 1 tbsp (16g)	1	1	0
1 Cup (255g)	15	8	0

	Total fat (g)	Saturated fat (g)	Cholesterol (mg)
Regular, 3½oz (100g)	52	10	17
Russian Dressing			
Low-calorie, 1 tbsp (16.3g)	1	0	1
1 Cup (260g)	10	2	16
Regular, 1 tbsp (15.3g)	8	1	3
1 Cup (245g)	125	18	44
Salad Cream			
Low-calorie, 8 Calories/tsp,			
1 tbsp (16g)	2	0	8
1 Cup (250g)	32	6	125
Regular, 1 tbsp (15g)	6	1	8
1 Cup (235g)	99	18	118
Sesame Seed Dressing			
1 tbsp (15.3g)	7	1	0
1 Cup (245g)	111	15	0
Thousand Island Dressing			
Low-calorie, 10 Calories/tsp,			
1 tbsp (15.3g)	2	0	2
1 Cup (245g)	26	4	37
Regular, 1 tbsp (15.6g)	6	1	4
1 Cup (250g)	89	15	65
Vinaigrette			
Home Recipe, 1 tbsp (15.6g)	8	1	0
1 Cup (250g)	125	23	0
Salami			
Bierwurst, 1 Slice (23g)	7	3	14
Pork, 1 Slice (10g)	3	1	8
Smoked, 1 Slice (28.35g)	6	3	18
Turkey, Cooked,			
1 Slice (28.4g)	4	1	23
Salsify			
Boiled, 1 Cup Slices (135g)	0	0	0
Fresh, 1 Cup Slices (133g)	0	0	0
Salt			
Table, 1 tsp (5½g)	0	0	0
Sandwich Spread			
Pork and Beef, 1 tbsp (15g)	3	1	6
1oz (28.35g)	5	2	11
With Chopped Pickle, Unspecified Oils,			
1 tbsp (15.3g)	5	1	12
1 Cup (245g)	83	13	186

	Total fat (g)	Saturated fat (g)	Cholesterol (mg)

SANDWICHES

Also see under Bread

Bacon
   1 Sandwich (74g)

| | 15 | 6 | 28 |

BLT (Bacon, Lettuce and Tomato)
   1 Sandwich (100g)

| | 23 | 9 | 50 |

Cheese and Tomato
   1 Sandwich (100g)

| | 25 | 15 | 71 |

Chicken
   Plain, 1 Sandwich (182g)

| | 29 | 9 | 60 |

Chicken and Cheese
   1 Sandwich (228g)

| | 39 | 12 | 76 |

Egg and Cheese
   1 Sandwich (156g)

| | 19 | 7 | 291 |

Egg Salad
   1 Sandwich (153g)

| | 24 | 8 | 264 |

Fish
   With Tartar Sauce,
     1 Sandwich (158g)

| | 23 | 5 | 55 |

   With Tartar Sauce and Cheese,
     1 Sandwich (183g)

| | 29 | 8 | 68 |

Ham
   1 Sandwich (113g)

| | 12 | 5 | 43 |

Ham and Cheese
   1 Sandwich (146g)

| | 15 | 6 | 58 |

Ham, Egg and Cheese
   1 Sandwich (143g)

| | 16 | 7 | 245 |

Ploughman's Lunch, with Cheese,
   French Bread, Butter and Pickle
   Made with 4oz (115g) Cheddar,
   3 Pats Butter

| | 52 | 32 | 153 |

Roast Beef
   Plain, 1 Sandwich (139g)

| | 14 | 4 | 52 |

Roast Beef and Cheese
   1 Sandwich (176g)

| | 18 | 9 | 77 |

Tuna
   1 Regular

| | 13 | 4 | 26 |

Sapodilla
   Fresh, 1 Fruit (170g)

| | 2 | 0 | 0 |

	Total fat (g)	Saturated fat (g)	Cholesterol (mg)

SAUCES

Barbecue

1 Cup (250g)	5	1	0

Bearnaise

Made with Milk and Butter, 1 Cup (254.8g)	68	42	189

Bechamel

Home Recipe, made with Butter, 1 Cup (255g)	24	7	145
Home Recipe, made with Margarine, 1 Cup (255g)	24	4	0

Cheese

Made with Milk, 1 Cup (279.2g)	17	9	53

Chilli

Bottled, 1 tbsp (15g)	0	0	0
1 Cup (273g)	1	0	0

Curry

Made with Milk, 1 Cup (272.3g)	15	6	35

Guava Sauce

1 Cup (238g)	0	0	0

Hollandaise

Dry Mix with Butterfat, made with Water, 1 Cup (259.2g)	20	12	52
Dry Mix with Vegetable Oil, made with Milk and Butter, 1 Cup (254.8g)	68	42	189

Mushroom

Dry Mix made with Milk, 1 Cup (266.7g)	10	5	35

Soubise

Home Recipe, 1 Cup (255g)	24	7	145

Sour Cream

Dry Mix made with Milk, 1 Cup (314.4g)	30	16	91

Soy

1 tbsp (18g)	0	0	0
1 Fl.oz (36g)	0	0	0

Spaghetti Sauce with Mushrooms

1 Cup (200g)	4	2	11

Stroganoff

Dry Mix made with Milk and Water, 1 Cup (296g)	11	7	39

	Total fat (g)	Saturated fat (g)	Cholesterol (mg)
Sweet and Sour			
Made with Water and Vinegar, 1 Cup (313.3g)	0	0	0
Tartar			
Low-calorie, 10 Calories/tsp, 1 tbsp (14g)	3	1	7
Regular, 1 tbsp (14g)	8	2	7
1 Cup (230g)	133	25	117
Teriyaki			
Dry Mix made with Water, 1 Cup (283g)	1	0	0
Ready-to-serve, 1 tbsp (18g)	0	0	0
1 Fl.oz (36g)	0	0	0
Tomato Ketchup			
Bottled, 1 tbsp (15g)	0	0	0
1 Cup (273g)	1	0	0
White			
Medium, 1 Cup (250g)	31	17	103
Thick, 1 Cup (250g)	39	21	125
Thin, 1 Cup (250g)	22	12	70
Dry Mix made with Milk, 1 Cup (263.8g)	14	6	34
Sauerkraut			
Juice, Tinned, 1 Cup (242g)	0	0	0
15oz Tin (453g)	0	0	0
Tinned, 1 Cup (236g)	0	0	0
Sausage Roll			
1 Sausage Roll (55g)	18	7	17
SAUSAGES			
Beerwurst			
Beef, 1 Slice (23g)	7	3	14
Pork, 1 Slice (23g)	4	1	14
Berliner			
1 Slice (28.35g)	5	2	13
Black Pudding (Blood Sausage)			
1 Slice (28.35g)	10	4	34
Bockwurst			
1oz (28.35g)	8	3	17
1 Link (65g)	18	7	38
Bologna			
Beef, 1 Slice (28.35g)	8	3	16
Beef and Pork, 1 Slice (28.35g)	8	3	16
Pork, 1 Slice (28.35g)	6	2	17

	Total fat (g)	Saturated fat (g)	Cholesterol (mg)
Turkey, 1 Slice (28.35g)	4	1	28
Bratwurst			
1oz (28.35g)	7	3	17
1 Link (85g)	22	8	51
Braunschweiger			
Smoked, 1 Slice (28.35g)	9	3	44
Brawn			
1 Slice (28.35g)	5	1	23
Brotwurst			
1oz (28.35g)	8	3	18
1 Link (70g)	20	7	44
Capicola or Capacola			
1 Slice (21g)	10	4	14
Cervelas			
Dry, 4 Slices (12g)	5	2	8
Chorizo			
1oz (28.35g)	11	4	25
1 Link (60g)	23	9	53
Italian			
Cooked, 1 Link (83g)	21	8	65
Raw, 1 Link (113g)	35	13	86
Kielbasa (Kolbassy)			
1 Slice (28.35g)	8	3	19
Knackwurst			
1oz (28.35g)	8	3	16
1 Link (68g)	19	7	39
Liver Pudding			
1 Slice (28.35g)	7	3	49
Liver Sausage			
Smoked, 1 Slice (28.35g)	9	3	44
Liverwurst			
Raw, 1 Slice (28.35g)	8	3	45
Luncheon Type			
1 Slice (28.35g)	6	2	18
Meatless (Vegetarian)			
1 Link (25g)	5	1	0
Mortadella			
1 Slice (15g)	4	1	8
2 Slices (28.35g)	7	3	16
Pepperoni			
1 Slice (5½g)	2	1	4
1 Sausage (251g)	110	41	198

	Total fat (g)	Saturated fat (g)	Cholesterol (mg)
Polish			
1 Slice (28.35g)	8	3	19
Polish-style			
1oz (28.35g)	8	3	20
1 Sausage (227g)	65	23	159
Pork and Beef			
1 Link (27g)	10	4	19
Pork Sausage Meat			
Cooked, 1 Link (27g)	8	3	22
Raw, 1 Link (57g)	23	8	39
Salami			
Beef and Pork, Cooked, 1 Slice (28.35g)	6	2	18
Beef and Pork, Dry, 1 Slice (10g)	3	1	8
Beef, Cooked, 1 Slice (28.35g)	6	3	18
Pork, Dry, 1 Slice (10g)	3	1	8
Smoked Sausage			
Pork, 1 Small Link (16g)	5	2	11
1 Large Link (68g)	22	8	46
Pork and Beef, 1 Small Link (16g)	5	2	11
1 Large Link (68g)	21	7	48
Thuringer			
1 Slice (28.35g)	8	3	21
Vienna			
Tinned, 1 Sausage (16g)	4	2	8
7 Sausages (113g)	29	11	59
Scone Dough			
Frozen, 3½oz (100g)	12	3	0
Scone Mix			
Dry Mix, 1 Cup (128g)	16	4	0
Scones			
From Dry Mix, made with Milk, 1 Scone (28g)	3	1	0
Home Recipe, made with Lard, 1 Scone (28g)	5	2	5
Home Recipe, made with Vegetable Shortening, 1 Scone (28g)	5	1	0
Scotch Egg			
1 Scotch Egg (115g)	24	9	253
Scotch Pancakes			
4 Pancakes (170g)	69	8	85

	Total fat (g)	Saturated fat (g)	Cholesterol (mg)
Scrambled Eggs			
1 Large Egg (64g)	7	3	248
1 Cup (220g)	24	10	854
Seaweed			
Agar, Dried, 3½oz (100g)	0	0	0
Agar, Fresh, 3½oz (100g)	0	0	0
Dulse, Fresh, 3½oz (100g)	3	0	0
Irishmoss, Fresh, 3½oz (100g)	0	0	0
Kelp, Fresh, 3½oz (100g)	1	0	0
Laver, Fresh, 3½oz (100g)	0	0	0
Spirulina, Dried, 3½oz (100g)	8	3	0
Spirulina, Fresh, 3½oz (100g)	0	0	0
Wakame, Fresh, 3½oz (100g)	1	0	0

SEEDS AND SEED PRODUCTS

Also see under Nuts; Spices

	Total fat (g)	Saturated fat (g)	Cholesterol (mg)
Breadfruit Seeds			
Boiled, 1oz (28.4g)	1	0	0
Fresh, 1oz (28.4g)	2	0	0
Roasted, 1oz (28.4g)	1	0	0
Cottonseed Kernels			
Roasted, 1 tbsp (10g)	4	1	0
1 Cup (149g)	54	15	0
Cottonseed Meal			
Partially Defatted, 1oz (28.4g)	1	0	0
3½oz (100g)	5	1	0
Lotus Seeds			
Dried, 1oz (28.4g)	1	0	0
1 Cup (32g)	1	0	0
Fresh, 1oz (28.4g)	0	0	0
Mustard Seeds			
Whole, Dried, 1oz (28.4g)	1	0	0
1 Cup (74g)	3	1	0
Pumpkin and Squash Seeds			
Kernels, Dried, 1oz (28.4g)	13	3	0
1 Cup (138g)	63	12	0
Kernels, Roasted, 1oz (28.4g)	12	2	0
1 Cup (227g)	96	18	0
Whole, Roasted, 1oz (28.4g)	6	1	0
1 Cup (64g)	12	2	0
Safflower Seed Kernels			
Dried, 1oz (28.4g)	11	1	0

	Total fat (g)	Saturated fat (g)	Cholesterol (mg)
Safflower Seed Meal			
Partially Defatted, 1oz (28.4g)	1	0	0
Sesame, Tahini			
From Fresh and Stone Ground Kernels, 1oz (28.4g)	14	2	0
From Roasted and Toasted Kernels, 1oz (28.4g)	15	2	0
From Unroasted Kernels, 1oz (28.4g)	16	2	0
Sesame Meal			
Partially Defatted, 1oz (28.4g)	14	2	0
Sesame Paste			
1oz (28.4g)	14	2	0
Sesame Seeds			
Kernels, Dried, 1 tbsp (8g)	4	1	0
1 Cup (150g)	82	12	0
Kernels, Toasted, 1oz (28.4g)	14	2	0
Whole, Dried, 1 tbsp (9g)	5	1	0
1 Cup (144g)	72	10	0
Whole, Roasted and Toasted, 1oz (28.4g)	14	2	0
Dry, Decorticated, 1 tbsp (8.0g)	4	1	0
Sunflower Seed Butter			
1oz (28.4g)	14	1	0
Sunflower Seed Kernels			
Dried, 1oz (28.4g)	14	2	0
1 Cup (144g)	71	8	0
Dry Roasted, 1oz (28.4g)	14	2	0
1 Cup (128g)	64	7	0
Oil Roasted, 1oz (28.4g)	16	2	0
1 Cup (135g)	78	8	0
Toasted, 1oz (28.4g)	16	2	0
1 Cup (134g)	76	8	0
Watermelon Seed Kernels			
Dried, 1oz (28.4g)	14	3	0
1 Cup (108g)	51	11	0
Sesbania Flowers			
Fresh, 1 Cup Flowers (20g)	0	0	0
Steamed, 1 Cup Flowers (104g)	0	0	0
Shakes – See under Milk Shakes			
Shallots			
Fresh, 1 tbsp Chopped (10g)	0	0	0
Shellfish – See under Fish/Shellfish			

	Total fat (g)	Saturated fat (g)	Cholesterol (mg)
Shepherd's Pie			
1 Serving (340g)	21	9	85
Snails			
Steamed or Boiled, 3oz (85g)	1	0	111
Raw, 3oz (85g)	0	0	55
Sorghum Grain			
All Types, 3½oz (100g)	3	0	0

SOUP

	Total fat (g)	Saturated fat (g)	Cholesterol (mg)
Bean			
With Bacon, Dry Mix made with Water,			
1 Cup (264.9g)	2	1	3
With Frankfurters, Tinned, Condensed,			
1 Cup (263g)	14	4	24
1 Tin (319g)	17	5	29
With Frankfurters, Tinned, Diluted,			
1 Cup (250g)	7	2	13
1 Tin (607g)	17	5	30
With Ham, Tinned, Chunky, Ready-to-serve,			
1 Cup (243g)	9	3	22
1 Tin (546g)	19	8	49
With Pork, Tinned, Condensed,			
1 Cup (269g)	12	3	5
1 Tin (326g)	14	4	7
With Pork, Tinned, Diluted, 1 Cup (253g)	6	2	3
1 Tin (614g)	14	4	6
Beef			
Tinned, Chunky, Ready-to-serve,			
1 Cup (240g)	5	3	14
1 Tin (539g)	12	6	32
Beef Broth			
Tinned, Condensed, 1 Cup (246g)	0	0	0
1 Tin (298g)	0	0	0
Tinned, Diluted, 1 Cup (241g)	0	0	0
1 Tin (586g)	0	0	0
Dry Mix made with Water, 1 Cup (244g)	1	0	0
Tinned, Ready-to-serve, 1 Cup (240g)	1	0	0
1 Tin (397g)	1	0	0
Beef Mushroom			
Tinned, Condensed, 1 Cup (251g)	6	3	13
1 Tin (305g)	7	4	15
Tinned, Diluted, 1 Cup (244g)	3	2	7

	Total fat (g)	Saturated fat (g)	Cholesterol (mg)
1 Tin (593g)	7	4	18
Beef Noodle			
Dry Mix made with Water, 1 Cup (251g)	1	0	3
Tinned, Condensed, 1 Cup (251g)	6	2	10
1 Tin (305g)	8	3	12
Tinned, Diluted, 1 Cup (244g)	3	1	5
1 Tin (593g)	8	3	12
Black Bean			
Tinned, Condensed, 1 Cup (257g)	3	1	0
1 Tin (312g)	4	1	0
Tinned, Diluted, 1 Cup (247g)	2	0	0
1 Tin (600g)	4	1	0
Cauliflower			
Dry Mix made with Water, 1 Cup (256.1g)	2	0	0
Cheese			
Tinned, Condensed, 1 Cup (257g)	21	13	59
1 Tin (312g)	25	16	72
Tinned, Prepared with Equal volume Milk, 1 Cup (251g)	15	9	48
1 Tin (609g)	35	22	116
Tinned, Prepared with Equal Volume Water, 1 Cup (247g)	11	7	30
1 Tin (600g)	25	16	72
Chicken			
Tinned, Chunky, Ready-to-serve, 1 Cup (251g)	7	2	30
1 Tin (305g)	8	2	37
Chicken Broth or Bouillon			
Dry Mix made with Water, 1 Cup (244g)	1	0	0
Tinned, Condensed, 1 Cup (251g)	3	1	3
1 Tin (305g)	3	1	3
Tinned, Diluted, 1 Cup (244g)	1	0	0
1 Tin (593g)	3	1	0
Chicken and Mushroom			
Tinned, Condensed, 1 Cup (251g)	18	5	20
1 Tin (305g)	22	6	24
Tinned, Diluted, 1 Cup (244g)	9	2	10
1 Tin (593g)	22	6	24
Chicken Noodle			
Dry Mix made with Water, 1 Cup (252.3g)	1	0	3
Tinned, Chunky, Ready-to-serve, 1 Cup (240g)	6	1	19

	Total fat (g)	Saturated fat (g)	Cholesterol (mg)
1 Tin (539g)	14	3	43
Tinned, Condensed, 1 Cup (246g)	5	1	12
1 Tin (298g)	6	2	15
Tinned, Diluted, 1 Cup (241g)	3	1	7
1 Tin (586g)	6	2	18
With Meatballs, Tinned, Chunky, Ready-to-serve, 1 Cup (248g)	4	1	10
1 Tin (567g)	8	2	23
Chicken Rice			
Dry Mix made with Water, 1 Cup (252.8g)	1	0	3
Tinned, Chunky, Ready-to-serve, 1 Cup (240g)	3	1	12
1 Tin (539g)	7	2	27
Chicken Vegetable			
Dry Mix made with Water, 1 Cup (250.7g)	1	0	3
Tinned, Chunky, Ready-to-serve, 1 Cup (240g)	5	1	17
1 Tin (539g)	11	3	38
Tinned, Condensed, 1 Cup (246g)	6	2	17
1 Tin (298g)	7	2	21
Tinned, Diluted, 1 Cup (241g)	3	1	10
1 Tin (586g)	7	2	23
Chicken with Dumplings			
Tinned, Condensed, 1 Cup (246g)	11	3	66
1 Tin (298g)	13	3	81
Tinned, Diluted, 1 Cup (241g)	6	1	34
1 Tin (586g)	13	3	82
Chilli Beef			
Tinned, Condensed, 1 Cup (263g)	13	7	26
1 Tin (319g)	16	8	32
Tinned, Diluted, 1 Cup (250g)	7	3	13
1 Tin (607g)	16	8	30
Consommé			
With Gelatin, Dry Mix made with Water, 1 Cup (249g)	0	0	0
Crab			
Tinned, Ready-to-serve, 1 Cup (244g)	2	0	10
1 Tin (369g)	2	1	15
Cream of Asparagus			
Dry Mix made with Water, 1 Cup (250.8g)	2	0	0
Tinned, Condensed, 1 Cup (251g)	8	2	10
1 Tin (305g)	10	3	12

	Total fat (g)	Saturated fat (g)	Cholesterol (mg)
Tinned, Prepared with Equal Volume Milk,			
1 Cup (248g)	8	3	22
1 Tin (602g)	20	8	54
Tinned, Prepared with Equal Volume Water,			
1 Cup (244g)	4	1	5
1 Tin (593g)	10	3	12
Cream of Celery			
Dry Mix made with Water, 1 Cup (254g)	2	0	0
Tinned, Condensed, 1 Cup (251g)	11	3	28
1 Tin (305g)	14	3	34
Tinned, Prepared with Equal Volume Milk,			
1 Cup (248g)	10	4	32
1 Tin (602g)	24	10	78
Tinned, Prepared with Equal Volume Water,			
1 Cup (244g)	6	1	15
1 Tin (593g)	14	3	36
Cream of Chicken			
Dry Mix made with Water,			
1 Cup (261.1g)	5	3	3
Tinned, Condensed, 1 Cup (251g)	15	4	20
1 Tin (305g)	18	5	24
Tinned, Prepared with Equal Volume Milk,			
1 Cup (248g)	12	5	27
1 Tin (602g)	28	11	66
Tinned, Prepared with Equal Volume Water,			
1 Cup (244g)	7	2	10
1 Tin (593g)	18	5	24
Cream of Mushroom			
Tinned, Condensed, 1 Cup (251g)	19	5	3
1 Tin (305g)	23	6	3
Tinned, Prepared with Equal Volume Milk,			
1 Cup (248g)	14	5	20
1 Tin (602g)	33	13	48
Tinned, Prepared with Equal Volume Water,			
1 Cup (244g)	9	2	2
1 Tin (593g)	22	6	6
Cream of Onion			
Tinned, Condensed, 1 Cup (251g)	11	3	30
1 Tin (305g)	13	4	37
Tinned, Prepared with Equal Volume Milk,			
1 Cup (248g)	9	4	32
1 Tin (602g)	23	10	78

	Total fat (g)	Saturated fat (g)	Cholesterol (mg)
Tinned, Prepared with Equal Volume Water,			
1 Cup (244g)	5	2	15
1 Tin (593g)	13	4	36
Cream of Potato			
Tinned, Condensed, 1 Cup (251g)	5	2	13
1 Tin (305g)	6	3	15
Tinned, Prepared with Equal Volume Milk,			
1 Cup (248g)	6	4	22
1 Tin (602g)	16	9	54
Tinned, Prepared with Equal Volume Water,			
1 Cup (244g)	2	1	5
1 Tin (593g)	6	3	12
Cream of Shrimp			
Tinned, Condensed, 1 Cup (251g)	10	7	33
1 Tin (305g)	13	8	40
Tinned, Prepared with Equal Volume Milk,			
1 Cup (248g)	9	6	35
1 Tin (602g)	23	14	84
Tinned, Prepared with Equal Volume Water,			
1 Cup (244g)	5	3	17
1 Tin (593g)	13	8	42
Cream of Tomato			
Home Made, 1 Serving (285g)	27	17	87
Cream of Vegetable			
Dry Mix made with Water, 1 Cup (260.1g)	6	1	0
Gazpacho			
Tinned, Ready-to-serve, 1 Cup (244g)	2	0	0
1 Tin (369g)	3	0	0
Irish Stew			
1 Serving (425g)	31	15	149
Leek			
Dry Mix made with Water, 1 Cup (253.9g)	2	1	3
Lentil with Ham			
Tinned, Ready-to-serve, 1 Cup (248g)	3	1	7
1 Tin (567g)	6	3	17
Minestrone			
Tinned, Condensed, 1 Cup (246g)	5	1	3
1 Tin (298g)	6	1	3
Tinned, Diluted, 1 Cup (241g)	3	1	2
1 Tin (586g)	6	1	6
Dry Mix made with Water,			
1 Cup (253.9g)	2	1	3

	Total fat (g)	Saturated fat (g)	Cholesterol (mg)
Tinned, Chunky, Ready-to-serve,			
1 Cup (240g)	3	2	5
1 Tin (539g)	6	3	11
Mushroom			
Dry Mix made with Water, 1 Cup (253g)	5	1	0
Mushroom Barley			
Tinned, Condensed, 1 Cup (251g)	5	1	0
1 Tin (305g)	6	1	0
Tinned, Diluted, 1 Cup (244g)	2	0	0
1 Tin (593g)	6	1	0
Mushroom with Beef Stock			
Tinned, Condensed, 1 Cup (251g)	8	3	15
1 Tin (305g)	10	4	18
Tinned, Diluted, 1 Cup (244g)	4	2	7
1 Tin (593g)	10	4	18
Onion			
Dry Mix made with Water, 1 Cup (246g)	1	0	0
Tinned, Condensed, 1 Cup (246g)	4	1	0
1 Tin (298g)	4	1	0
Tinned, Diluted, 1 Cup (241g)	2	0	0
1 Tin (586g)	4	1	0
Oxtail			
Dry Mix made with Water, 1 Cup (253.1g)	3	1	3
Oyster Stew			
Home Recipe, 1 Part Oysters to 2 Parts Milk,			
1 Cup (240g)	15	7	86
Home Recipe, 1 Part Oyster to 3 Parts Milk,			
1 Cup (240g)	13	7	70
Tinned, Condensed, 1 Cup (246g)	8	5	27
1 Tin (298g)	9	6	33
Tinned, Prepared with Equal Volume Milk,			
1 Cup (245g)	8	5	32
1 Tin (595g)	19	12	77
Tinned, Prepared with Equal Volume Water,			
1 Cup (241g)	4	3	15
1 Tin (586g)	9	6	35
Pea, Green			
Dry Mix made with Water, 1 Cup (271g)	2	0	3
Tinned, Condensed, 1 Cup (263g)	6	3	0
1 Tin (319g)	7	3	0
Tinned, Prepared with Equal Volume Milk,			
1 Cup (254g)	7	4	18

	Total fat (g)	Saturated fat (g)	Cholesterol (mg)
1 Tin (616g)	17	10	43
Tinned, Prepared with Equal Volume Water,			
1 Cup (250g)	3	1	0
1 Tin (607g)	7	3	0
Pea, Split Pea with Ham			
Tinned, Chunky, Ready-to-serve,			
1 Cup (240g)	4	2	7
1 Tin (539g)	9	4	16
Tinned, Condensed, 1 Cup (269g)	9	4	16
1 Tin (326g)	11	4	20
Tinned, Diluted, 1 Cup (253g)	4	2	8
1 Tin (614g)	11	4	18
Scotch Broth			
Tinned, Condensed, 1 Cup (246g)	5	2	10
1 Tin (298g)	6	3	12
Tinned, Diluted, 1 Cup (241g)	3	1	5
1 Tin (586g)	6	3	12
Tomato			
Cream of, Home Recipe, 1 Serving (285ml)	27	17	87
Dry Mix made with Water, 1 Cup (265g)	2	1	0
Tinned, Condensed, 1 Cup (251g)	4	1	0
1 Tin (305g)	5	1	0
Tinned, Prepared with Equal Volume Milk,			
1 Cup (248g)	6	3	17
1 Tin (602g)	15	7	42
Tinned, Prepared with Equal Volume Water,			
1 Cup (244g)	2	0	0
1 Tin (593g)	5	1	0
Tomato with Beef and Noodles			
Tinned, Condensed, 1 Cup (251g)	9	3	8
1 Tin (305g)	10	4	9
Tinned, Diluted, 1 Cup (244g)	4	2	5
1 Tin (593g)	10	4	12
Tomato Bisque			
Tinned, Condensed, 1 Cup (257g)	5	1	10
1 Tin (312g)	6	1	13
Tinned, Prepared with Equal Volume Milk,			
1 Cup (251g)	7	3	23
1 Tin (609g)	16	8	55
Tinned, Prepared with Equal Volome Water,			
1 Cup (247g)	3	1	5
1 Tin (600g)	6	1	12

	Total fat (g)	Saturated fat (g)	Cholesterol (mg)
Tomato Rice			
Tinned, Condensed, 1 Cup (257g)	5	1	3
1 Tin (312g)	7	1	3
Tinned, Diluted, 1 Cup (247g)	3	1	3
1 Tin (600g)	7	1	6
Tomato Vegetable			
Dry Mix made with Water, 1 Cup (253g)	1	0	0
Turkey Noodle			
Tinned, Condensed, 1 Cup (251g)	4	1	10
1 Tin (305g)	5	1	12
Tinned, Diluted, 1 Cup (244g)	2	1	5
1 Tin (593g)	5	1	12
Turkey Vegetable			
Tinned, Condensed, 1 Cup (246g)	6	2	3
1 Tin (298g)	7	2	3
Tinned, Diluted, 1 Cup (241g)	3	1	2
1 Tin (586g)	7	2	6
Turkey			
Chunky, Ready-to-serve, 1 Cup (236g)	4	1	9
1 Tin (532g)	10	3	21
Vegetable			
Tinned, Chunky, Ready-to-serve, 1 Cup (240g)	4	1	0
1 Tin (539g)	8	1	0
Vegetarian Tinned, Condensed, 1 Cup (246g)	4	1	0
1 Tin (298g)	5	1	0
Vegetarian, Tinned, Diluted, 1 Cup (241g)	2	0	0
1 Tin (586g)	5	1	0
Vegetable Beef			
Dry Mix made with Water, 1 Cup (253.1g)	1	1	0
Tinned, Condensed, 1 Cup (251g)	4	2	10
1 Tin (305g)	5	2	12
Tinned, Diluted, 1 Cup (244g)	2	1	5
1 Tin (593g)	5	2	12
Vegetable with Beef Broth			
Tinned, Condensed, 1 Cup (246g)	4	1	3
1 Tin (298g)	5	1	3
Tinned, Diluted, 1 Cup (241g)	2	0	2
1 Tin (586g)	5	1	6

	Total fat (g)	Saturated fat (g)	Cholesterol (mg)
Soured Cream			
1 tbsp (12g)	3	2	5
1 Cup (230g)	48	30	102
Imitation, Non-dairy, Cultured, 1oz (28g)	6	5	0
1 Cup (230g)	45	41	0
Soursop			
Fresh, 1 Fruit (625g)	2	0	0
Soy Milk			
1 Cup (240g)	5	1	0
Soy Sauce			
1 tbsp (18g)	0	0	0
¼ Cup (58g)	0	0	0
Spaghetti			
In Tomato Sauce with Cheese, Home Recipe, 1 Cup (250g)	9	2	8
In Tomato Sauce with Cheese, Tinned, 1 Cup (250g)	2	0	8
1 Tin (432g)	3	0	13
Noodles, Boiled, 1 Cup (140g)	1	0	0
and Meat Balls, in Tomato Sauce, Home Recipe, 1 Cup (248g)	12	3	74
1 Portion (537g)	25	7	161
and Meat Balls, in Tomato Sauce, Tinned, 1 Cup (250g)	10	2	23
1 Tin (425g)	17	4	38

SPICES

	Total fat (g)	Saturated fat (g)	Cholesterol (mg)
Allspice			
Ground, 1 tsp (1.9g)	0	0	0
1 tbsp (6.0g)	1	0	0
Anise Seed			
1 tsp (2.1g)	0	0	0
1 tbsp (6.7g)	1	0	0
Basil			
Ground, 1 tsp (1.4g)	0	0	0
1 tbsp (4½g)	0	0	0
Bay Leaf			
Crumbled, 1 tsp (0.6g)	0	0	0
1 tbsp (1.8g)	0	0	0
Caraway Seed			
1 tsp (2.1g)	0	0	0

	Total fat (g)	Saturated fat (g)	Cholesterol (mg)
1 tbsp (6.7g)	1	0	0
Cardamon			
Ground, 1 tsp (2.0g)	0	0	0
1 tbsp (5.8g)	0	0	0
Celery Seed			
1 tsp (2.0g)	1	0	0
1 tbsp (6½g)	2	0	0
Chervil			
Dried, 1 tsp (0.6g)	0	0	0
1 tbsp (1.9g)	0	0	0
Chilli Powder			
1 tsp (2.6g)	0	0	0
1 tbsp (7½g)	1	0	0
Cinnamon			
Ground, 1 tsp (2.3g)	0	0	0
1 tbsp (6.8g)	0	0	0
Cloves			
Ground, 1 tsp (2.1g)	0	0	0
1 tbsp (6.6g)	1	0	0
Coriander Leaf			
Dried, 1 tsp (0.6g)	0	0	0
1 tbsp (1.8g)	0	0	0
Coriander Seed			
1 tsp (1.8g)	0	0	0
1 tbsp (5.0g)	1	0	0
Cumin Seed			
1 tsp (2.1g)	1	0	0
1 tbsp (6.0g)	1	0	0
Curry Powder			
1 tsp (2.0g)	0	0	0
1 tbsp (6.3g)	1	0	0
Dill Seed			
1 tsp (2.1g)	0	0	0
1 tbsp (6.6g)	1	0	0
Dill Weed			
Dried, 1 tsp (1.0g)	0	0	0
1 tbsp (3.1g)	0	0	0
Fennel Seed			
1 tsp (2.0g)	0	0	0
1 tbsp (5.8g)	1	0	0
Fenugreek Seed			
1 tsp (3.7g)	0	0	0

	Total fat (g)	Saturated fat (g)	Cholesterol (mg)
1 tbsp (11.1g)	1	0	0
Garlic Granules or Powder			
1 tsp (2.8g)	0	0	0
1 tbsp (8.4g)	0	0	0
Ginger			
Ground, 1 tsp (1.8g)	0	0	0
1 tbsp (5.4g)	0	0	0
Mace			
Ground, 1 tsp (1.7g)	1	0	0
1 tbsp (5.3g)	2	1	0
Marjoram			
Dried, 1 tsp (0.6g)	0	0	0
1 tbsp (1.7g)	0	0	0
Mustard Seed			
Yellow, 1 tsp (3.3g)	1	0	0
1 tbsp (11.2g)	3	0	0
Nutmeg			
Ground			
1 tsp (2.2g)	1	1	0
1 tbsp (7.0g)	3	2	0
Onion Powder			
1 tsp (2.1g)	0	0	0
1 tbsp (6½g)	0	0	0
Oregano			
Dried, 1 tsp (1½g)	0	0	0
1 tbsp (4½g)	1	0	0
Paprika			
1 tsp (2.1g)	0	0	0
1 tbsp (6.9g)	1	0	0
Parsley			
Dried, 1 tsp (0.3g)	0	0	0
1 tbsp (1.3g)	0	0	0
Pepper			
Black, 1 tsp (2.1g)	0	0	0
1 tbsp (6.4g)	0	0	0
Red or Cayenne, 1 tsp (1.8g)	0	0	0
1 tbsp (5.3g)	1	0	0
White, 1 tsp (2.4g)	0	0	0
1 tbsp (7.1g)	0	0	0
Poppy Seed			
1 tsp (2.8g)	1	0	0
1 tbsp (8.8g)	4	0	0

	Total fat (g)	Saturated fat (g)	Cholesterol (mg)
Poultry Seasoning			
1 tsp (1½g)	0	0	0
1 tbsp (3.7g)	0	0	0
Rosemary			
Dried, 1 tsp (1.2g)	0	0	0
1 tbsp (3.3g)	1	0	0
Saffron			
1 tsp (0.7g)	0	0	0
1 tbsp (2.1g)	0	0	0
Sage			
Dried, 1 tsp (0.7g)	0	0	0
1 tbsp (2.0g)	0	0	0
Savory			
Dried, 1 tsp (1.4g)	0	0	0
1 tbsp (4.4g)	0.	0	0
Tarragon			
Dried, 1 tsp (1.6g)	0	0	0
1 tbsp (4.8g)	0	0	0
Thyme			
Dried, 1 tsp (1.4g)	0	0	0
1 tbsp (4.3g)	0	0	0
Turmeric			
Ground, 1 tsp (2.2g)	0	0	0
1 tbsp (6.8g)	1	0	0
Spinach			
Boiled, 1 Cup (180g)	1	0	0
Fresh, 1 Cup Chopped (56g)	0	0	0
Soufflé, Home Recipe,			
1 Cup (136g)	18	7	184
Tinned, 1 Cup (234g)	1	0	0
Sponge Cake			
1 Slice (55g)	15	5	72
Squab – See under Pigeon			
Squash			
Also see under Marrow; Pumpkin			
Acorn Squash			
Baked, 1 Cup Cubes (205g)	0	0	0
Boiled, 1 Cup Mashed (245g)	0	0	0
Fresh, 1 Cup Cubes (140g)	0	0	0
1 Squash,			
4-inch Diameter (431g)	0	0	0

	Total fat (g)	Saturated fat (g)	Cholesterol (mg)
Butternut Squash			
Baked, 1 Cup Cubes (205g)	0	0	0
Boiled, 1 Cup Mashed (240g)	0	0	0
Butternut, Fresh,			
1 Cup Cubes (140g)	0	0	0
Spaghetti Squash			
Boiled or Baked, 1 Cup (155g)	0	0	0
Fresh, 1 Cup Cubes (101g)	1	0	0
Summer Squash			
Boiled , 1 Cup Slices (180g)	1	0	0
Fresh, 1 Cup Slices (130g)	0	0	0
Starfruit, Fresh			
1 Fruit (127g)	0	0	0
Steak			
Also see under Beef			
Flank, Grilled, 3oz (85g)	14	6	60
Gammon, Extra Lean, Grilled,			
1 Slice (56.7g)	2	1	26
Porterhouse, Grilled, 3oz (85g)	18	8	71
Sirloin, Grilled, 3oz (85g)	15	6	77
T-bone, Grilled, 3oz (85g)	21	9	71
Tenderloin, Grilled, 3oz (85g)	15	6	72
Steak and Kidney Pie, Home Recipe			
1 Serving (170g)	31	13	213
Stock			
Also see under Gravy; Soup			
Beef Stock Cube			
Made with Water, 1 Cup (241.3g)	0	0	0
Chicken Stock Cubes			
Made with Water, 1 Cup (243g)	0	0	0
Dry Mix			
Made with Water, 1 Cup (246.1g)	1	0	0
Tinned			
1 Cup (238.4g)	1	0	0
1 Tin (298g)	1	0	0
Strawberries			
Fresh, 1 Cup (149g)	1	0	0
1 Pint (320g)	1	0	0
Frozen, 1 Cup (255g)	0	0	0
Tinned, 1 Cup (254g)	1	0	0
Strawberry Flavour Beverage Mix			
Powder, 2–3 Heaped tsp (21.6g)	0	0	0

	Total fat (g)	Saturated fat (g)	Cholesterol (mg)
Made with Milk, 1 Cup Milk and 2–3 Heaped tsp Powder (266g)	8	5	32
Sugar			
Beet or Cane, Brown, 1 Cup (145g)	0	0	0
Beet or Cane, Granulated, 1 tsp (4g)	0	0	0
1 Cup (200g)	0	0	0
Beet or Cane, Icing, 1 Cup (120g)	0	0	0
Swedes			
Boiled, 1 Cup Cubes (170g)	0	0	0
1 Cup Mashed (240g)	0	0	0
Fresh, 1 Cup Cubes (140g)	0	0	0
Sweetcorn			
Boiled, 1 Ear (77g)	1	0	0
Frozen Cob, Boiled, 1 Ear (63g)	1	0	0
Frozen Kernels, Boiled, 1 Cup (164g)	0	0	0
Fresh, 1 Ear (90g)	1	0	0
Tinned, Cream Style, 1 Cup (256g)	1	0	0
1 Tin (482g)	2	0	0
Tinned, Drained Solids, 1 Cup (164g)	2	0	0
1 Tin (298g)	3	1	0
Tinned, Solids and Liquid, 1 Cup (256g)	1	0	0
1 Tin (482g)	2	0	0
Tinned with Red and Green Peppers, 1 Cup (227g)	1	0	0
Sweet Potatoes			
Baked in Skin, 1 Sweet Potato (114g)	0	0	0
Boiled, without Skin, 1 Cup Mashed (328g)	1	0	0
Glazed, 1 Serving (105g)	3	1	8
Leaves, Fresh, 1 Cup Chopped (35g)	0	0	0
Leaves, Steamed, 1 Cup (64g)	0	0	0
Raw, 1 Sweet Potato (130g)	0	0	0
Tinned, Mashed or Pieces, 1 Cup (255g)	1	0	0
1 Tin (496g)	1	0	0

SWEETS

Also see under Chocolate

Butterscotch			
1oz (28g)	1	1	3
Caramels			
Chocolate Flavoured, 1oz (28g)	3	1	0
Plain or Chocolate, 1oz (28g)	3	2	1
Plain or Chocolate with Nuts, 1oz (28g)	5	2	1

	Total fat (g)	Saturated fat (g)	Cholesterol (mg)
Chocolate Coated			
Almonds, 1oz (28g)	12	2	0
1 Cup (165g)	72	12	2
Chocolate Fudge Centre, 1oz (28g)	5	2	1
Chocolate Fudge Centre with Nuts, 1oz (28g)	6	2	1
Coconut Centre, 1oz (28g)	5	3	0
Mint Fondant, 1 Large Mint (35g)	4	1	0
1 Small Mint (2.4g)	0	0	0
Fudge, Peanuts and Caramel Centre, 1oz (28g)	7	2	1
Hard Sweet Filled with Peanut Butter, 1oz (28g)	6	2	0
Nougat and Caramel, 1oz (28g)	4	1	1
Peanuts, 1oz (28g)	12	3	0
1 Cup (170g)	70	18	2
Raisins, 1oz (28g)	5	3	3
1 Cup (190g)	33	18	19
Vanilla Creams, 1oz (28g)	5	1	1
Chocolate			
Bitter, 1oz (28g)	11	6	0
Plain, 1oz (28g)	10	6	0
Sweet, 1oz (28g)	10	6	0
Fondant			
1 Cup Mints, Uncoated (110g)	2	1	0
1 Cup (200g)	4	1	0
Fudge			
Chocolate, 1oz (28g)	3	1	0
Chocolate, with Nuts, 1oz (28g)	5	1	0
Vanilla, 1oz (28g)	3	1	1
Vanilla, with Nuts, 1oz (28g)	5	1	1
Wine Gums			
1oz (28g)	0	0	0
Jelly Babies			
1oz (approx 10) (28g)	0	0	0
1 Cup (approx 75) (220g)	1	0	0
Marshmallows			
1 Large (7.2g)	0	0	0
1 Cup Miniature (46g)	0	0	1
Milk Chocolate			
Plain, 1oz (28g)	9	5	6
With Almonds, 1oz (28g)	10	5	5
With Peanuts, 1oz (28g)	11	4	4

	Total fat (g)	Saturated fat (g)	Cholesterol (mg)
Peanut Bars			
1oz (28g)	9	2	0
Peanut Brittle			
1oz (28g)	3	1	0
Rock			
1oz (28g)	0	0	0
Sugar-coated Almonds			
1oz (28g)	5	0	0
1 Cup (195g)	36	3	0
Sugar-coated Chocolate Discs			
1oz (28g)	6	3	3
1 Cup (197g)	39	22	24
Syrup			
Golden, 1 Cup (328g)	0	0	0
Taco			
With Meat Filling, Salad and Sauce,			
1 Small (171g)	21	11	57
1 Large (263g)	32	17	87
Taco Salad			
With Chilli con Carne, 1½ Cups (261g)	13	6	4
Tahini			
From Ground Sesame Seeds,			
1 tbsp (15g)	7	1	0
1 Cup (227g)	109	15	0
Tamari			
1 tbsp (18g)	0	0	0
¼ Cup (58g)	0	0	0
Tamarinds			
Fresh, 1 Fruit (2g)	0	0	0
1 Cup Pulp (120g)	1	0	0
Tangerines			
Fresh, 1 Fruit (84g)	0	0	0
1 Cup Sections (195g)	0	0	0
Tinned, 1 Cup (249g)	0	0	0
Tapioca Dessert			
1 Cup (250g)	0	0	0
Tapioca			
Dry, 1 tbsp (8.4g)	0	0	0
1½ Cup (227g)	1	0	0
Taro			
Boiled or Baked, 1 Cup Slices (132g)	0	0	0

	Total fat (g)	Saturated fat (g)	Cholesterol (mg)
Fresh, 1 Cup Slices (104g)	0	0	0
Leaves, Fresh, 1 Cup (28g)	0	0	0
Leaves, Steamed, 1 Cup (145g)	1	0	0
Taro Chips			
1 Cup (10 Chips) (23g)	6	2	0
Tea			
Brewed, 6 Fl.oz (178g)	0	0	0
Herb, Brewed, 6 Fl.oz (178g)	0	0	0
Instant, Prepared, 1 Cup Water and 1 tsp Powder (237g)	0	0	0
Tempeh			
1 Serving (83g)	6	1	0
1 Cup (166g)	13	2	0
Texturized Vegetable Protein (TVP)			
Dry, 1oz (28g)	1	0	0
1 Cup (88g)	3	0	0
Tofu			
Firm, 1 Serving (81g)	7	1	0
3½oz (100g)	9	1	0
Freeze-dried, 1 Piece (17g)	5	1	0
3½oz (100g)	30	4	0
Fried, 1 Slice (13g)	3	0	0
3½oz (100g)	20	3	0
Okara, 1 Serving (61g)	1	0	0
3½oz (100g)	2	0	0
Salted and Fermented, 1 Piece (11g)	1	0	0
3½oz (100g)	8	1	0
Silken or Soft, 1 Serving (116g)	6	1	0
3½oz (100g)	5	1	0
Tomato Juice			
Cocktail, Tinned or Bottled, 1 Cup (243g)	0	0	0
Tinned, 1 Cup (240g)	0	0	0
Tomato Ketchup			
Bottled, 1 tbsp (15g)	0	0	0
1 Cup (273g)	1	0	0
Tomato Paste			
Tinned, 1 Tin (170g)	2	0	0
Tomato Purée, Tinned			
1 Cup (250g)	0	0	0
1 Tin (822g)	1	0	0
Tomato Sauce			
Tinned, 1 Cup (245g)	0	0	0

	Total fat (g)	Saturated fat (g)	Cholesterol (mg)
Tinned or Bottled, for Spaghetti,			
1 Cup (249g)	12	2	0
1 Jar (439g)	21	3	0
Tinned, Italian Style, 1 Cup (240g)	1	0	0
1 Tin (425g)	1	0	0
Tinned, with Herbs and Cheese,			
1 Cup (240g)	5	2	0
1 Tin (425g)	8	3	0
Tinned, with Mushrooms, 1 Cup (245g)	0	0	0
Tinned, with Onions, 1 Cup (245g)	1	0	0
Tinned, with Onions, Green Peppers and			
Celery, 1 Cup (240g)	2	0	0
1 Tin (411g)	3	1	0
Tinned, with Tomato Chunks,			
1 Cup (240g)	1	0	0
1 Tin (425g)	2	0	0
Tomato Soup			
Cream of, Home Recipe,			
1 Serving (285g)	27	17	87
Tomatoes			
Green, Fresh, 1 Tomato (123g)	0	0	0
Red, Ripe, Boiled, 1 Cup (240g)	1	0	0
Red, Fresh, 1 Tomato (123g)	0	0	0
1 Cup Chopped (180g)	0	0	0
Red, Tinned, Chopped in Tomato Juice,			
1 Cup (261g)	0	0	0
Red, Tinned, Stewed, 1 Cup (255g)	0	0	0
Red, Tinned, Whole, 1 Cup (240g)	1	0	0
Tostada, with Beans and Cheese,			
1 Tostada (144g)	10	5	30
Tostada			
With Beans, Beef and Cheese,			
1 Tostada (225g)	17	11	75
With Beef and Cheese, 1 Tostada (163g)	16	10	41
With Guacamole, 1 Tostada (131g)	12	5	20
With Salad and Cheese, 1 Tostada (144g)	11	5	18
Treacle			
1 Cup (328g)	0	0	0
Tripe			
Pickled, 3½oz (100g)	1	1	68
Raw, 4oz (113g)	5	2	107
Trout – See under Fish/Shellfish			

	Total fat (g)	Saturated fat (g)	Cholesterol (mg)

TURKEY

DISHES

Diced and Seasoned

| Light and Dark Meat, 1oz (28.35g) | 2 | 1 | 16 |
| 1 Cup (227g) | 14 | 4 | 125 |

Frozen Turkey and Gravy

| 1 Cup (240g) | 6 | 2 | 43 |

Luncheon Meat

| Cured, 1 Slice (28.4g) | 1 | 1 | 16 |
| Loaf, Breast Meat, 2 Slices (42½g) | 1 | 0 | 17 |

Patties

Breaded, Battered, Fried,

| 1 Regular Patty (64g) | 12 | 3 | 40 |
| 1 Large Patty (94g) | 17 | 4 | 58 |

Potted Turkey

| 1 Tin (156g) | 30 | 14 | 122 |
| 1 Cup (225g) | 43 | 20 | 176 |

Pre-basted Breast

| Meat and Skin, Roasted, ½ Breast (864g) | 30 | 9 | 363 |
| 1 Breast (1728g) | 60 | 17 | 726 |

Pre-basted Thigh

| Meat and Skin, Roasted, 1 Thigh (314g) | 27 | 8 | 195 |
| 2 Thighs (629g) | 54 | 17 | 390 |

Pressed Breast Meat

| 1 Slice (21g) | 0 | 0 | 9 |

Sticks

| Breaded, Battered, Fried, 1 Stick (64g) | 11 | 3 | 41 |
| 2 Sticks (128g) | 22 | 6 | 82 |

Tinned Turkey Meat

| With Broth, 1 Tin (142g) | 10 | 3 | 94 |

Turkey Loaf

| 1 Slice (28.35g) | 4 | 1 | 28 |

Turkey Pastrami

| 1 Slice (28.4g) | 2 | 1 | 15 |

Turkey Pie

| Frozen, 3½oz (100g) | 10 | 4 | 9 |
| Home Recipe, 1 Portion, ⅓ of Pie (232g) | 31 | 11 | 72 |

Turkey Roast

Boneless, Frozen, Seasoned, Light and Dark Meat, Raw, 1 Portion

| (284g) | 6 | 2 | 151 |
| 1 Roast (1134g) | 25 | 8 | 601 |

	Total fat (g)	Saturated fat (g)	Cholesterol (mg)
Boneless, Frozen, Seasoned, Light and Dark Meat, Roasted,			
1 Portion (196g)	11	4	104
1 Roast (782g)	45	15	415
Turkey Roll			
1 Slice (28.35g)	2	1	16
Turkey Salami			
1 Slice (28.4g)	4	1	23
LARGE CLASS: WHOLE BIRD			
Meat and Skin and Giblets and Neck			
Roasted, 1 Turkey (4023g)	380	111	3822
Raw, 1 Turkey (5554g)	432	122	4332
Meat and Skin			
Roasted, 1 Portion (240g)	23	7	197
½ Turkey (1857g)	181	53	1523
Raw, 1 Portion (332g)	27	8	226
½ Turkey (2565g)	206	58	1744
Meat Only			
Roasted, 1 Portion (208g)	10	3	158
½ Turkey (1610g)	80	26	1231
Raw, 1 Portion (281g)	8	3	183
½ Turkey (2174g)	62	21	1413
Dark Meat and Skin			
Roasted, 1 Portion (104g)	12	4	93
½ Turkey (808g)	93	28	719
Raw, 1 Portion (152g)	13	4	109
½ Turkey (1176g)	104	30	847
Dark Meat			
Roasted, 1 Portion (91g)	7	2	77
½ Turkey (704g)	51	17	595
Raw, 1 Portion (132g)	6	2	91
½ Turkey (1017g)	45	15	702
Light Meat and Skin			
Roasted, 1 Portion (136g)	11	3	103
½ Turkey (1050g)	88	25	798
Raw, 1 Portion (180g)	13	4	117
½ Turkey (1388g)	102	28	902
Light Meat			
Roasted, 1 Portion (117g)	4	1	81
½ Turkey (906g)	29	9	628
Raw, 1 Portion (150g)	2	1	90
½ Turkey (1156g)	18	6	694

	Total fat (g)	Saturated fat (g)	Cholesterol (mg)
LARGE CLASS: PART BIRDS			
Back, Meat and Skin			
Roasted, 1 Portion (34g)	5	1	31
½ Back (262g)	38	11	238
Raw, 1 Portion (47g)	6	2	35
½ Back (361g)	47	13	267
Breast, Meat and Skin			
Roasted, 1 Portion (112g)	8	2	83
½ Breast (864g)	64	18	639
Raw, 1 Portion (146g)	10	3	95
½ Breast (1132g)	80	22	736
Giblets			
Simmered, with some Giblet Fat, Giblets (145g)	7	2	606
Raw, Giblets (244g)	10	3	688
Gizzard			
Simmered, 1 Cup (145g)	6	2	336
Raw, 1 Gizzard (113g)	4	1	179
Heart			
Simmered, 1 Cup (145g)	9	3	328
Raw, 1 Heart (29g)	2	1	33
Leg, Meat and Skin			
Roasted, 1 Portion (71g)	7	2	60
1 Leg (546g)	54	17	464
Raw, 1 Portion (105g)	7	2	75
1 Leg (816g)	55	17	579
Liver			
Simmered, 1 Cup (140g)	8	3	876
Raw, 1 Liver (102g)	4	1	475
Neck			
Meat Only, Simmered, 1 Neck (152g)	11	4	185
Meat Only, Raw, 1 Neck (180g)	10	3	142
Skin Only			
Raw, 1 Portion (51g)	19	5	46
½ Turkey (392g)	145	38	357
Roasted, 1 Portion (32g)	13	3	36
½ Turkey (248g)	98	26	280
Wing, Meat and Skin			
Roasted, 1 Wing (186g)	23	6	151
Raw, 1 Wing (256g)	32	8	179

	Total fat (g)	Saturated fat (g)	Cholesterol (mg)
ROASTERS: WHOLE BIRDS			
Meat and Skin and Giblets and Neck			
Roasted, 1 Turkey (1772g)	100	29	2091
Raw, 1 Turkey (2410g)	102	29	2217
Meat and Skin			
Roasted, 1 Portion (229g)	13	4	241
½ Turkey (808g)	46	13	848
Raw, 1 Portion (310g)	13	4	251
½ Turkey (1093g)	47	13	885
Meat Only			
Roasted, 1 Portion (195g)	5	2	191
½ Turkey (687g)	18	6	676
Raw, 1 Portion (272g)	4	1	199
½ Turkey (960g)	15	5	701
Dark Meat and Skin			
Roasted, 1 Portion (106g)	8	2	124
½ Turkey (374g)	26	8	438
Raw, 1 Portion (151g)	7	2	131
½ Turkey (532g)	26	8	463
Dark Meat Only			
Roasted, 1 Portion (91g)	4	1	102
½ Turkey (320g)	14	5	359
Raw, 1 Portion (136g)	4	1	110
½ Turkey (479g)	13	4	388
Light Meat and Skin			
Roasted, 1 Portion (123g)	6	2	117
½ Turkey (433g)	20	5	411
Raw, 1 Portion (159g)	6	2	121
½ Turkey (561g)	21	6	426
Light Meat Only			
Roasted, 1 Portion (104g)	1	0	89
½ Turkey (367g)	4	1	317
Raw, 1 lb Ready To Cook Turkey (136g)	1	0	90
½ Turkey (481g)	2	1	318
PART BIRDS			
Back			
Roasted, 1 Portion (37g)	4	1	40
½ Back (130g)	13	4	140
Raw, 1 Portion (52g)	4	1	45
½ Back (183g)	13	4	157
Meat Only, Roasted, 1 Portion (27g)	2	1	26

	Total fat (g)	Saturated fat (g)	Cholesterol (mg)
½ Back (96g)	5	2	91
Meat Only, Raw, 1 Portion (43g)	2	1	32
½ Back (150g)	5	2	111
Breast			
Meat and Skin, Roasted, 1 Portion (98g)	3	1	88
½ Breast (344g)	11	3	310
Meat and Skin, Raw, 1 Portion (123g)	3	1	86
½ Breast (433g)	12	3	303
Meat Only, Roasted, 1 Portion (87g)	1	0	72
½ Breast (306g)	2	1	254
Meat Only, Raw, 1 Portion (111g)	1	0	69
½ Breast (390g)	3	1	242
Leg			
Meat and Skin, Roasted, 1 Portion (70g)	4	1	49
1 Leg (245g)	13	4	172
Meat and Skin, Raw, 1 Portion (99g)	4	1	86
1 Leg (349g)	13	4	304
Meat Only, Roasted, 1 Portion (64g)	2	1	76
1 Leg (224g)	8	3	267
Meat Only, Raw, 1 Portion (93g)	2	1	78
1 Leg (329g)	8	3	276
Skin Only			
Roasted, 1 Portion (34g)	8	2	49
½ Turkey (121g)	28	7	174
Raw, 1 Portion (38g)	9	2	53
½ Turkey (133g)	31	8	185
Wing			
Meat and Skin, Roasted, 1 Portion (25g)	3	1	29
1 Wing (90g)	9	2	104
Meat and Skin, Raw, 1 Portion (36g)	3	1	35
1 Wing (128g)	10	3	125
Meat Only, Roasted, 1 Portion (17g)	1	0	17
1 Wing (60g)	2	1	61
Meat Only, Raw, 1 Portion (26g)	0	0	21
1 Wing (90g)	1	0	73
YOUNG COCK: WHOLE BIRD			
Meat and Skin and Giblets and Neck			
Roasted, 1 Turkey (5957g)	525	154	5719
Raw, 1 Turkey (8399g)	606	172	6803
Meat and Skin			
Roasted, 1 Portion (239g)	22	6	196

	Total fat (g)	Saturated fat (g)	Cholesterol (mg)
½ Turkey (2750g)	249	73	2255
Raw, 1 Portion (338g)	25	7	243
½ Turkey (3895g)	289	82	2804
Meat Only			
Roasted, 1 Portion (206g)	10	3	159
½ Turkey (2376g)	111	37	1833
Raw, 1 Portion (286g)	8	3	195
½ Turkey (3302g)	89	29	2245
Dark Meat and Skin			
Roasted, 1 Portion (103g)	11	3	94
½ Turkey (1184g)	129	39	1077
Raw, 1 Portion (152g)	12	4	117
½ Turkey (1758g)	139	41	1354
Dark Meat Only			
Roasted, 1 Portion (90g)	6	2	79
½ Turkey (1033g)	72	24	907
Raw, 1 Portion (133g)	6	2	100
½ Turkey (1532g)	63	21	1149
Light Meat and Skin			
Roasted, 1 Portion (136g)	11	3	102
½ Turkey (1566g)	121	34	1175
Raw, 1 Portion (185g)	13	4	124
½ Turkey (2137g)	150	41	1432
Light Meat Only			
Roasted, 1 Portion (117g)	3	1	81
½ Turkey (1344g)	39	12	931
Raw, 1 Portion (154g)	2	1	96
½ Turkey (1771g)	28	9	1098
PART BIRDS			
Back, Meat and Skin			
Roasted, 1 Portion (33g)	5	1	31
½ Back (380g)	52	15	357
Raw, 1 Portion (45g)	5	1	36
½ Back (524g)	58	17	414
Breast			
Meat and Skin, Roasted, 1 Portion (115g)	9	2	86
½ Breast (1329g)	98	28	997
Meat and Skin, Raw, 1 Portion (155g)	10	3	104
½ Breast (1789g)	113	31	1199

	Total fat (g)	Saturated fat (g)	Cholesterol (mg)
Leg			
Meat and Skin, Roasted,			
1 Portion (70g)	7	2	63
1 Leg (805g)	78	24	725
Meat and Skin, Raw, 1 Portion (107g)	7	2	81
1 Leg (1234g)	78	24	938
Skin Only			
Roasted, 1 Portion (32g)	12	3	37
½ Turkey (374g)	139	36	438
Raw, 1 Portion (51g)	18	5	49
½ Turkey (592g)	205	53	562
Wing			
Meat and Skin, Roasted,			
1 Portion (21g)	2	1	17
1 Wing (237g)	27	7	192
Meat and Skin, Raw, 1 Portion (30g)	3	1	22
1 Wing (348g)	39	10	251
YOUNG HEN: WHOLE BIRD			
Meat and Skin and Giblets and Neck			
Roasted, 1 Turkey (3300g)	348	102	3102
Raw, 1 Turkey (4457g)	391	111	3254
Meat and Skin			
Roasted, 1 Portion (243g)	26	8	190
½ Turkey (1524g)	166	49	1189
Raw, 1 Portion (327g)	30	8	206
½ Turkey (2052g)	187	53	1293
Meat Only			
Roasted, 1 Portion (212g)	12	4	155
½ Turkey (1328g)	73	24	968
Raw, 1 Portion (276g)	9	3	166
½ Turkey (1731g)	55	18	1039
Dark Meat and Skin			
Roasted, 1 Portion (106g)	14	4	89
½ Turkey (665g)	85	26	559
Raw, 1 Portion (152g)	16	5	99
½ Turkey (953g)	98	29	620
Dark Meat Only			
Roasted, 1 Portion (93g)	7	2	74
½ Turkey (580g)	45	15	460
Raw, 1 Portion (130g)	6	2	81
½ Turkey (812g)	40	13	503

	Total fat (g)	Saturated fat (g)	Cholesterol (mg)
Light Meat and Skin			
Roasted, 1 Portion (137g)	13	4	101
½ Turkey (859g)	81	23	636
Raw, 1 Portion (175g)	14	4	109
½ Turkey (1099g)	89	24	681
Light Meat Only			
Roasted, 1 Portion (119g)	5	1	81
½ Turkey (748g)	28	9	507
Raw, 1 Portion (147g)	2	1	85
½ Turkey (919g)	15	5	533
PART BIRDS			
Back			
Meat and Skin, Roasted, 1 Portion (35g)	6	2	30
½ Back (217g)	34	10	185
Meat and Skin, Raw, 1 Portion (47g)	8	2	32
½ Back (298g)	48	13	203
Breast			
Meat and Skin, Roasted, 1 Portion (109g)	9	3	79
½ Breast (686g)	54	15	494
Meat and Skin, Raw, 1 Portion (139g)	12	3	86
½ Breast (874g)	73	20	542
Leg			
Meat and Skin, Roasted, 1 Portion (71g)	8	2	58
1 Leg (448g)	47	15	367
Meat and Skin, Raw, 1 Portion (105g)	8	2	66
1 Leg (656g)	49	15	413
Skin Only			
Roasted, 1 Portion (31g)	14	4	33
½ Turkey (196g)	87	23	208
Raw, 1 Portion (51g)	21	5	41
½ Turkey (321g)	130	34	260
Wing			
Meat and Skin, Roasted, 1 Portion (28g)	4	1	22
1 Wing (174g)	23	6	134
Meat and Skin, Raw, 1 Portion (36g)	5	1	23
1 Wing (224g)	31	8	146

	Total fat (g)	Saturated fat (g)	Cholesterol (mg)
Turnip Greens			
Boiled, 1 Cup Chopped (180g)	0	0	0
Fresh, 1 Cup Chopped (55g)	0	0	0
Turnips			
Boiled, 1 Cup Cubes (156g)	0	0	0
1 Cup Mashed (230g)	0	0	0
Fresh			
1 Cup Cubes (130g)	0	0	0
Turtle			
Green, Raw, 3½oz (100g)	1	0	50
Green, Tinned, 3½oz (100g)	1	0	50

VEAL

	Total fat (g)	Saturated fat (g)	Cholesterol (mg)
Composite Cuts			
Fat Class			
Raw, (excluding Kidney and Kidney Fat), 3½oz (100g)	16	8	71
Raw, (including Kidney and Kidney Fat), 3½oz (100g)	19	9	71
Medium Fat Class			
Raw, (excluding Kidney and Kidney Fat), 3½oz (100g)	12	6	71
Raw, (including Kidney and Kidney Fat), 3½oz (100g)	14	7	71
Thin Class			
Raw, (excluding Kidney and Kidney Fat), 3½oz (100g)	8	4	71
Raw, (including Kidney and Kidney Fat), 3½oz (100g)	10	5	71
Parts			
Best End			
Fat Class, Raw, 3½oz (100g)	15	7	71
Medium Fat Class, Grilled, 1 Portion (90g)	12	6	91
Medium Fat Class, Raw, 3½oz (100g)	11	5	71
Thin Class, Raw, 3½oz (100g)	8	4	71
Fillet			
Fat Class, Raw, 3½oz (100g)	12	6	71
Medium Fat Class, Grilled, 1 Portion (82g)	9	4	83
Medium Fat Class, Raw, 3½oz (100g)	9	4	71

	Total fat (g)	Saturated fat (g)	Cholesterol (mg)
Thin-class, Raw, 3½oz (100g)	6	3	71
Flank (Tendron)			
Fat Class, Raw, 3½oz (100g)	36	17	71
Medium Fat Class, Stewed, 3½oz (100g)	32	16	101
Medium Fat Class, Raw, 3½oz (100g)	27	13	71
Thin Class, Raw, 3½oz (100g)	18	9	71
Foreshank			
Fat Class, Raw, 3½oz (100g)	10	5	71
Medium Fat Class, Stewed, 3½oz (100g)	10	5	101
Medium Fat Class, Raw, 3½oz (100g)	8	4	71
Thin Class, Raw, 3½oz (100g)	5	2	71
Middle Neck			
Fat Class, Raw, 3½oz (100g)	19	9	71
Medium Fat Class, Roasted, 1 Portion (80g)	14	7	81
Medium Fat Class, Raw, 3½oz (100g)	14	7	71
Thin Class, Raw, 3½oz (100g)	9	4	71
Scrag End			
Fat Class, Raw, 3½oz (100g)	23	11	71
Medium Fat Class, Stewed, 1 Portion (79g)	17	8	80
Medium Fat Class, Raw, 3½oz (100g)	17	8	71
Thin Class, Raw, 3½oz (100g)	12	6	71
Shoulder			
Fat Class, Raw, 3½oz (100g)	13	6	71
Medium Fat Class, Raw, 3½oz (100g)	10	5	71
Medium Fat Class, Braised, 1 Portion (80g)	10	5	81
Thin Class, Raw, 3½oz (100g)	6	3	71
Veal Escalopes à la Viennoise			
1 serving, 3oz (85g)	28	11	137
VegeBurger®			
Meatless Burger, Grilled or Baked, 1 Patty	10	0	0
Vegetable Juice Cocktail			
Tinned, 1 Cup (240g)	0	0	0
Vegetable Oyster			
Fresh, 1 Cup Slices (133g)	0	0	0
Vegetable Protein (TVP)			
Dry, 1oz (28g)	1	0	0

	Total fat (g)	Saturated fat (g)	Cholesterol (mg)
1 Cup (88g)	3	0	0
Vegetables			
See under individual entries			
Mixed, Frozen, Boiled			
1 Cup (182g)	0	0	0
Mixed, Tinned			
1 Cup (245g)	1	0	0
Vegetarian Bacon Substitute			
1 Strip (8g)	2	0	0
1 Cup Pieces (144g)	43	7	0
Vegetarian Meat			
Tinned, Peanuts and Soya, 3½oz (100g)	17	4	0
Tinned, Wheat and Soy Protein, 3½oz (100g)	1	0	0
Tinned, Wheat and Soy Protein, Soy and Other Vegetable Oils, 3½oz (100g)	6	1	0
Tinned, Wheat Protein, 3½oz (100g)	1	0	0
Tinned, Wheat Protein, Nuts or Peanuts, 3½oz (100g)	7	2	0
Tinned, Wheat Protein, Vegetable Oil, 3½oz (100g)	10	3	0
Vegetarian Sausage			
Meatless, 1 Link (25g)	5	1	0
1 Patty (38g)	7	1	0
Venison			
Lean Meat Only, Raw, 3oz (85g)	3	2	55
Vinegar			
Cider, 1 tbsp (15g)	0	0	0
1 Cup (240g)	0	0	0
Distilled, 1 tbsp (15g)	0	0	0
1 Cup (240g)	0	0	0
Waffle Mix			
Dry Form, 3½oz (100g)	19	4	0
Plain and Buttermilk, Dry, 1 Cup (147g)	3	0	0
Waffles			
Home Recipe, 1 Waffle, 9-inch Square (200g)	20	6	250
Made from Mix with Water, 3½oz (100g)	14	3	0
Frozen, 1 Waffle (34g)	2	1	43
Waterchestnuts			
Tinned, 4 Waterchestnuts (28g)	0	0	0

	Total fat (g)	Saturated fat (g)	Cholesterol (mg)
½ Cup Slices (70g)	0	0	0
Fresh, 4 Waterchestnuts (36g)	0	0	0
½ Cup Slices (62g)	0	0	0
Watercress			
Fresh, 1 Cup Chopped (34g)	0	0	0
Watermelon			
Fresh, 1 Cup Diced Pieces (160g)	1	0	0
1 Slice,10 Diam (482g)	2	0	0
Welsh Rarebit			
1 Serving (232g)	32	17	100
Whale Meat			
Raw, 3½oz (100g)	8	1	50
Wheat Bran			
Crude, 3½oz (100g)	5	1	0
Wheat Flour – See under Flour			
Wheat Germ			
Crude, 3½oz (100g)	11	2	0
Wheat			
Whole Grain, Durum, 3½oz (100g)	3	0	0
Whole Grain, 3½oz (100g)	2	0	0
Whey			
Acid, Dried, 1 tbsp (2.9g)	0	0	0
1 Cup (57g)	0	0	2
Acid, Fluid, 1 Cup (246g)	0	0	1
Sweet, Dried, 1 tbsp (7½g)	0	0	1
1 Cup (145g)	2	1	9
Sweet, Fluid, 1 Cup (246g)	1	1	5
Wiener Schnitzel			
1 serving, 3oz (85g)	28	11	137
Wild Rice			
Raw, 1 Cup (160g)	1	0	0
Wine – See under Alcohol			
Yam			
Boiled or Baked, 1 Cup Cubes (136g)	0	0	0
Fresh, 1 Cup Cubes (150g)	0	0	0
Yeast Extract			
1oz (28g)	0	0	0
Yeast			
Bakers, Compressed, 1oz (28g)	0	0	0
Bakers, Dry, Active, 1oz (28g)	0	0	0
Brewers, Debittered, 1oz (28g)	0	0	0

	Total fat (g)	Saturated fat (g)	Cholesterol (mg)
Yoghurt			
Fruit, Low Fat, 1 Small Container (113g)	2	1	6
1 Medium Container (227g)	3	2	13
Plain, Low Fat, 1 Small Container (113g)	2	1	7
1 Medium Container (227g)	4	2	14
Plain, Skimmed Milk, 1 Small			
Container (113g)	0	0	2
1 Medium Container (227g)	0	0	4
Plain, Whole Milk, 1 Small Container (113g)	4	2	14
1 Medium Container (227g)	7	5	29
Vanilla, Low Fat, 1 Small Container (113g)	1	1	6
1 Medium Container (227g)	3	2	11
Yorkshire Pudding			
2 Puddings (55g)	6	3	39

APPENDIX ONE:
A BRIEF GLOSSARY OF
MEDICAL WORDS

Anemia – a shortage of red blood cells, and therefore haemoglobin, in your blood.

Aneurysm – a weak point in the wall of an artery which bulges and may burst, or rupture.

Angina (pectoris) – a distinct, gripping pain in the chest indicating that the muscle of your heart is not receiving enough oxygen.

Artery – the channel, or vessel, which carries blood away from your heart.

Atheroma – from the Greek, meaning 'porridge'. Atheroma is the mixture of fat, blood and calcium which builds up in deposits along the artery walls.

Atherosclerosis – a hardening and narrowing of the arteries due to build up of atheroma.

Atrium (plural = atria) – the 'waiting rooms' of your heart. The two upper chambers of your heart which collect blood prior to it being pumped out of the heart again.

Calcification – a feature of advanced atherosclerosis, the addition of calcium to the deposits (atheroma) causing them to harden.

Calorie – a measure of a unit of heat or energy. Food converts into energy and the amount of energy each food gives is measured in calories.

Carbon Monoxide – a very poisonous gas present in car exhaust and cigarette smoke.

Carboxy-haemoglobin – the substance which takes the place of oxygen in the red blood cells in those who smoke. Carbon monoxide combines with haemoglobin to create carboxy-haemoglobin.

Cardiac – having to do with the heart.

Cardiovascular – having to do with the heart and the blood vessels.

Cerebrovascular – having to do with the brain and the blood vessels. In particular with the supply of blood to the brain.

Cholesterol – a fatty substance found in all animal fats.

Coronary – relating to the heart. Some people say 'he's had a coronary' when referring to someone who has had a heart attack.

Coronary Heart Disease – a term used to describe the group of symptoms which result from diseased coronary arteries. These include angina, heart attack and sudden death.

Coronary Thrombosis – a coronary artery blocked by a blood clot.

Diastole – the lowest blood pressure reading. From the point in your heart beat when the heart muscle is relaxed.

Embolism – blockage of an artery (usually quite sudden) by a break-away atheroma deposit, blood clot or foreign body.

Erythrocytes – red blood cells.

Fatty Acid – the substances in fat that give it its unique flavour, texture and melting point.

Glucose – also called blood sugar, this is the final product from your body's breakdown of carbohydrate food.

Haemoglobin – the pigment of your red blood cells, containing iron, which carries oxygen and carbon dioxide.

Hardening of the arteries – the process of atherosclerosis with calcification.

Heart Attack – see myocardial infarction.

Haemorrhage – an abnormal discharge of blood, internally or externally.

Hormone – a chemical secreted by your glands which travels through your tissue fluid to an organ where it triggers a specific effect on your metabolism.

Hypercholesterolemia – high blood cholesterol.

Hypertension – abnormally high blood pressure.

Infarct – an area of dead tissue, or scar tissue. An infarction is the death of tissue due to loss of oxygen supply.

Ischaemic (heart disease) – having to do with lack of blood supply, therefore causing lack of oxygen supply.

Leucocytes – white blood cells.

Lipid – a fat substance.

Metabolism – the chemical process of assimilating food by turning it into energy and substances which will repair and replace body tissues. Your metabolism includes all of the stages and features of this process.

Myocardial Infarction – also known as heart attack. The death of heart muscle after its supply of blood, and therefore oxygen, has been interrupted.

Myocardium – the heart muscle itself. The muscle wall of the heart.

Obesity – the state of being excessively overweight.

Serum – as in serum cholesterol, that measured in the blood.

Stroke – a cerebrovascular accident. Damage to an area of brain due to the blockage or rupture of a blood vessel in the brain.

Systole – the highest blood pressure reading. From the point in your heart beat when your heart muscle is contracting, or pumping.

Thrombus (thrombosis) – a blood clot. Thrombosis is the formation of a blood clot.

Tissue – cells of a particular kind which group together for a specific function, i.e. muscle tissue, skin tissue, bone tissue.

Toxic – having the effect of a poison. The amount of a substance which may be toxic will vary depending on individual tolerances for it.

Vascular – having to do with blood vessels or blood supply.

Veins – blood vessels or channels that return blood to the heart.

Ventricle (plural = ventricles) – the two lower chambers of the heart which pump blood out of the heart into the arteries.

APPENDIX TWO: FURTHER READING

Relaxation East and West: A Manual of Poised Living, James Hewitt, Rider, London 1982

Vegan Nutrition, Dr. Michael A. Klaper, Vegan Society Publications, Oxford 1988

Vegan Nutrition, Gill Langley, Vegan Society Publications, Oxford 1988

The New Why You Don't Need Meat, Peter Cox, Bloomsbury Publishing Ltd., London 1994

APPENDIX THREE:
USEFUL ADDRESSES

Action on Smoking and Health (ASH), 16 Fitzhardinge Street, London W1H 9PL, telephone 0171-314-1360

British Cardiac Society, 7 St. Andrew's Place, London W1, telephone 0171-383-3887

British Heart Foundation, 9 Fitzroy Square, London W1H 4DH, telephone 0171-935-0185 NOTE: there are eleven regional offices for the BHF. Please look in your phone directory for that nearest to you.

British Wheel of Yoga, 80 Leckhampton Road, Cheltenham, Gloucestershire GL53 0BN

The Coronary Artery Disease Research Association (CORDA), 121 Sydney Street, London SW3 6ZA, telephone 0171-349-8686

Coronary Prevention Group, 42 Store Street, London WC1E 7DB, telephone 0171-580-1070

Coronary Prevention in Children Project, Exeter Health Authority, Exeter

Alcohol Advisory Service, 309 Grays Inn Road, London WC1X 8QF, telephone 0171-530-4820

The Health Education Authority, Hamilton House, Mabledon Place, London WC1A 1AH, telephone 0171-383-3833

The Keep Fit Association, National Secretary, Francis House, Francis Street, London SW1P 1DE, telephone 0171-233-8898

Northern Ireland ASH, c/o The Ulster Cancer Foundation, 40 Eglantine Avenue, Belfast BT9 6DX

Northern Ireland Coronary Prevention Group, Bryson House, 28 Bedford Street, Belfast BT2 7FJ

Scottish ASH, Royal College of Physicians, 9 Queen's Street, Edinburgh EH2 1JQ

Scottish Health Education Group, Health Education Centre, Woodburn House, Canaan Lane, Edinburgh EH10 4SG

The Vegan Society, 7 Battle Road, St Leonard's on Sea, East Sussex TN37 7AA, telephone 0424-427393

The Women's League of Health and Beauty, Streatham centre,

Dunraven, Leigham Court Road, London SW16, telephone 0181-659-1478

NOTE: the following organizations each have regional offices, please look in your phone book for that nearest to you. Ring or write for advice on first aid courses that may help you save the life of someone having a heart attack.

Ambu International, Head Office, Charlton Road, Midsomer Norton, Bath BA3 4DR

The British Red Cross Society, Head Office, 9 Grosvenor Crescent, London SW1X 7EJ, telephone 0171-235-5454

The Royal Life-saving Society, Head Office, Mountbatten House, Studley, Warwickshire

St. Andrew's Ambulance Association, Head Office, Milton Street Glasgow G4 0HR

St. John's Ambulance, Head Office, 1 Grosvenor Crescent, London SW1X 7EF, telephone 0171-235-5231